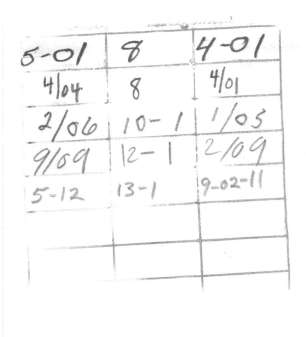

Cape Bulbs

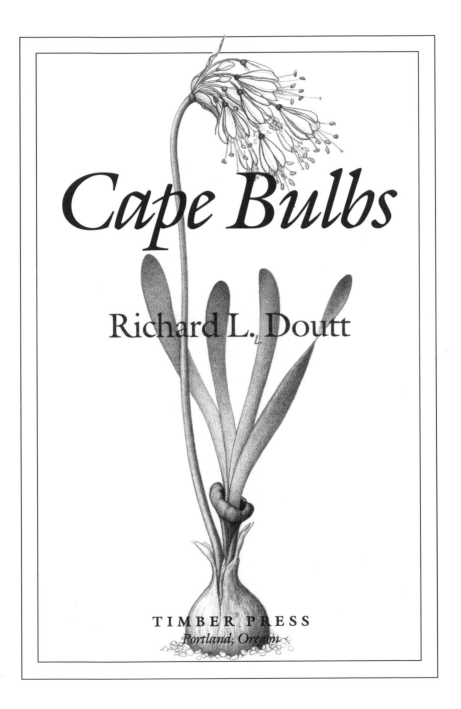

Cape Bulbs

Richard L. Doutt

TIMBER PRESS
Portland, Oregon

ISBN 0-88192-245-5

Printed in Hong Kong

TIMBER PRESS, INC.
The Haseltine Building
133 S.W. Second Ave., Suite 450
Portland, Oregon 97204-3527, U.S.A.

Library of Congress Cataloging in Publication Data
Doutt, Richard L.
    Cape bulbs / Richard L. Doutt.
        p.   cm.
    Includes bibliographical references and index.
    ISBN 0-88192-245-5
    1. Cape bulbs. I. Title.
SB425.D73   1994
635.9´34324—dc20   93-17655
                                        CIP

635.934324

Contents

Color photographs follow page 64

To Lucinda and Betty, who have so enriched my life

Preface

South African friends introduced me to Cape bulbs in the 1980s, and I am eager to share my enthusiasm for these flowers. To this end I have given talks and published articles. Now I have written this book to compile the widely scattered literature on Cape bulb species and to share the things I have learned from growing them in my garden and from studying them in their natural habitats in the South African veld.

Researching the literature for this book took me through many obscure publications that were a joy to read. They were full of surprising discoveries, which made the work continually exciting. The amount of literature on Cape bulbs is substantial and impressive, but unfortunately, much of it is very difficult to obtain; information that is of enormous value to gardeners frequently remains effectively buried in publications of very limited distribution and access. Nuggets of gardening information mined from arcane literature are included with the genus or species of Cape bulbs to which they specifically apply throughout the text. Although most of the Cape bulbs in my collection are to be treasured, some are of little horticultural value, and a few are potentially weedy and noxious. Along with my own garden experiences, I recount the appraisal of other collectors and the many uses gardeners have found for these unusual and delightful flowers.

The inherent charm and wildness of Cape bulbs no longer exist in the hybridized, manipulated, and thoroughly domesticated products mass-produced in Holland for sale in the garden outlets of supermarkets. The wild, ancestral, African genes for fragrance, gracefulness of form, and delicacy of color in the *Gladiolus*, for example, have been replaced by genes for stiff and scentless spikes, spectacular but disappointing.

From field research, I was thrilled to find the South African veld a wonderful treasure house of glorious bulbs awaiting discovery and recognition by gardeners. These wild bulbs are opportunists that radiated into a mosaic of different, isolated habitats to evolve into hundreds of remarkably interesting and lovely species.

Cape bulbs are tough and tenacious survivors of an ancient climatic shift from ample rainfall to increasing aridity. Growing in the wild, these flowers are concentrated in the Cape Province of South Africa, which is blessed with a Mediterranean climate that is characterized by an annual climatic rhythm of rain falling only during the mild winter, followed by a long summer drought. Nature has adapted Cape bulbs to survive a long, dry summer, so they are conditioned to flourish in any area of the world with this rare climatic pattern, including California, central Chile, and parts of Australia.

In spite of compatible climatic conditions, I find that much written about Cape bulbs is substantially different from my experiences with them in my California garden. And my gardening books all seem to have been written somewhere else, alluding to frozen ground and frigid winters of which I know nothing. I know only dry summers where the grasses and forbs turn golden brown in May, and the parched hillsides bake under a hot summer sun until the first good autumn rain suddenly and refreshingly turns them green for the mild winter. Although much of California enjoys this phenomenal Mediterranean climate, conditions for gardening are certainly not uniform. Instead, the state is a complex mixture of localities that vary enormously when it comes to temperature, rainfall, wind, fog, sunshine, altitude, soil type, often within only a few miles.

I gardened in the San Francisco Bay Area on a wind-swept hill in El Cerrito that received the brunt of the cold summer fogs coming through the Golden Gate. That garden situation was considerably different from the much warmer gardens of friends in nearby Berkeley. I also tried container gardening on a deck cantilevered from my home in Mill Valley surrounded by tall, second-growth coast redwoods native to the shady site at the foot of Mount Tamalpais. For several years I farmed in the San Joaquin Valley near Fresno, where grim winter tule fogs can hover for days, blocking out the sun, and where the low temperatures can stagnate day after day. Yet this is an area where the summers sizzle, and on every July day the thermometer can reach 100°F (38°C). I once grew a vegetable garden in Riverside. There the summers are hot and dry and desert-like, and the winters are often crisp, but without the depressing, bone-chilling tule fogs of the central San Joaquin Valley. Now I write this book from a riparian oak-woodland in Montecito, a suburb of Santa Barbara, on a narrow coastal strip sandwiched between the Santa Ynez Mountains a mile to the north and the Pacific Ocean a mile to the south. The conditions here are much milder than in any of the other places I have gardened, suitable for commercial orchards of tender crops such as avocados and cherimoyas. But paradise it is not, for water is in short supply, and my water allocation is limited. So I grow my garden in a xeriscape where Cape bulbs are fully compatible, for they are adapted to survive the rainless summer when water must be conserved.

Had I grown Cape bulbs in any one of the widely different garden situations described above they would have flourished, for they would in each instance have had the requisite dry summer and a comparatively mild but rainy winter. And, while I identify with gardeners who practice their art under many different conditions in California, I do not write this book solely for the 30 million fellow citizens of my native state, nor do I write it only for those who live in other regions that have a Mediterranean climate. Instead, I have been made keenly aware of the worldwide interest in Cape bulbs. This awareness came from international correspondence, from research, from membership in the Indigenous Bulb

Growers Association of South Africa, and from comments by foreign visitors. These sources reveal that Cape bulbs are also grown and enjoyed by ingenious gardeners in places with harsh winters and rainy summers.

The range of interest in Cape bulbs is very gratifying, and it is my hope that this book will encourage participation in the conservation efforts being made by both the National Botanical Institute of South Africa and individual gardeners worldwide. Cultivation of rare and unusual flowers is of utmost importance: tragically, some species no longer exist in nature, and others are threatened with extinction. I believe that concerned gardeners can prevent the total loss of these flowers through their cultivation and dissemination, enjoying their beauty at the same time.

Acknowledgments

In South Africa I received warm hospitality and generous assistance from many individuals. These included my former associates in entomology: Sarel Broodryk, Stefan Neser, and the late David P. Annecke. In the Cape Province my visits were helped in countless ways by Johan Loubser, Paul F. X. Von Stein, Pauline Perry, Carol Turnley-Jones, and Graham Duncan at Kirstenbosch. My hostess at Kamieskroon was Colla Swart, whose invitation to return to Namaqualand is almost irresistible. I am especially indebted to Jim Holmes, who guided me through much of the best bulb areas of the Cape and introduced me to Neil MacGregor, who was my very gracious host for two memorable days on his farm, Glenlyon, at Nieuwoudtville.

In California I am grateful to Barbara Barton, author of "Gardening by Mail" who encouraged me to submit my manuscript for publication. My wife, Betty Mann Doutt, has been a continuing source of support and of special assistance with the intricacies of the computer. It has been my good fortune to have Shari Smith do the botanically accurate and esthetically pleasing illustrations. Finally, Suzy Blackaby, the editor assigned to me by Timber Press, has used her considerable professional skills to polish and make presentable a very raw manuscript. I thank them all.

Cape Bulbs

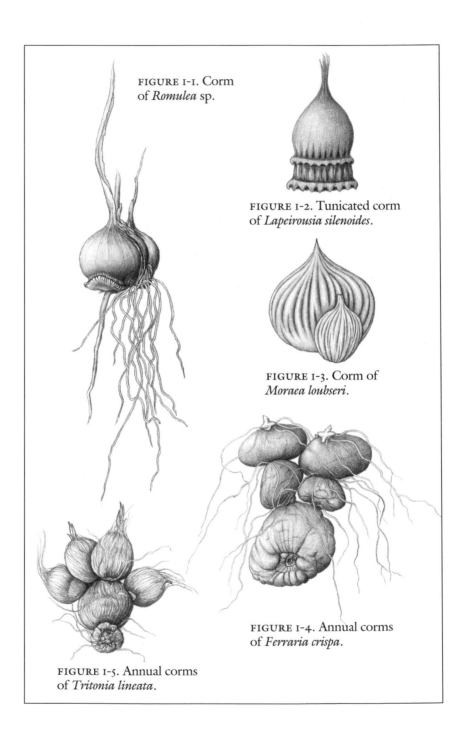

FIGURE 1-1. Corm of *Romulea* sp.

FIGURE 1-2. Tunicated corm of *Lapeirousia silenoides*.

FIGURE 1-3. Corm of *Moraea loubseri*.

FIGURE 1-4. Annual corms of *Ferraria crispa*.

FIGURE 1-5. Annual corms of *Tritonia lineata*.

CHAPTER 1

A South African Treasure House

THE PHYSICAL ENVIRONMENT OF CAPE BULBS

Gold and diamonds are dug from the South African earth, but the truly unique treasures of that country are the bulbs, corms, rhizomes, and tubers that flower in profusion each year. Technically such plants are *geophytes* or *geophytic petaloid monocots*, but, like most gardeners, I simply call all of them bulbs and treat them alike horticulturally (see Figures 1-1 through 1-8).

The richness of the Cape flora is known worldwide. The Cape floral kingdom has about 8550 species of flowering plants in 957 genera, with an impressive 73 percent of the species being endemic to the region. In fact, the world's greatest concentration of indigenous bulbs is in the Cape Province of South Africa, where there are a total of about 1336 species, or 16 percent of the Cape flora (see Plates 1, 2). This quantity is unparalleled anywhere else in the world (Goldblatt, 1978).

Among these bulbs are some of the choicest wildflowers of the region and some of the most threatened. The richness and beauty of the Cape bulbs are remarkable, yet most are little known to gardeners, who, in growing them, might help to save them from extinction. The diversity among these bulbs allows selections for almost any garden situation. Many are natural container plants, thriving in narrow crevices in the Precambrian granite boulders of the Cape, and are of a size suitable to the

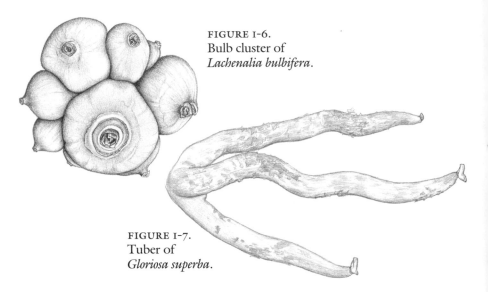

FIGURE 1-6.
Bulb cluster of
Lachenalia bulbifera.

FIGURE 1-7.
Tuber of
Gloriosa superba.

scale of a small patio or container garden. Others are robust plants reaching 5 feet (1.5 m) tall, and there are intermediate varieties of every description.

In 1980 I began to grow as many species of Cape bulbs as I could obtain because I wanted to test them under the outdoor conditions of my garden in Santa Barbara. Actually, South African plants are so prevalent in Santa Barbara that when Professor J. R. Compton, then head of the Botanic Garden of the Cape Colony, visited the area in the late 1920s, he saw far more native South African plants in our gardens than at home (de Forest and de Forest, 1930). Successful cultivation of South African plants is possible in California because it shares a Mediterranean climate—characterized by winter rainfall and summer drought—with part of the Cape Province. This type of climate is a rarity, occurring in only three other places in the world, namely, southern and western Australia, central Chile, and portions of the countries bordering the Mediterranean Sea (see Figure 1-9). In total, the areas constitute only about one percent of the earth's land surface. In South Africa, only a very small region actually enjoys a Mediterranean climate. This winter-rainfall area is in the southwesternmost part of the country, extending from the Cape of Good

FIGURE I-8.
Root stock of *Clivia miniata*, resembling a rhizome, is a bulb-like thickening of leaf bases. Fruiting bodies are characteristic.

Hope approximately 300 miles (483 km) northward along the Atlantic coast, and inland for 50 to 70 miles (80 to 113 km) (see Figure 1-10).

A Mediterranean climate produces vegetation adapted to survival during the summer drought and genetically programmed for active growth during the winter when the rains occur. In California, this vegetation is termed *chaparral*, while in the Cape it is called *fynbos* (pronounced fane-bose), meaning "fine bush" in Afrikaans. The plant species comprising the chaparral and fynbos are entirely different, but in adapting to the rigors of similar climates, they have produced vegetation that looks and functions in much the same way. Scientists term this process *convergent evolution*.

The annual summer drought of a Mediterranean climate encourages the evolution of a bulb, enabling the plant to survive the months

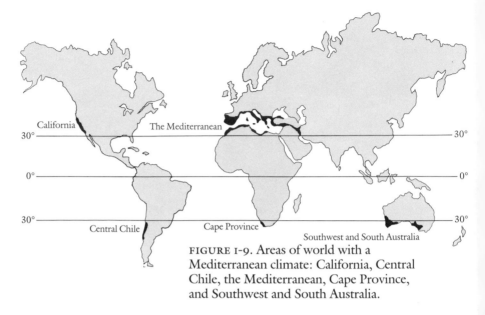

FIGURE 1-9. Areas of world with a
Mediterranean climate: California, Central
Chile, the Mediterranean, Cape Province,
and Southwest and South Australia.

when no water is available for maintenance and growth. I will repeatedly emphasize the vital importance of this annual rhythm in the culture of Cape bulbs.

Northward from Cape Town to Namaqualand, the coastal strip and winter-rainfall region becomes increasingly arid and eventually turns into the Namib Desert. Eastward from Cape Town in the area known as the Little Karoo and the southern Cape, rain may occur at any season of the year. Still further east in the Cape Province is the Great Karoo and eastern Cape, where there is seasonal rainfall during the summer months.

The cold Benguela current flows north along the Cape Province with an upwelling of cold water at the coast. In summer, fog often forms over these cold coastal waters when the warm, moisture-laden marine air reaches the dewpoint as it moves across the zone of cold surface water. In the arid northern area, such fogs or sea mists are ecologically significant for those plants able to capture and utilize the moisture. Where advective sea fog is prevalent, plants may intercept the moisture even though no precipitation in the form of rainfall is recorded at the time.

The precipitation on Table Mountain, just back of Cape Town, is extraordinary. Most of it is the result of condensation as mist blows over

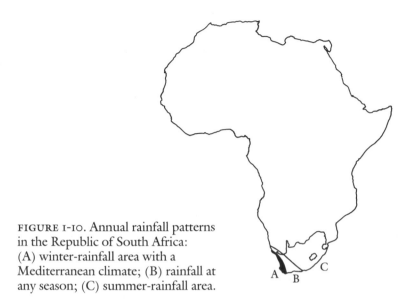

FIGURE 1-10. Annual rainfall patterns in the Republic of South Africa: (A) winter-rainfall area with a Mediterranean climate; (B) rainfall at any season; (C) summer-rainfall area.

the plateau at its summit during summer. The mist forms the famous "table cloth" of Table Mountain as seen from Cape Town. The condensation intercepted each year is enormous, estimated at several times the winter rainfall (Schulze and McGee, 1978). This phenomenon led South Africa's early botanist, Dr. Rudolph Marloth, to conclude that the climate of the mountain top was that of a swamp. Rock hollows almost continuously filled with clear brown water and fringed with damp moss are one of the features of Table Mountain.

In the Cape there are mountains lying roughly parallel to the narrow coastal strip. These separate long interior valleys that are in the rain shadow of the mountains. Because of this rugged topography there exist within very short distances great variations in patterns of rainfall, temperature, wind, and fog. When these elements are combined with different edaphic factors, a complicated mixture of microclimates and habitats results. These isolated sites, like miniature ecological islands, encourage the evolution of a diversity of endemic bulbs in a remarkably limited geographic area. However, when the entire wild population of a species exists in such a restricted location, it is at great risk of extinction.

There are varying degrees of aridity throughout the Cape area. Precipitation can differ substantially over short distances, particularly with changes in altitude. As noted above, Table Mountain, which rises steeply above Cape Town, receives annual precipitation (fog plus rainfall) of approximately 71 inches (1810 mm), while about 30 miles (50 km) south at Cape Point, annual precipitation is about 14 inches (360 mm).

Historical geology was important in the evolution of Cape geophytes. Africa split off from the ancient supercontinent of Gondwanaland in the late Jurassic or early Cretaceous era (King, 1978), so the Cape vegetation has been isolated for well over 100 million years. This has permitted products of many ancient and distinctive evolutionary lines to survive (Axelrod and Raven, 1978). The glaciation in the Northern Hemisphere did not occur in the Cape because there was no Pleistocene ice age in Africa. The sea surface water was warmer then; the Benguela current was neither as strong nor as cold as it is now. As ice spread over Antarctica about 5 million years ago, there was a trend toward aridity. There is no evidence that the Mediterranean climate existed in South Africa before the formation of the major Antarctic ice sheet.

The Cape Province is geologically very old, and the region is studded with ancient outcroppings of Precambrian granite. These rocky hills, *klipkoppies* or simply *koppies*, are the treasure houses of Cape bulbs (see Plate 3). Koppies often have rounded domes caused by the exfoliation process so common in granite, and below them are huge jumbled masses of boulders. The granite domes and large boulders often have crevices that fill with humus and detritus from disintegrating rock and become the restricted habitats of rare bulbs. The hilly koppies are like islands; most are separated by intervening valley areas that in summer are very dry, hot, and more inhospitable to plants than the koppies themselves. The deep, rocky crevices on the koppies in which the bulbs occur can remain cooler and more moist than the open, baking veld.

Some botanists believe that a different Cape flora was once widespread in areas that are presently semidesert or desert. As aridity increased in the Cape region, the plants that required summer rain were gradually restricted eastward, opening the environment for taxa with a genetic tolerance to summer drought. Axelrod and Raven (1978) suggested that, in effect, a new island habitat was being created within the area of an established vegetation type. Plant groups able to survive had great opportunity for evolutionary radiation and production of hundreds of new, localized species. In other words, as the Cape region became increasingly dry, the plant species requiring summer rainfall failed to survive, permitting plants that could survive an annual summer drought to evolve into many species occupying the local ecological niches. Bulb formation was simply nature's way of helping plants survive the summer drought.

HABITAT DESTRUCTION

While the bulb flora in the Cape area is perhaps the richest in the world, it may also be the most threatened. The South African population is rapidly growing. Much of this growth is centered in the Cape Province, where it has eliminated many wildflower habitats, and the destruction continues with urban, industrial, and agricultural expansion. When a species is destroyed it cannot be replaced. Irreversible extinction erases millions of years of evolution. While conservation efforts are made by dedicated people in worthy organizations, they are never enough, and many species hang on precariously. However, gardeners can keep the precious genes of some threatened species alive, and a single individual can do wonders.

NEIL MACGREGOR, CONSERVATIONIST

On a visit to the Cape Province in 1987, I met Neil MacGregor of the tiny community of Nieuwoudtville in arid Namaqualand. Neil has a farm, Glenlyon, on which he profitably raises very fine Merino sheep. This would seem incompatible with wildflower conservation, for sheep and goats can decimate the vegetation of any area. Neil thought there should be a better way, "Nature's Way." He imagined what the vegetation was once like and what stress it was subjected to when the roaming herds of antelope-like animals grazed the area before the arrival of Europeans. He envisioned the animals feeding selectively on the vegetation and then moving on. His Merino sheep are aliens to the South African landscape, but Neil believed that by selective grazing, good range management, and timing the sheep's pasturage to coincide with dormant season of wildflowers, he could raise sheep and conserve wildflowers, too. He decided to let the flowers grow in the spring, produce seed, and store food in the bulbs. Then he would let his sheep graze the area. Using this procedure, the plants are saved: the hooves help to plant the seeds; the droppings fertilize the area; and the bulbs, being underground, are not affected.

It took about ten years to achieve what Neil now has at Glenlyon. In the spring his land is ablaze with color and filled with rare bulbous plants. His farm is the type locality for scores of species that were first found there and described by the country's professional botanists, for whom he is a generous host. He assists them in every way, even providing lodging in his guest cottage. He also welcomes lay visitors, who ride in his farm truck while he gives them a tour of his wildflower preserve and explains the ecological miracle of rare bulbs flourishing on a working sheep ranch. He lets people roam at will through the flowers; Neil doesn't believe in "don't boards," signs that would confine people to paths or restrict their enjoyment of the flowers. He is unsurpassed in his dedication to preserve one of the most beautiful concentrations of wildflowers in the world, and he has created a true national treasure for South Africa. Among the many bulb genera being conserved at Glenlyon are *Brunsvigia*, *Bulbinella*, *Gladiolus*, *Hesperantha*, *Lachenalia*, *Lapeirousia*, *Romulea*, and *Sparaxis*.

COMMUNITY WILDFLOWER SHOWS

Among the delightful events of the spring season in the Cape are the wildflower shows held annually in several rural farming communities. Each show lasts three days and in a typical year the first takes place in the town of Vredendal about 20 August. Shows are scheduled over successive weekends at Picketberg, Clanwilliam, Riversdale, Caledon, Darling, Kirstenbosch, Hermanus, Tulbagh, Worcester, Villiersdorp, and Porterville, ending at Ceres about 10 October. Each is a community effort run by eager volunteers, and each has its own special charm and selection of wildflowers because the species composition varies tremendously from town to town, reflecting the astonishing richness of the Cape flora.

All the shows I have seen feature mass displays of wildflowers, and some have a section of carefully identified specimens. Some people believe that mass displays may seriously deplete the wild populations needing protection. Doreen Court, an authority on South African succulents, has forcefully expressed this view. She does not believe that the flower pickers know which species are endangered or rare and which bulbs are delicate and may be set back or even destroyed by having the whole flowering stem removed. She writes, "We pot, bag and cut our treasures, many of which are swept out with the dust after the public have gone home." She concludes, "We should think again, and, wherever possible, leave the plants where they belong. To my way of thinking, this would be true conservation" (Court, 1983).

To investigate the controversy I chose a representative wildflower show at Caledon, a small wheat and barley farming community about an hour's drive east of Cape Town. The Caledon show, which began in 1892, is widely respected, and the organizers kindly permitted me to observe their preparations, accompany the pickers in the veld, and attend the opening to view the public's reaction.

When I asked the Secretary of the Caledon Horticultural and Wildflower Society to respond to the negative view of these shows, she said that the shows create a special awareness of these precious flowers. Farmers take pride in having rarities on their land and are fiercely protective of their habitat. She added that the Caledon Wildflower Society, which sponsors the show, must first get permits from the Cape Province officials and must then obtain each landowner's permission and a license to transport the flowers to the show. The Province's regulations require the name of each farmer-landowner, the names of the flower pickers, and the names of the drivers transporting the flowers. The rules also require that no more than one-third of the flowers be picked from a bush and that one-third of the stem be left on bulbous plants. Furthermore, the flower stems are to be cut with scissors to prevent the bulb from being inadvertently plucked from the ground.

I accompanied the pickers to a mountain farm set aside by a local man solely for the natural production of wildflowers. They were after the famous Caledon bluebell, *Gladiolus bullatus*, which occurs as scattered, single plants. I winced at the size of the picked bunch of lovely blue flowers, which I thought excessive, and I was not reassured that the plants would rejuvenate. The required scissors were not used, and I saw at least one plant with its corm uprooted. Such mistakes notwithstanding, my impression of the Caledon citizens is that they are serious conservationists. To their credit they have set aside a special reserve to protect the rare and striking *Moraea insolens*, and they support a large community wildflower preserve.

The community wildflower shows sometimes make unexpected contributions to the knowledge of the Cape flora with the discovery of new species. Such is the story of *Moraea atropunctata*. It was brought in 1978 and 1979 to the Caledon show, where it was recognized as being new. Ion Williams, a botanist from Hermanus, preserved the specimens and established that the flowers came from the farm Vleitjies on the slopes of the Eseljacht Mountains. There it was later recollected, described, and named by Peter Goldblatt (1982). I have been growing it in my garden since 1987 from seeds made available by the National Botanical Institute at Kirstenbosch.

I attended a delightful show at Darling, where the local species were displayed in a natural but spectacular fashion without mass picking of the veld. At the show I met Frieda Duckitt, whose family has farmed the area for many generations and has been active in the show since its inception in 1917. The Duckitt family has established wildflower reserves on its farms. Visitors to the show may ride on tractor-drawn farm wagons along roads that wind through one of the Duckitts' flower reserves. This reserve has many species of bulbs, including species of *Bulbinella*, *Geissorhiza*, *Gladiolus*, *Ixia*, *Moraea*, *Ornithogalum*, *Romulea*, *Sparaxis*, *Watsonia*, and *Zantedeschia*. Thousands of citizens come to the Darling show by car, bus, or on a special steam train run for old time's sake from Cape Town just for a Sunday show, and they enjoy a truly splendid experience.

The last show I attended was sponsored by the Botanical Society of South Africa at Kirstenbosch. It features specimen flowers, many of which in the wild are seriously threatened or on the endangered list, grown by Society members in their private gardens or by the Kirstenbosch staff. The atmosphere is more sedate than the bustling activity of the community shows, but it provides another tribute to the precious Cape flora and emphasizes the role that concerned gardeners may play in conserving species.

In my garden are several species that either no longer exist in nature or are reduced to a few individuals in a tiny remnant of their shrinking habitat. Examples are *Gladiolus aureus*, *Gladiolus citrinus*, and *Moraea loubseri*. The Botanical Society of South Africa stresses the important role that gardeners can play in the conservation of rare and endangered species through dissemination and cultivation. Members of the Botanical Society of South Africa receive an annual list of available, free seeds. For information about membership write The Executive Secretary, Botanical Society of South Africa, Kirstenbosch, 7735 Claremont, Republic of South Africa. The National Botanical Institute issues a wholesale seed catalog. For information on this catalog write The Director: Gardens, National Botanical Institute, Kirstenbosch, Private Bag X7, Claremont 7735, Republic of South Africa.

In regard to conservation, the International Bulb Society (formerly The American Plant Life Society) has published concerns about the harvesting of threatened or endangered species from the wild for the world's bulb trade. Some in the conservation movement express the sentiment that wild species should not be cultivated or kept in private hands. The unrestricted commercial exploitation of wild populations must be stopped, but a ban on cultivation is not the answer. Conscientious gardeners can and should obtain their bulbs from reputable dealers who sell only cultivated stock. Harold Koopowitz, director of the arboretum at the University of California at Irvine, has unimpeachable credentials as a conservationist. In 1983 Koopowitz and Kaye published a book calling attention to the alarming global crisis in plant extinction. Less than a decade later, Koopowitz (1990, page 22) concluded that

> many bulbous plants are endangered but often they prove easy to cultivate and propagate. Examples of such species are *Gladiolus aureus*, *G. watermeyeri*, *G. citrinus*, *Moraea loubseri*, *M. atropunctata*, and *Ixia maculata*, which have been saved from the brink of extinction by being brought into cultivation.

As a gardener I grow all these species from seeds obtained from cultivated sources. This is conservation through cultivation.

THE ANNUAL CYCLE OF BULBS

As a grower of Cape bulbs, I am fascinated by these drought evaders, these superb survivors. When I plant winter-growing Cape species in late summer or early fall, they are dry, dormant, brown, and seem almost lifeless, but with the first good autumn rain they respond immediately. They quickly absorb the refreshing rainwater and exuberantly throw up their fresh green foliage, which is soon followed by an explosion of flowers. Later, as the spring rains taper off and the days lengthen after the vernal equinox, the bulbs ripen, harden, and prepare to aestivate. This biological rhythm is basic and beautiful, and it reminds the gardener that the plants have their own physiological clock, schedule, and calendar.

When a winter-growing bulb is moved from the Cape to the Northern Hemisphere, it is in synchrony with the rhythm of its native land (six months out of phase with the northern latitudes). Its physiological clock must be reset, a problem the gardener can avoid by growing the plants from seeds. If seeds received from South Africa are planted in late summer

26

or fall in the north, the seedlings respond to the photoperiod and immediately adjust to the climatic cycle of the Northern Hemisphere. They grow during their first northern winter, then go dormant in the northern summer and revive in autumn. The adjustment is not so easily accomplished with an imported bulb. One method is to hold the bulb for a protracted period until the northern growing season arrives. Another method is to restrict its dormancy, which shortens its growing period but avoids the loss of vitality and risk of lethal dessication from being stored too long.

Corms acclimatize better than true bulbs or rhizomes, which seem to have some memory of their Cape habitat in the plant parts that developed there; this retards acclimatization (Du Plessis and Duncan, 1989).

CHAPTER 2

Cape Bulb Culture

In general, the cultivation of Cape bulbs is not difficult, though sometimes it seems that the most beautiful and desirable species are also the most finicky, frustrating, and temperamental. They certainly pose the greatest challenge to the gardener.

After growing Cape bulbs for several years, I became painfully aware that I had much to learn about their proper care and treatment throughout the year. Some species would grow like weeds and were always vigorous, prolific, and seemingly indestructible; others would sulk, and I could never make them happy; few, to my great dismay, simply died. To dispel my ignorance I decided to make another visit to the Cape Province to see and photograph the bulbs in their native habitats, to record data about the conditions of their existence in the veld, and to discuss their culture with knowlegeable people, especially the members of the Indigenous Bulb Growers Association of South Africa (IBSA).

To supplement the field data, I have perused the literature in search of growing hints. Specialized techniques for growing a particular genus of Cape bulbs are appropriately discussed in Chapter 3 with the plant to which they specifically apply.

CAPE BULB HABITATS

The natural conditions under which most of the Cape bulbs grow vary tremendously, and even the most inhospitable-looking localities have bulbs. Desertlike conditions north of Springbok in Namaqualand have *Galaxia, Gethylis, Ornithogalum, Romulea,* and other species growing on scree-like slopes consisting of sun-baked rocks with hard, thin, and very gritty soil. Usually these are very tiny plants with leaves that are gray, hirsute, or corkscrew shaped.

I found bulbs such as *Babiana, Freesia, Lapeirousia,* and *Veltheimia* in narrow crevices of huge rock outcroppings. Other bulbs, including *Lachenalia* and *Spiloxene,* were growing along the base of rock faces where water runoff concentrates and where there is some partial shade (see Plates 4, 5). Especially beautiful flowers such as *Bulbinella latifolia, Hesperantha vaginata,* and *Romulea monantha* grow in heavy, adobe-type soil. When wet, it sticks to one's boots in great masses; when dry in the summer, it is as hard as a brick, and it shrinks, causing deep cracks.

I found bulbs such as *Boophane, Moraea,* and *Romulea* growing in what seemed to be pure sand—sometimes fine, but usually very coarse and often full of small stones—in locations that are blisteringly hot in summer.

A number of bulbs grow around seasonal pools on hardpan clay or in springtime marshy seeps (*vleis* in Afrikaans). The pools dry completely in summer. Other flowers, such as *Crinum, Watsonia,* and *Zantedeschia,* grow near or actually in ephemeral streams that also are completely dry in summer (see Plate 6).

Dry summers are conducive to wildfires, and there are many Cape bulbs that flourish after an area is burned; *Cyrtanthus ventricosus* is commonly known as fire lily, reflecting its amazing post-fire response. Field observations indicate that many Cape bulbs may remain in a vegetative state for years without producing a single flower but bloom profusely within a few weeks following a burn. This flowering often occurs at an earlier-than-normal date for the species, and the flowering declines markedly over the two subsequent post-fire seasons. The ability of amaryllids such as *Cyrtanthus* and *Haemanthus* to flower so quickly after a fire suggests that flower initials form on the bulb every year, but they simply abort and remain as a papery sheath between the leaf scales unless a stimulus triggers them into growth.

It has been suggested that the heat of the fire, the destruction of competing vegetation, or the presence of soluble potassium salts in the ash deposit may be responsible for stimulating the dramatic post-fire effects observed, but these theories are not totally convincing. Tompsett (1985) suggests that ethylene and carbon monoxide gases in the smoke provide the real stimulus. Smoke treatments of bulbs of *Ornithogalum thyrsoides* and *Freesia* corms in England were shown to break dormancy.

Another Cape bulb well known for its spectacular mass flowering following summer or autumn wildfires is *Watsonia borbonica* (syn. *W. pyramidata*). According to le Maitre (1984), the mass flowering and consequent heavy seed production overwhelm the seed predators, which are primarily weevils (Curculionidae). Many seeds are overlooked by the satiated beetles, resulting in a large population of post-fire seedlings.

Although it may be difficult to generalize about Cape bulbs that thrive naturally in such different situations and habitats, two things are essential to successful culture: good drainage and a dry resting period. The latter, so critical to the winter-growing Cape bulbs, is provided by the veld's hot, rainless summer. Although summer temperatures are high, the bulbs do not need to bake. On the contrary, they are often quite deep in the soil or in rock crevices, where temperatures are much cooler than at the surface, and many grow in the shelter of shrubs that provide at least partial shade and attendant coolness.

All successful growers of Cape bulbs provide good drainage and a dry resting period, but otherwise the culture of the bulbs by proven experts varies considerably, and there seem to be about as many different ways to grow the bulbs as there are gardeners. Bulb enthusiasts seeking the best way to grow their plants do a good deal of experimenting, and trial and error often yield excellent results.

SOUTH AFRICAN CULTIVATION METHODS

At Kirstenbosch's famous bulb house, Graham Duncan, the leading authority on propagating South African bulbs, successfully raises thousands of rare bulbs that make collectors sinfully envious (see Plate 7). He uses sand as the major soil ingredient, mixing two parts industrial sand to one part loam and one part compost. Sometimes the loam is omitted, adjusting the formula to three parts sand and one part decomposed compost. This mix drains well and is not overly rich. Winter-growing Cape bulbs are not heavy feeders, although bonemeal can be applied rather freely. Organic fertilizers derived from kelp are useful, but caution is advised in the application of inorganic fertilizer that can easily overfeed the bulbs. It is easier to add fertilizer than to correct a medium that contains excessive nutrients.

At Kirstenbosch the bulbs are grown either in long, narrow, concrete-walled and sand-filled beds or in containers and pots. All the plants are under a roof shelter of transluscent plastic that keeps out the occasional summer rains. In fact, all the growers I visited in South Africa have the plants under some kind of shelter, usually shade cloth. Shade cloth is also used at the arboretum of the University of California at Irvine, which has a substantial collection of Cape bulbs. The shade cloth may function as a substitute for the shelter that shrubs provide to many bulbs in the veld. Bulbous flowers are often found thrusting up through a sheltering plant, though the bulb's survival may be due more to the protection from grazing animals afforded by a prickly bush than to its sheltering shade. In California I grow most bulbs in the open, but the surrounding coast live oak and sycamore trees do shade them for part of the day. I have found that newly emerged seedlings survive far better in partial shade than in full sun.

I encountered an ingenious bulb grower in Porterville, South Africa, who used the local sand as a growing medium in all manner of containers retrieved from rubbish heaps. It is not easy to get conventional flower pots and other standard containers in the remote outlying farm areas of the Cape Province. On top of the sand this man sprinkled a very thin layer of dried, well-rotted cow manure. His *Gethylis* seedlings were vigorous, and those in one particular container that he watered four to five times daily were well ahead of the other seedlings. I was surprised that such frequent watering would produce such a response from the plants, though it is possible the sand dried too quickly otherwise. To space his seeds, this creative gardener rolled an old rusty gear wheel over the surface of the sand and dropped a seed into each of the indentations made by the cogs.

Among the healthiest plants I saw in the Cape were those grown by Carol Turnley-Jones. Her pots of gorgeous flowers win high awards at competitive flower shows. She uses sand with compost at about a three-to-one ratio. Pots and mix are sterilized with either boiling water or a commercial product containing carbolic acid. Bulbs in storage are dusted with a fungicide and covered with vermiculite. When thrips are attacking foliage, Turnley-Jones uses a pyrethrum insecticide. Her growing medium in containers is layered, beginning with small stones, then some peat, and finally the sand/compost into which she mixes bonemeal. She feeds the plants every three to four weeks with seaweed extract and at some point gives them a product containing the trace elements iron, copper, and manganese. Turnley-Jones commented that the local soil is often deficient in boron; in California the opposite is sometimes the case.

CALIFORNIAN CULTIVATION METHODS

In my nursery in Santa Barbara, California, I grow many of the bulbs in large plastic tubs in a sterile medium and continually experiment with various combinations of sand, peat moss, perlite, vermiculite, and various soil amendments sold as mulch or humus. Sand is inexpensive, gives excellent drainage, and is the major component used by the most successful indigenous bulb growers in South Africa, but it makes the containers very heavy. In the past I have substituted perlite for some of the sand to reduce weight; its white granules give a good indication of how uniformly the medium's ingredients are mixed: if the perlite appears to have the same concentration throughout the medium, then presumably the other components do, too. Some growers believe that the perlite may be mildly toxic because of fluorides it contains and that the phytotoxicity is exacerbated if the medium is at all acid. I have no proof of its possible phytotoxic effects, but I have generally discontinued the use of perlite because it tends to float to the surface over time, which I find esthetically objectionable.

The peat moss is light, retains moisture, and may give the medium a slightly acid pH to more closely duplicate Cape soil. The vermiculite is also light and tends to balance or stabilize the retention of moisture, which is lost more quickly from sand than from peat moss. I add nutrients to the sterile medium when the bulbs are first planted rather than when the medium is first mixed.

My bulb collection is now of a size that requires bulk mixing of the bulb-planting medium, which I accomplish in a cement mixer. When I had fewer things to grow, I mixed the ingredients by hand in a plastic tub or on a tarp spread on the ground. Most gardeners need only small batches, which can easily be mixed for a few pots at a time.

The recipe for the bulb-planting medium I am now using is two parts washed river sand and two parts commercial soil amendment much like compost. I am often tempted to increase the proportion of sand because of its dominant use by the successful South Africans. In practice, I alter this formula frequently; whenever a species is not doing well, I change its medium. Most bulb growers use good garden loam or compost in their mixes. These ingredients have considerable merit if they are sterilized but otherwise are not recommended because of the severe weed problem or losses from harmful microorganisms that may result. The mix I use is sterile, drains well, and has air space for roots, but it requires nutrients. In the past when planting bulbs, I added only bonemeal or superphos to the medium, but now I use a granular fertilizer that has a 6–10–6 proportion of N–P–K.

CULTURE OF CAPE BULBS IN COLD WINTER AREAS

All my experience in growing Cape bulbs has been under southern California conditions very much like those in the environment at Cape Town, where winters are mild. In December 1990, Santa Barbara had a record freeze; the temperature in my garden dropped to 20°F ($-7°$ C). Although foliage and some bulbs were damaged, some individuals of all species survived what turned out to be the coldest winter in almost a century. The cold snap in my region, however, was nothing compared to normal winters throughout most of the United States, and I have been unable to advise friends who garden in much colder areas on the culture of Cape bulbs during truly frigid winters. It was, therefore, a welcome revelation to read Dr. Maurice Boussard's 1985 account of over 25 years of growing many species (no hybrids) of South African Iridaceae in his garden in the northeast corner of France.

Dr. Boussard gardens at Verdun, where winters are often fairly severe, with spells of days that are either cool but gloomy or sunny but cold. There are about 90 nights of frost a year. Springs and autumns are usually cool to mild, with sudden heat waves in spring or freezes in late autumn. Summers are warm to hot and dry with some showers. Annual rainfall is about 27.5 inches (699 mm), with 75 percent falling from autumn to spring, including three to ten days of snowfall. Extreme temperatures recorded since 1961 are similar to those of many midwestern and eastern regions in the United States, ranging from -10 to 105°F (-22 to 41°C). The mean winter temperature (December to February) is 35°F (2°C) with summer temperatures normally ranging from 71 to 89°F (22 to 32°C).

Most of the Cape bulbs in Dr. Boussard's garden are grown under frames protected by movable glass. The glass cover is removed during the growth season of the winter-growing Cape bulbs from October until May but replaced in case of snow or frost. The ground in Dr. Boussard's garden may become hard-frozen to a depth of 1–2 inches (2.5–5.1 cm) for a week or sometimes two. Under these conditions, Dr. Boussard reports that the corms are unharmed even if the foliage is injured. He found that all his winter-growing Cape irids withstood a few degrees of frost, and several—*Gladiolus floribundus, G. tristis, Moraea bellendenii,* and some *Ixia* and *Sparaxis*—were quite hardy. In the glasshouse the air is moved by fans when the weather is too cold to open vents. Dr. Boussard uses extra fluorescent light for species that grow in Cape areas with strong winter sunshine, including *Anomalesia saccata, Gladiolus equitans,* and *Moraea bolusii.*

Dr. Boussard's garden has a light, neutral (pH = 7.2), well-drained soil. He grows most of his plants (except for seedlings) in the ground, since he perceives that pot culture often prevents flowering, does not allow a full spreading of the roots, and induces dying down too early.

Dr. Boussard plants irid corms at a depth three times their greatest dimension but reports that they often adjust themselves to their proper depth, which may range from 1 to 2 inches (2.5 to 5.1 cm) for small ones such as *Anomatheca* or *Romulea* down to an astonishing 12 inches (30.5 cm) for *Antholyza.* He leaves the corms undisturbed thoughout the year except to divide them and to treat species susceptible to pests with a pesticide at the end of the growing season. Treated corms are then replanted.

In early autumn, Dr. Boussard sows the seeds of the Cape natives. The light, well-drained medium is composed of 50 percent loam, 30 percent sand, 10 percent peat, and 10 percent vermiculite. It is kept slightly but constantly moist. Germination usually occurs within 36 weeks of sowing, though seed of some species may not germinate until the following season. Dr. Boussard keeps planted but ungerminated seeds at least two years before discarding them. Seedlings of winter-growing irids are grown in the cold house during their two first seasons. Dr. Boussard (1985, page 61) remarked that "failures exist indeed, but there are not too many."

GROWING CAPE BULBS FROM SEEDS

With only a few exceptions, my collection of species has been grown from seeds obtained from South African sources. Starting from seeds takes patience, since some species require a considerable number of years to flower. But I have found this method to be rewarding, because each year a new plant blooms for the first time in my garden, quite an exciting prospect, especially when the newcomer is a species I have never before seen in bloom. After nurturing a seedling for several years, I watch the bud formation with eager anticipation, hoping each morning that the day will be bright and warm enough to encourage the flower to open. With camera in place on its tripod I watch the event with the birds singing and the warmth of the spring sun on my back. Such an ambience in the garden makes the long wait worthwhile even on the rare occasion when the flower does not quite live up to expectations.

There are good reasons for growing Cape bulbs from seeds:

1. Bulbs imported to the Northern Hemisphere from South Africa are six months out of phase, and their acclimatization is sometimes difficult, whereas South African seeds planted in the Northern Hemisphere autumn produce seedlings in synchrony with the annual climatic cycle.

2. Growing bulbs from seeds is an inexpensive way to build stocks for mass planting.

3. Some bulbs do not readily multiply vegetatively and so are best increased from seeds.

4. Some species are not easy to maintain and decrease each year for reasons that are as yet unclear. In such cases it is a good idea to collect and plant seeds on a routine basis to ensure the continued presence of these species in a collection.

5. In the effort to conserve Cape bulbs through cultivation, the dissemination of species to gardeners throughout the world is best accomplished through seed exchanges, the practice followed by the Botanical Society of South Africa and the National Botanical Institute at Kirstenbosch.

In California I plant seeds of most of the Cape bulb species in the autumn. This gives them time as winter-growing plants to make as large a bulb as possible before they naturally go into a resting mode in late spring. The summer-growing species may be planted in the spring.

I prefer to use pots instead of seed flats because the corms of many seedlings produce two types of roots: fibrous roots and enlarged, fleshy, contractile roots that shorten to pull the corm to a given, often surprising depth (see Figure 2-1). *Babiana* corms, for example, are at the bottom of the pots by the end of their first growing season. I leave the seedlings undisturbed in the pots for at least two and often three years until they reach a size that enables them to be safely transferred to permanent containers or into the garden. The bulbs of some species are only the size of a pinhead at the end of their first season and are easily lost or overlooked.

For a seed-planting mix I use two parts washed river sand, one part screened peat moss, one part vermiculite, and one part screened forest humus, a commercial product resembling compost. The mix is put into 7-inch plastic pots with many drainage holes. I fill the pots with the planting medium, firm it down, plant the seeds, and cover them with a light layer of the medium, sand, or vermiculite. I then either sprinkle the pot very gently or float it in a tub of water until the water works up through the mix and glistens on the surface. The pots are placed in a shady location and kept moist until the seeds germinate, which with most Cape species requires a month or more. It is useful to treat the soil surface with a fungicide to discourage damping off.

After the seeds germinate I feed the seedlings every six weeks with a liquid fertilizer that has an N–P–K ratio of 16–4–2 and that contains trace elements of chelated iron, zinc, and manganese. This fertilizer is best used at half strength. The nitrogen does not appear to be detrimental to *Nerine* seedlings, though some say it is not advised. During the first couple of months the seedling pots are kept in partial shade; then they are moved into a sunnier location, where they remain during their first summer. A note of caution here: To avoid burning tender shoots, do not abruptly move a plant from shade to full sun if it is in an early growth stage.

FIGURE 2-1. Growth of seedling *Babiana villosa* with early, fleshy contractile root and later fibrous roots.

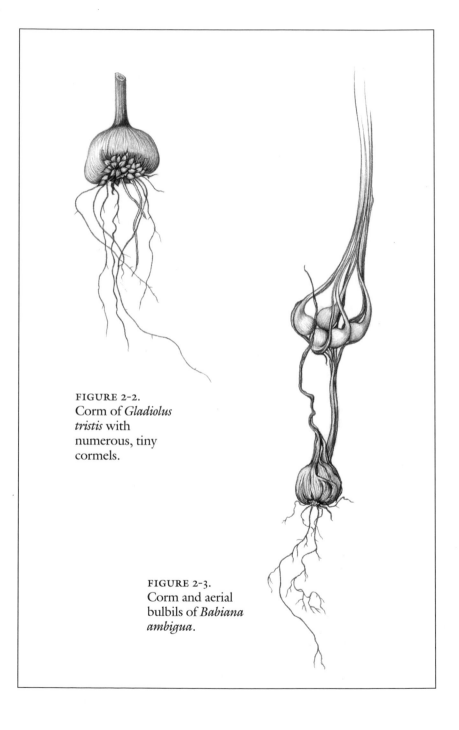

FIGURE 2-2.
Corm of *Gladiolus
tristis* with
numerous, tiny
cormels.

FIGURE 2-3.
Corm and aerial
bulbils of *Babiana
ambigua*.

Numerous tiny offsets, called cormels, are formed on the seedling corms sometime prior to flowering, usually during the second year (see Figure 2-2). Cormels are regularly formed by a mature plant, developing between the old and the new corm. The more shallowly placed corms produce the most cormels. The cormels can be separated from the mother corm and planted in the same manner as seeds, though somewhat deeper. During their first season they produce only grasslike foliage and a new corm; the cormel itself does not increase in size. The plant may bloom the second season. In the wild, the survival value of cormels is that they are numerous and in the proper site for the bulb's growth. They have little if any role in dispersal of the species, seeds being the major agents of dispersal of the Cape bulbs.

In addition to offsets and cormels, toward the end of the season many Cape bulb species form small bulbils in the leaf axils (see Figure 2-3). In the wild, these are freed as the foliage decomposes in the habitat. Under cultivation they can be removed and planted and perform in the same manner as cormels.

Survival of the clone is aided by cormels and bulbils. Dispersion and colonization in a new location are effected by seeds. Martyn Rix (1983, page 5) makes the observation that three parts of the plant evolved independently: "the bulbs in relation to climate and soil moisture, the flowers in response to pollinators, and seed dispersal in relation to habitat."

The seedlings as well as mature bulbs enjoy water during their growing season. In South Africa these bulbs grow in places that are damp during the winter and early spring. Often the soil was almost boggy as I sloshed through masses of Cape bulbs that grow in much drier conditions in my garden.

GARDENING IS THE ART OF WATERING

Correct watering is especially important in the cultivation of Cape bulbs. Delpierre and Du Plessis (1973, page 17), for example, write that it should be clear . . . that the way water is used is the determining factor in the successful cultivation of winter-growing Gladioli, and this is further confirmation of the fact that the art of gardening is largely a matter of how watering is carried out.

Certainly there is widespread agreement that proper watering of container-grown bulbs is critical to success. Generations of gardeners have been aware that capricious watering of Cape bulbs is their bane: They should be watered fairly frequently while they are making leaves, more sparingly after they are grown, and not at all when they are at rest.

The timely application and proper amount of water are very important in the culture of Cape bulbs. Watering practices should be adjusted to prevent the plant from being stressed for lack of available moisture, and at the same time to avoid continuous saturation of the soil mass in the pot. Normally the soil should be fairly dry before the plant is watered, then irrigation should be heavy—a practice that not only provides moisture but also tends to leach excess salts from the soil, thus preventing a saline build up.

Unfortunately, there are no precise indicators of water stress, so much depends upon the skill and good judgment of the gardener. When I was in South Africa I visited a former student who was managing an enormous farm under sprinkler irrigation. He had tensiometers and other advanced, state-of-the-art devices for measuring the moisture condition of the soil. I asked him which technique he relied on, and without saying a word, he grinned and handed me a shovel—the same technique I use when I scratch and probe into the bulbs' potting mix with my index finger.

THE OUTDOOR BED METHOD
IN THE NETHERLANDS

It is instructive to note some techniques for growing deciduous bulbs in outdoor beds. One technique used in the Netherlands is to plant into beds made by excavating to a depth of 14 inches (36 cm). The soil is replaced with a mixture of one part leaf mold, one part sand, and one part peat moss to which bonemeal is added. This mixture provides good drainage and some water retention for the bulbs. If the beds are used for seedlings, a light pre-plant application of a complete fertilizer (6–6–6 or 10–10–10) is broadcast over the beds, followed by watering to wash the fertilizer into the root zone. The seeds are planted, and the young seedlings are lifted at the end of the second season's growth and replanted at wider spacing where they will flower during their third year. Often the beds are under the shade of deciduous trees.

BULB CULTURE THROUGHOUT THE YEAR

After the spring flowers have finished blooming, their stalks should be removed unless seeds are to be harvested. However, the foliage still has a very important function. The green leaves continue to manufacture food materials that are stored in the new corm. Flower production in bulbs depends particularly upon the food materials stored in the corm after bloom (Hartmann and Kester, 1975). So the aging foliage should not be removed early. It is best to wait until the leaves have died back at least halfway before shearing them off at the ground level.

It is tricky to control weeds in beds of flowering bulbs. Hand pulling is still the most effective way to remove weeds, but other techniques can ameliorate the situation. Before bulbs are planted or before their growth begins, weed seeds can be germinated by thoroughly watering the beds; they can then be pulled or hoed before the first bulb shoots emerge. Chemical weed killers can be used, but many growers are averse to this approach. Instead it may be preferable to spread a fine mulch over the bulbs to deter weed growth. The bulbs have no problem growing through a layer of mulch, and it does deter most weeds. The weeds that do come up very conspicuously remind the gardener to pull them.

Just for a change of pace, the miniature Cape bulbs such as selected species of *Anomatheca*, *Lachenalia*, or *Lapeirousia* can temporarily be brought indoors. When the Cape bulbs are brought indoors, they last best in a cool, bright place. If kept continuously in a very warm house, the flowers will last only a few days. Small pots dry out fast indoors, so the soil moisture should be checked by means of the finger test almost daily. After the flowers fade, the container should be moved outdoors.

The small scale of the miniature Cape bulb species is particularly appropriate for the compact spaces often found in courtyards, entries, or raised beds around patios. Cape bulbs are especially effective plants for any site that will be viewed from close up, such as window boxes, entry containers, or planting beds along the top of a low wall. Planting in containers or pots makes it easier to move the plants into the limelight at the height of their bloom.

Most of the Cape bulbs bloom early in the spring and then die back for the summer. In the Northern Hemisphere, they will be well into their resting season by the end of June. This is the time to do the digging and dividing that will increase the bulbs' number and quality. It is advisable to dig and replant about a third of the bulbs each year. As they are unearthed, some are joined together and others are fully divided. If they do not separate easily and naturally, leave them joined together. The bulbs are best stored in a cool, dry place, certainly out of the sun. If different species or varieties are grown, the bulbs should be labeled. The stored bulbs can be dusted with an insecticidal or fungicidal dust. In northern latitudes, most Cape bulbs are ready to be replanted in containers or in the garden in early September. It is advisable to inspect the bulbs for signs of growth earlier, for some are ready to replant as early as August. I am always surprised to find roots developing and shoots starting to grow when I have scarcely removed the July page from the calendar.

Initially I was puzzled to find that in my garden not all the mature bulbs in the population of a particular species will become active. Instead it seems as if Mother Nature gives a few individuals a sabbatical leave, and they sit it out for the year, not even producing foliage. They are perfectly sound and healthy, and in a subsequent year they will perform perfectly. This is probably a survival trait that always leaves some individuals in reserve should there be a catastrophic year that wipes out plants that are growing and exposed above ground. I have noticed this occurring with some species of *Moraea*, and Dr. Boussard (1985) reported the same phenomenon with *Ferraria* and *Lapeirousia*. The phenomenon has been known in *Ferraria* since 1759 according to Miriam De Vos (1979), who suggested that it may be an adaptation to drought conditions. Perry et al. (1979) reported that only about 10 percent of *Drimia altissima* bulbs flower at the Karoo Botanic Garden each year. They also reported a paucity of flowers in *Brunsvigia josephinae*; a population of 20 bulbs produced no flowers in 1977, but following good rains and a good 1978 growing season, 14 of the bulbs flowered. This skipping a season and remaining dormant for a year may be much more common in Cape bulbs than we now know. It is probable that it occurs in the species from the more arid locations of the Cape (Namaqualand and the Karoo), where coping with a hostile environment is essential for survival.

LEAF CUTTINGS

I have found leaf cuttings to be a useful propagation technique with some *Lachenalia* species that are slow to increase vegetatively, such as *L. rubida* and *L. trichophylla*. Leaf cuttings have also proved successful with *Scadoxus* (*Haemanthus*) and are perhaps worth exploring with other genera. In this technique, the leaf is cut squarely across its base and is put into moist sand. If conditions are right, it will produce small bulbs.

In New Zealand, Terry Hatch (1987b, page 22) described his success with leaf cuttings of *Scadoxus albiflos*: "I detached three mature leaves and dipped the base in softwood hormone powder, then set each leaf into a pot of sand. These whole-leaf cuttings set a few bulbs at the base—about 20 in all." The next time he tried the technique he cut a single leaf into three parts, used the hormone powder, and set the cut leaf portions into a tray of sand under his propagation bench in a cool, shady spot. The top portion of the leaf produced the most bulbs, the middle produced fewer, and the bottom produced the least. From these cuttings he potted 67 strong bulbs and understandably concluded that he had found a fast way of increasing *S. albiflos*.

PESTS AND DISEASES

Fundamental tactics for control of Cape bulb pests and diseases occur in a sequence: (1) exclusion, (2) sanitation, (3) resistance, (4) removal, and (5) treatment. In each instance, correct identification of the pest or disease is essential for effective control.

Exclusion has several aspects. Major pest problems often result from the accidental transport of diseased, pest-infested, or potentially noxious plant material from one area of the world to another. Legal barriers in the form of quarantine laws now restrict such free and unrestrained movement of alien plant material into many countries. In the United States, the federal regulations are promulgated and enforced by the Animal and Plant Health Inspection Service (APHIS). Another type of exclusion is inadvertent, which is the situation with bulbous plants that are mostly transported either as seeds or as bulbs, precluding the importation of many bulb diseases or pests that have their life cycle above ground. Such pathogens or insect pests are transported only with foliage. Finally, the individual gardener can exclude pests and diseases by carefully selecting and buying only healthy bulbs or by growing a Cape bulb collection from seeds.

Sanitation is an important garden practice. Cleaning up debris that can harbor slugs, snails, or pest insects is advisable, as is the removal of weeds that can be the source of viruses and insect vectors of viruses.

Resistance to pests and diseases is enhanced in vigorous plants. Vigor is encouraged by good cultural practices. Overcrowding, overfeeding, wrong exposure, poor drainage, and similar bad environmental conditions weaken plants and increase susceptibility to pests and diseases. These conditions also invite physiological deficiencies, which are diseases in the broad sense.

Removal is the deliberate handpicking and disposal of pest organisms such as snails, slugs, beetles, caterpillars, or mealybugs from the foliage. This removal tactic also encompasses the individual roguing out of a virus-infected or otherwise unfit bulbous plant.

Treatment for pest control is usually chemical, although physical heat is used in some situations. Gardeners everywhere are now aware of the global contamination by pesticides, which resulted from their unrestrained use in the decades immediately following World War II. Gardeners understand that any toxic material must be used with prudence and caution and that it is wise to select a product having the least risk to the gardener and to the environment. I have an aversion to pesticides because I have spent 30 years advocating natural, nonchemical, biological control with prudent use of insecticides only when absolutely necessary. This environmentally correct approach is now called integrated pest management (IPM).

Pests have not been a serious problem in my garden. The insects and plant diseases that plague the South African gardeners seem mercifully to be absent. While Cape bulbs have fewer pest and disease problems than many other plant groups, they are by no means immune and exempt from such troubles.

One common problem, shared by all growers of *Gladiolus*, is foliage and flower injury caused by thrips. These are minute, slender-bodied insects with narrow, fringed wings. A hand lens is necessary to see their morphological characteristics. There are many species (about 180 in California alone). Some are cosmopolitan in distribution, and a few are vectors of virus. They feed on both flowers and foliage. Their sucking mouthparts leave white spots and streaks. *Taeniothrips simplex*, the *Gladiolus* thrips, injures the leaves and reduces the size, development, and color of *Gladiolus* flowers. Thrips are more damaging to the summer-growing *Gladiolus* species than to the winter-growing species that flower during the colder weather when the thrips are not so active. Stored *Gladiolus* corms can harbor thrips, so I treat stored corms with an insecticidal dust.

Aphids are also common pests of Cape bulbs throughout the world. They are small, delicate, somewhat pear-shaped green or black insects with long legs and antennae. Unlike other insects, they have a pair of tubelike structures called *cornicles* projecting backward near the posterior end of the body. Aphids form colonies of numerous individuals on the succulent shoots and leaves. Most of the aphids in the colony will be wingless. They have sucking mouthparts, and a plant suffers from loss of plant juices. Aphids excrete a sticky substance called honeydew, which becomes the substrate for a black fungus termed sooty mold. Aphids can also transmit viruses (usually the mosaic viruses).

Aphids can be washed off the foliage, but to remove them I gently rub the infested leaf between thumb and forefinger or with a damp cloth. When they are among the flowers in a dense raceme or spike, there is little that can be done except to use some insecticidal spray. Aphids do attack the inflorescence of *Bulbinella*. They have many natural enemies, the most familiar being ladybugs (Coccinelid beetles), the larvae of syrphid flies, and tiny parasitic wasps. Any of these can and do wipe out aphid colonies.

Spider mites are also worldwide pests of bulb foliage. These tiny creatures that vary in color from yellow to orange to red damage plants by sucking fluids from leaf tissue. Injury from mites shows as very fine whitish to yellowish stippling on the upper leaf surface. Fine webbing is often present on the underside of a leaf. Frequent and forceful spraying with water on the underside of the leaf helps to control mites. If an insecticide is used, frequent applications may be necessary. Spider mites are not a problem for me in the outdoor garden, but I occasionally find them in the greenhouse.

Mealybugs are soft, slow-moving, elongate-oval insects covered with a mealy or cottony wax secretion. They tend to clump together in colonies that detract from the plant's appearance. They withdraw plant sap through their threadlike mouth parts, which diminishes plant vigor. In the garden they are suppressed by natural enemies, but they sometimes occur on greenhouse plants. I remove them by handpicking or with a swab of rubbing alcohol. Chemical pesticides can be used, in which case the potted plant should be taken outdoors for the treatment.

Whiteflies are listed as pests of Cape bulbs by Du Plessis and Duncan (1989). These are not flies (Diptera) but are close relatives of aphids and mealybugs. The adults have four powdery, white wings. When disturbed they take flight for a few seconds and quickly settle back on the foliage. Their larvae are found on the underside of leaves. These immature stages are flattened, oval, and sessile, remaining in one place to suck out the plant sap. Whiteflies tend to be greenhouse pests. Pesticides, if used, must be applied to the underside of leaves to be effective. Natural enemies depress outdoor whitefly populations.

In South Africa, Du Plessis and Duncan (1989) also reported problems with the larvae of several moth species, including cutworms and boll worms. We have these Lepidoptera in North America, but they have never troubled my collection of Cape bulbs.

Widespread in Africa is a black, yellow-banded caterpillar (*Brithys pancratii*) called the lily borer, *Amaryllis* lily borer, or *Crinum* borer. These common names suggest the range of its plant hosts. The larva feeds as it moves down the leaf stalk and later attacks the bulb. It can be hand-picked or treated with an insecticide.

The one insect most damaging to my collection is *Stenopelmatus fuscus*, the subterranean Jerusalem cricket, which is neither a cricket nor from Jerusalem. These insects are also called potato bugs. The species, an Orthopteran belonging to the family Stenopelmatidae, is indigenous to the western states and common on the West Coast. It enters the tubs through the side drainage holes. Fortunately it seems to be territorial, for I rarely find more than a single individual per tub. These pests are more than an annoyance because the loss of a rare bulb is far more serious than the cosmetic injury caused by thrips or aphids. The best opportunity to remove any Jerusalem cricket is when the bulbs are lifted from a tub.

Nematodes are minute worms that attack the roots of many plants. They are managed by using sterilized soil.

Finally, among the other important invertebrate pests are slugs and snails. An effective control program begins with sanitation. Removing boards, stones, litter, and other debris that serve as shelters is the first step. Consistent handpicking is effective, particularly if done after dark. For disposal they can be bagged. The bag is then crushed before being deposited in the trash can. Snails and slugs can be trapped under boards or flower pots where they seek shelter during the day. A saucer or pan placed in a depression in the ground with its lip at the surface and filled with beer to which some yeast is added will attract and trap snails and slugs. Each morning they should be removed and disposed of. Poisoned baits may also be used.

In addition to pests, the Cape bulbs are susceptible to disease. The pathogens may be bacteria, fungi, or viruses. Included with diseases are physiological disorders.

Viruses may be transmitted mechanically by the use of infected cutting tools, but most transmission is by insect vectors such as aphids and thrips. Insect vectors transmit the virus by feeding on a virus-infested Cape bulb plant and then moving to feed on a healthy one. Symptoms of a virus infection include deformed leaves or mottled and streaked leaves or flowers. Similar conditions may not be caused by a viral infection but may instead result from feeding damage by insects or mites or from physiological disorders. When the diagnosis clearly indicates a viral disease, the plant must be destroyed.

Bacteria can cause root rot and reduce rootstocks of Cape bulbs to a soggy mess. A diseased plant must be removed and the soil sterilized to prevent spread of the bacteria. Conditions favorable for such rot are induced by moisture and warmth during the summer when the aestivating Cape bulb should have a dry environment. Bacteria can cause necrotic lesions on leaves, which should then be cut off and destroyed.

Fungi may also cause leaf spots, especially during wet weather, and fungal infections can cause root rot, which good drainage helps to prevent. Stored bulbs are susceptible to attack by such molds as *Botrytis*, *Fusarium*, and *Penicillium*. Commercial bulb growers have developed carefully regulated heat treatments for their control. Fungicidal dusts are useful in their control and may be the best option for most gardeners.

Damping-off is the fungus disease that can devastate young seedlings. It is mostly caused by *Pythium,* which attacks the base of the young shoot, causing it to collapse. Crowded seedlings are the most susceptible because the fungus spreads progressively through them. To discourage damping-off, the seeds should be sown sparsely and the seedlings kept well ventilated. Water only in the morning so that the soil will be drier overnight.

During prolonged periods of cloudy, cool, rainy, humid, and moist conditions, Cape bulbs are susceptible to powdery mildew (*Oidium*), which appears as a gray powder on the leaves. The same conditions encourage the growth of rust fungi such as *Uromyces* and *Phragmidium* (Du Plessis and Duncan, 1989). Repeated sprays of fungicides are suggested for control in these situations.

HYBRIDIZING

Cape bulbs have been used extensively in breeding programs to develop modern cultivars, particularly those of *Freesia, Gladiolus, Lachenalia, Nerine, Ornithogalum,* and *Sparaxis.* Intergeneric crosses of *Homoglossum* and *Gladiolus* have produced the interesting "homoglads" (Ingram, 1977). *Amaryllis belladonna* has been crossed with *Brunsvigia, Crinum,* and *Nerine* to produce hybrids called *Brunsdonna,* × *Amacrinum,* × *Crinodonna,* and *Amnerine.* Intrageneric breeding projects are in progress on *Lachenalia, Ornithogalum,* and *Zantedeschia* (Brown, 1990; Meyer et al., 1990).

The gene pools of the Cape bulb species offer exciting possibilities to the hybridizer for developing an array of splendid garden flowers. Fortunately, hybridizing is an activity in which any patient and interested gardener can participate.

The procedure for hybridizing is basically simple. First, the anthers are excised from the flower selected as the seed parent so that it will not self-pollinate. This is best done with tweezers or forceps. If the species is self-sterile, removal of the anthers is not strictly necessary. Next, pollen is collected on a small brush from the anthers of the flower selected as the male (pollen) parent. This is then carried to the flower of the seed parent and placed on its stigma. The pollinated flower should then be bagged to exclude pollinators, such as bees, that could carry other pollen to the stigma. The flower should be labeled with a tag indicating the date and the cross involved in the following manner: seed parent species × pollen parent species. In practice, an example is *Gladiolus tristis* × *Homoglossum huttonii*. After the seed capsule matures, the seeds are removed, propagated, and grown to maturity. Their flowers are hybrids that may exhibit genetic features inherited from both parent flowers. This is the first filial generation, which is abbreviated as the F_1 generation.

A sustained plant-breeding program is more sophisticated and has more complications. It involves genetic principles, definite goals, technical planning, and perseverance. The plant breeder has specific aims and selects carefully among the hybrid individuals for desirable characteristics. A good plant breeder must have a keen eye for the traits in plants to be preserved and a hard heart to discard and incinerate everything else.

Species or varieties or other good candidates for hybridization experiments often flower at different times. In such cases it is sometimes necessary to store pollen until the flowers of the female parent are available. Marcia Wilson (1982) described a technique for storing amaryllid pollen, a procedure that may also be applicable to many Cape bulbs. As she pointed out, sophisticated methods have been developed for commercial freezing or storage of various pollens, but for the average hobbyist, who is primarily concerned with safe storage of pollen for just one season of bloom, the following suggestions are useful.

For pollen storage, use small containers such as glassine envelopes obtained from a stamp dealer or stationery store, or empty gelatin capsules from a pharmacy or natural food store. Place the clipped anther (pollen sac) into the appropriately labeled container, which should be kept open until the anther dries and shrinks and the pollen becomes powdery. This does not take long; the pollen can mature and become powdery after a single night in a warm room. Next, close the small container and store it in a refrigerator in a small glass jar with a tight-fitting lid. No special drying agent is necessary if the pollen is to be used within three months. For longer storage sufficient for one season, place 0.5–1 inch (1.3–2.5 cm) of powdered milk or silica gel in the jar. To preserve viable pollen for six months to a year, keep the air-tight jar with drying agent in the freezer. When this aged pollen is used, it should be lavishly applied with a small brush to an obviously receptive (sticky) stigma.

CUT FLOWERS

Many Cape flowers, with their fragile beauty, are fine and sought-after additions to cut-flower arrangements. Some, such as *Ornithogalum thyrsoides,* have a naturally long vase life, but the longevity of other cut flowers occasionally needs assistance.

A very effective method for extending the life of cut flowers is to keep their stems in a liquid medium consisting of two tablespoons of lemon juice and one tablespoon of sugar mixed into one quart of water, with a slight amount (one-half teaspoon) of household bleach added. Cutting the stems a second time after they are in this solution will help them continue to absorb water and nutrients.

CHAPTER 3

A Cape Bulb Encyclopedia

CAPE BULB NOMENCLATURE AND CLASSIFICATION

Cape flowers have been variously named from prehistoric to modern times by the Bushmen, Dutch, English, Hottentots, and Portugese (Smith, 1966). The many common or vernacular names were essential for communication among and between the indigenous peoples and earliest immigrants from Europe. Scientific names for the Cape bulbs came into being when botanists arrived to explore the Cape and applied to its flora the binomial system of nomenclature used internationally in the biological sciences. This system was developed in Sweden by Carl Linnaeus. His master work, *Species Plantarum,* published in 1753, is universally recognized as the starting point for the nomenclature of flowering plants.

Linnaeus named hundreds of Cape flowers, including many Cape bulbs. According to Conrad Lighton (1973, page 13), "it is almost impossible to traverse any part of the [Cape] Floral Kingdom today without finding species of plants personally named by Linnaeus."

Linnaeus had a sporadic correspondence in Latin with Ryk Tulbagh, governor of the Cape from 1751 until 1771. In one remarkable letter published by Coombs (1948, page 104) and later by Lighton (1973, page 15), Linnaeus wrote:

> May you be fully aware of your fortunate lot in being permitted . . .
> to enjoy . . . that paradise on earth, the Cape of Good Hope, which

the Beneficent Creator has enriched with His choicest wonders. Certainly if I were at liberty to change my fortune for that of Alexander the Great, or of Solomon, Croesus or Tulbagh, I should without hesitation prefer the latter. May you long enjoy your enviable situation.

Governor Tulbagh sent many plants, bulbs, and seeds to Linnaeus, who named the Cape bulb genus *Tulbaghia* in his honor. *Amaryllis, Cyanella,* and *Moraea* are other Linnaean genera. Many species named by Linnaeus were gathered by two Swedish plant collectors—Anders Sparrman and Carl Peter Thunberg, a brilliant pupil of Linnaeus—who arrived at Cape Town just four days apart in April 1772.

Sparrman dispatched his Cape collection to Linnaeus in November 1772 just before he signed on with Captain James Cook, whose ship, *Resolution*, was then anchored in Table Bay. Cook was embarked on his second great voyage around the world. Apparently Sparrman took the place of Francis Masson, the Scottish botanist from Kew, who had arrived aboard the *Resolution*. Masson and Thunberg explored the Cape peninsula on foot in 1773 and went into the Karoo by ox-drawn wagon. These three early collectors—Sparrman, Thunberg, and Masson—found many of the Cape bulbs we know today and a few that are now extinct.

The Linnaean system of nomenclature uses a generic name followed by a specific epithet. The genus name is capitalized, the species name is not. This botanical or scientific name is used for the particular species throughout the world, permitting accurate communication among botanists regardless of their native language and helping to avoid the confusion caused by the multiplicity of vernacular names. For example, in the Cape there are about 85 species of the genus *Gladiolus*. Each has been separately described, named, and published by a botanist. Thus *G. debilis* and *G. carneus* refer to plants with distinct identities though both go by the common name painted lady.

Gardeners who feel intimidated by scientific names may learn to appreciate not only their precision but also the information they convey about the plant's history. For the most part, species names represent attempts to describe an outstanding characteristic of the plant in the most abbreviated way possible, a single word. Sometimes the species epithet honors some historic figure in botany, reminding us of a particular contribution and period in botanical history or plant exploration; an example is *Freesia sparrmanii*. Other species names reflect the geographic location from which the plants were obtained, such as *Lachenalia capensis* from the Cape or *L. namaquensis* from Namaqualand. Still others reflect human error or confusion, as in mistakenly giving a bulb from South Africa the species name *canadensis*. The origins of scientific names are often fascinating, and I have gone to some effort to include them in the following encyclopedic listing of Cape bulbs.

Many gardeners find to their chagrin that no sooner is a scientific name accepted and widely used than some taxonomic botanist finds it necessary to change it because he or she has discovered an earlier name for that species. This is the law of priority. To taxonomists, it is as immutable as the law of gravity: If two or more names have been applied to a single species, the one first published prevails, and all later names are considered synonyms. In the following encyclopedia, plants are listed under the names currently considered correct, and synonyms are indicated in parentheses where approrpriate.

Until recently the Cape bulbs were principally placed taxonomically in three plant families: the Amaryllidaceae, the Iridaceae, or the Liliaceae *sensu lato*. (In taxonomy *sensu lato* means the taxon is considered in the broadest sense.) These three families are distinguished by differences in the reproductive structures of their flowers.

To determine which family a Cape bulb belongs to, first count the male (pollen-producing) structures, or *stamens*. A stamen consists of the *filament*, a slender stalk bearing at its apex the *anther*, which contains the grains of pollen. If there are three stamens, the plant belongs to the Iridaceae. If there are six stamens, look next at the female structure, or *pistil*, to determine whether the flower belongs to the Amaryllidaceae or the Liliaceae *sensu lato*. The pistil consists of the basal *ovary*, which contains the seeds, then a stalk-like extension of the ovary, the *style*, that is capped by the *stigma*, which receives the pollen. If the ovary is beneath the free portions of the other flower parts, or *inferior*, the plant belongs to the Amaryllidaceae. If the ovary is above them, or *superior*, the plant belongs to Liliaceae *sensu lato*. Using this information, a simple key to the major family concepts of Cape bulbs can be constructed.

Key to Major Families of the Cape Bulbs

1 Three stamens .... Iridaceae
  Six stamens 2
    2 Ovary inferior .... Amaryllidaceae
      Ovary superior .... Liliaceae *sensu lato*

The arrangement of flowers on a stalk is important in classification. The simplest is a single flower at the end of the stalk, or *peduncle*. Alternately, individual flowers may have a *pedicel* (stem). When the pedicels of all the flowers arise from a single point on a central stalk, the *inflorescence* (flower cluster) is an *umbel,* which gives the flower head the globelike appearance seen in *Agapanthus, Amaryllis, Brunsvigia,* and *Nerine.* When the flowers are without pedicels and are borne along a central stalk, as in *Onixotis,* the arrangement is called a *spike*. When the flowers grow along a single stalk but each flower has its own short pedicel, as in *Lachenalia*, the inflorescence is called a *raceme*.

Cape bulb flowers do not have the common architecture and familiar flower arrangement of petals forming a corolla subtended by sepals forming the calyx. Instead, in Cape bulbs there is no clear separation of calyx and corolla, but together they form a tubelike structure, the *perianth* (Figure 3-1). The apex of the perianth is usually divided into several *segments, lobes,* or *tepals*, terms used interchangeably by many growers; the term *segment* is used here. If the segments are evenly arranged and radiate from the flower center, the flower is regular, or *actinomorphic*. If the segments are arranged otherwise, the flower is irregular, or *zygomorphic*.

Some taxonomists considered the concept of Liliaceae to be too broad and therefore extensively and fundamentally restructured it by segregating several distinct and valid families. Bond and Goldblatt (1984) believed that as presently structured, Liliaceae itself is strictly a Northern Hemisphere family, so they did not include it in the Cape flora. Instead they recognized the segregates Alliaceae, Asparagaceae, Asphodelaceae, Colchicaceae, Dracaenaceae, Eriospermaceae, and Hyacinthaceae—four of which contain Cape bulbs—and I have followed their arrangement here. A simplified key to these four segregated families (adapted from Perry, 1985) follows.

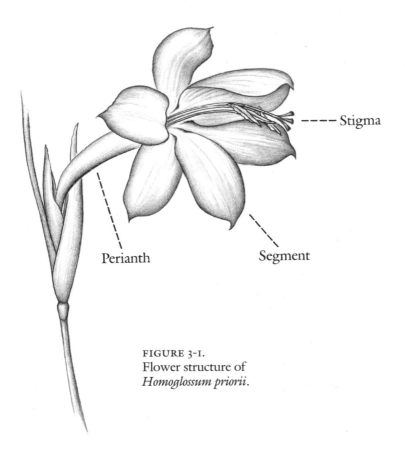

Stigma

Perianth

Segment

FIGURE 3-1.
Flower structure of
Homoglossum priorii.

Key to Cape Bulb Families

1 Stigma with three branches, rootstock a corm .... Colchicaceae
Stigma entire, rootstock a bulb, rhizome, or fleshy roots 2
   2 Plant with fibrous or tuberous rhizome .... Asphodelaceae
   Plant with bulb or swollen, fleshy roots, not a rhizome 3
      3 Inflorescence a raceme .... Hyacinthaceae
      Inflorescence an umbel-like cluster .... Alliaceae

THE CAPE BULBS: *AGAPANTHUS* TO *ZANTEDESCHIA*

The following encyclopedic listing of Cape bulbs is arranged alphabetically by genus, with the taxonomic family noted. Terminology used in the entries is explained in the Glossary.

Agapanthus (Alliaceae)

Agapanthus is in the Alliaceae, a family segregated from Liliaceae by Bond and Goldblatt (1984). Professional botanists are not in agreement on this particular family placement, and some very respected authors put this genus in the Amaryllidaceae. According to Robert Haller, a professor of botany at the University of California at Santa Barbara, it depends on to whom you talk. *Agapanthus* has a superior ovary, which keys it out to Liliaceae *sensu lato*. In accordance with the current interpretation of South African flora, it then segregates to Alliaceae. Another view is that all liliaceous plants with flowers in an umbel should be placed in the Amaryllidaceae. This uncertainty among taxonomists shows that taxa are often artificial and subjective, being imperfect human efforts to organize the complexities of the natural world.

The name *Agapanthus* is derived from the Greek *agape*, "love," and *anthos*, "flower," so it could be translated romantically as "flower of love." The verb *agapeo* also means "to be well contented with" (Jackson and MacGregor, 1985). The common name is lily of the Nile, although there is no connection whatsoever with that river. *Agapanthus* is South African, but only three of the ten species are Cape bulbs, and they are absent from the arid areas.

Agapanthus has been used by the Bantus in magic and medicine, and pieces of root were worn by Xhosa brides to ensure fertility.

The first plants introduced from the Cape to Europe were those that were readily available and grew near Cape Town, so it is understandable that *Agapanthus africanus* was, in 1679, the first species of the genus to be cultivated and illustrated. It was then called the African hyacinth (Duncan, 1985).

In *Agapanthus* the two major foliage groups are evergreen and deciduous and the two types of flowers are pendulous tubular flowers and open, bell or trumpet-shaped flowers in an umbel. The two species from the southwestern Cape are *Agapanthus africanus*, which blooms profusely after wildfires, and the rare *A. walshii*, which is the only evergreen species that has pendulous flowers. I have not grown *A. walshii* because I have never found it available. According to Duncan (1985a), it grows in a very restricted area in the Steenbras mountains, Caledon District, specifically near Steenbras Dam, where it occurs as a single plant or in very small clumps. Duncan (1983b) describes a white form of *A. walshii*.

The third species, *Agapanthus praecox*, is found in the eastern Cape, where rains are more frequent than in the southwestern Cape. It is quite variable and is the species most commonly grown worldwide.

The differences between *Agapanthus africanus* and *A. praecox* as given in the key by Frances Leighton (1965) seem minimal, being based on the texture of the perianth and its shade of blue. But Leighton made her revision of the genus only after intensive study, and she is the recognized authority (and therefore persuasive voice) on the classification of *Agapanthus* species. Her key reads as follows:

Perianth thick in texture, deep blue in color: inflorescence few, many-flowered but not dense .... *A. africanus*
Perianth thin in texture, pale–medium blue in color: inflorescence few, many-flowered or dense .... *A. praecox*

Agapanthus praecox (*praecox* means "precocious") was separated into three subspecies by Leighton (1965): *A. praecox* subsp. *praecox*, *A. praecox* subsp. *minimus*, and *A. praecox* subsp. *orientalis*. Except for the dwarf *A. praecox* subsp. *minimus*, it is difficult to differentiate these subspecies of *A. praecox* with confidence. Most bulb catalogs sell *A. praecox* as *A. orientalis*. The many cultivars are available in varying shades of light to deeper blue, and there is a white form. *Agapanthus praecox* subsp. *minimus* grows from 12 to 18 inches (30 to 46 cm). *Agapanthus praecox* subsp. *orientalis* differs from *A. africanus*. It is taller, growing easily to 4 feet (122 cm), and it has more flowers in the umbel (see Figure 3-2). *Agapanthus africanus* is about 2 feet (61 cm) and is typically of a somewhat darker blue. It, too, has a white variety.

Agapanthus is easily grown from seeds. My garden records show germination of *A. africanus* in 24–30 days, *A. campanulatus* in 28 days, *A. caulescens* in 19 days, *A. comptonii* (Plate 8) in 20–25 days, *A. inapertus* in 26 days, and *A. praecox* in 23–28 days. Seedlings may take three to four years to flower. Generally, *Agapanthus* species are best increased by dividing the clumps, preferably in the spring, but the evergreen species can also be divided in the fall. When grown in containers, the mass of rhizomes and fleshy roots can more easily be split using a sharp spade. The plants do not mind crowding and will bloom well in containers. The clumps should be divided every four to six years. They respond to summer feeding and do best if kept in rich moist soil, but they can stand some drying in the winter. On the west coast of California they do well in full sun, but where summers are hotter, some shade is advisable. *Agapanthus* is used extensively in parkways and around municipal buildings in southern California. It is reported that some can withstand the winters in USDA zone 7. The deciduous species, which I have never grown, go dormant in the winter. They may be grown in colder climates but need mulch in the winter.

The tall stalks of *Agapanthus praecox* subsp. *orientalis* make it a good accent plant. The foliage is glossy and attractive. It flowers in summer over an extended period. It is sometimes effectively planted under

FIGURE 3-2.
Agapanthus praecox
subsp. *orientalis*, flowers
in an umbel.

Jacaranda trees because they bloom simultaneously, and the colors harmonize. Inter-plantings of *Agapanthus* and *Amaryllis belladonna* are often seen. The evergreen foliage of *Agapanthus* hides the bare bases of the *Amaryllis* flower stalks and provides skirts for the naked ladies. Graham Duncan (1985) at Kirstenbosch suggests *Agapanthus* be used in mixed plantings with the tall, stately, yellow-flowered *Chasmanthe floribunda* var. *duckittii*.

All *Agapanthus* are good cut flowers. There is much to recommend both *A. africanus* and *A. praecox* subsp. *orientalis*, the two outstanding species from the Cape Province.

Albuca (Hyacinthaceae)

According to Ray Genders (1973), *Albuca* takes its name from *albus,* "white," but John Bryan (1989) says that *albucus* was the name given by the Greeks to a white species of *Asphodelus*, a genus of bulbs that does not occur in South Africa. Bond and Goldblatt (1984) list 11 species of *Albuca* in the Cape flora.

The flower shape is characteristic for all the Cape species of *Albuca*. The flowers may be hanging or erect, but they always have three straight outer perianth segments held at an angle of about 45 degrees. The three inner segments form a slightly inflated tube. These inner segments with their hoodlike knobbed tips each enclose a fertile stamen and have earned the plant the quaint common name of sentry in a box.

The color of the *Albuca* flowers is hardly striking. Perry and Bayer (1980) think of it as a camouflage greenish yellow that merges into the surrounding foliage.

Albuca altissima lives up to its name, for it is a tall plant reaching about 36 inches (91 cm). It is the most widespread and common species in the Cape, where it is found growing in areas of deeper soil. It blooms over a period of several months from late winter into spring. The flowers are white and green. The outer stamens are sterile. The foliage is lanceolate, bluish green, and fleshy. Frankly, these flowers lack excitement.

PLATE 1. Richness of Cape flora.

PLATE 2. Namaqualand in flower.

PLATE 3. A Precambrian granite klipkoppie, a treasure house of Cape bulbs.

PLATE 4. *Babiana* sp. growing in granite outcrop.

PLATE 5. *Lapeirousia silenoides* and *Lachenalia* sp. growing in granite rock crevice.

PLATE 6. Cape bulbs growing in wet location in the Cape veld.

PLATE 7. Bulb house at Kirstenbosch.

PLATE 8. *Agapanthus comptonii*.

PLATE 9. *Albuca namaquensis.*

PLATE 10. *Amaryllis* 'Multiflora', white form.

PLATE 11. *Anapalina caffra*.

PLATE 12. *Anomalesia cunonia*.

PLATE 13. *Antholyza plicata.*

PLATE 14. *Aristea ecklonii*.

PLATE 15. *Babiana nana*.

PLATE 16. *Babiana villosa*.

PLATE 17. *Brunsvigia litoralis*.

PLATE 18. *Bulbinella latifolia*.

PLATE 19. *Chasmanthe floribunda*
var. *duckittii*.

PLATE 20. *Chasmanthe floribunda* var. *antholyzoides*.

PLATE 21. *Clivia miniata*.

PLATE 22. *Clivia miniata* var. *citrina*.

PLATE 23. *Cyanella lutea*.

PLATE 24. *Cyrtanthus hybrid*.

PLATE 25. *Dierama pendulum*.

PLATE 26. *Ferraria densepunctulata*.

PLATE 27. *Freesia occidentalis*.

PLATE 28. *Galtonia candicans*.

PLATE 29. *Geissorhiza radians*.

PLATE 30. *Geissorhiza splendidissima*.

PLATE 31. *Gladiolus alatus.*

PLATE 32. *Gladiolus uysiae.*

PLATE 33. *Gladiolus carneus*, white form.   PLATE 34. *Gladiolus aureus*.

PLATE 35. *Gladiolus citrinus*.

PLATE 36. *Gladiolus caryophyllaceus*.

PLATE 37. *Gladiolus undulatus*.

PLATE 38. *Hesperantha vaginata*.

PLATE 39. *Homeria collina*.

PLATE 40. *Homeria comptonii*.

PLATE 41. *Homoglossum priorii*.

PLATE 42. *Ixia dubia*.

PLATE 43. *Ixia conferta*.

PLATE 44. *Ixia viridiflora*.

PLATE 45. *Lachenalia viridiflora*.

PLATE 46. *Lachenalia bulbifera*.

PLATE 47. *Lachenalia aloides* var. *quadricolor*.

PLATE 48. *Lachenalia mutabilis*.

PLATE 49. *Lachenalia framesii.*

PLATE 50. *Lachenalia namaquensis*.   PLATE 51. *Lachenalia rosea*.

PLATE 52. *Massonia angustifolia*.

PLATE 53. *Melasphaerula ramosa*.

PLATE 54. *Moraea aristata*.

PLATE 55. *Moraea gigandra*.

PLATE 56. *Moraea tricolor*, a dwarf species.

PLATE 57. *Moraea neopavonia*.

PLATE 58. *Nerine alta.*

PLATE 59. *Onixotis triquetra.*

PLATE 60. *Ornithogalum thyrsoides.*

PLATE 61. *Ornithogalum dubium*.

PLATE 62. *Ornithhogalum fimbri-marginatum*.

PLATE 63. *Polyxena ensifolia*.

PLATE 64. *Romulea sabulosa.*

PLATE 65. *Romulea hantamensis.*

PLATE 66. *Romulea tortuosa*.

PLATE 67. *Romulea flava*.

PLATE 68. *Sparaxis elegans*.

PLATE 69. *Sparaxis tricolor*.

PLATE 70. *Spiloxene canaliculata*.

PLATE 71. *Synnotia villosa*.

PLATE 72. *Veltheimia capensis*.

PLATE 73. *Watsonia coccinea*.

PLATE 74. *Watsonia wilmaniae*.

PLATE 75. *Zantedeschia elliotiana*.

Albuca canadensis is wrongly named and a classic example of a mistake in nomenclature. This strictly South African species was originally and erroneously thought to grow in Canada. The name will continue indefinitely, reflecting a puzzling act on the part of its author, Linnaeus. According to Bryan (1989), Linnaeus knew of the true origin but nevertheless named the species *canadensis* because it was listed by Jacques Nornutus in a book of Canadian plants. It is a coastal dune plant in the Cape but can also be found inland, where it grows on rocky slopes. The bulbs are reportedly edible (Du Plessus and Duncan, 1989). The flowers are pale yellowish green with green stripes. Three of the stamens are sterile. The species grows less than 24 inches (61 cm) in height and blooms in early spring. It is easy to grow from seeds, which germinate in 23–29 days.

Perry and Bayer (1980) report that *Albuca canadensis* and *A. namaquensis* grow side by side in parts of the Karoo Garden Veld Reserve. *Albuca canadensis* covers a wider area, growing on rocky slopes, and it flowers slightly earlier; *A. namaquensis* (Figure 3-3) has more leaves, some with curled tips (see Plate 9).

Leaves with coiled tips are characteristic of *Albuca spiralis*, and they give the species some interest. The flowers, which bloom in spring, are yellow with a green median stripe to each perianth segment. All the stamens are fertile. The plants are rather small, reaching about 12 inches (30 cm). The flat black seeds germinate in 21 days.

There are a number of *Albuca* species in the Cape region yet to be described and named. It is interesting that while eight different species of *Albuca* are sympatric and bloom simultaneously, there is no evidence of natural hybridization in the wild according to Perry and Bayer (1980).

Propagation of *Albuca* is by offsets or seeds. The seeds are black, flat, light for their size, and copiously produced. They germinate readily. *Albuca aurea* has germinated for me in just 10 days. While some seedlings may bloom their first season, most flower in their second year.

These flowers may be of more interest to bulb collectors than to gardeners because their usefulness is limited. They are not showy, though

FIGURE 3-3.
Characteristic sentry-
in-a-box flowers of
Albuca namaquensis.

they can provide a contrast to more colorful plants in a bulb border; Una Van Der Spuy (1976) considers them to be charming flowers for pots or window boxes where they can be seen at eye level.

Amaryllis (Amaryllidaceae)

Amaryllis is named after a shepherdess who appears in Theocritus, Virgil, and Ovid (Jackson and MacGregor, 1987).

Though the genus is monotypic, containing the single species *Amaryllis belladonna*, it seems to have had more written about it than any other Cape bulb. Much of this literature stems from a great fuss about nomenclature. Some taxonomists, including Traub (1963), have contended that Linnaeus had a different plant in mind when he named *Amaryllis belladonna* and that the species should be called *Brunsvigia rosea*. However, this theory is no longer accepted, and Les Hannibal (1980) commented that the use of *B. rosea* for this Cape species should be relegated to the dust bin. Actually, the issue was resolved by an international committee, and its official decision to have the name *Amaryllis* reserved for *A. belladonna* alone was reported in *Taxon*, volume 3, part 8, page 231 (1954).

The bronzy green stems of *Amaryllis belladonna*, each topped with a large, spearpoint-shaped flower bud, burst suddenly out of the heat-baked soil of summer and grow rapidly to more than 24 inches (61 cm) in a few days. This explosive growth has caused some folks to call the plants surprise lilies. The species epithet *belladonna* means "beautiful lady." The sudden appearance of the tall, bare flower stalk without any foliage accounts for its most common name, naked ladies. They are also called belladonna lilies or March lilies, for that is the month of their peak bloom in the Cape.

The flower bud quickly opens with eight to twelve pale pink, trumpet-shaped flowers that radiate from a central point to form a slightly one-sided umbel. The heavily scented flowers are over 4 inches (10 cm) long and apically flare open about 3 inches (8 cm). The inflorescence tends to face the direction that receives the greatest exposure to the sun.

The winter-growing foliage, which appears after the flowers have gone to seed, is a lush green and resembles that of *Agapanthus*. In fact, a mixed bed of blue *Agapanthus* and pink *Amaryllis belladonna* is an esthetically successful combination, and the evergreen leaves of *Agapanthus* provide skirts for the flowering naked ladies.

The plants tolerate quite arid conditions in the southwestern Cape, where *Amaryllis belladonna* is primarily a plant of the mountains. According to Creasey (1939), it almost invariably grows protected from the full heat of the sun by ground-covering plants. It is reported that when thickly overgrown by bushes and trees the bulbs may remain barren for many years but flower profusely after a wildfire. *Amaryllis belladonna* can be grown under a ground cover of Cape weed *Arctotheca calendula*, which also does not need summer water.

I find the bulbs to be almost indestructible and to thrive on benign neglect. For example, they grew *en masse* in a sunny but neglected area of poor soil along the driveway of the house where my mother was born in 1890. They were still flourishing there when I was born in that same house 26 years later. However, that doesn't mean they should go a quarter of a century without being lifted and thinned out. They are best moved just after flowering and before the winter foliage appears. When disturbed, their flowering may be set back a year.

Amaryllis belladonna will flourish in containers. Strout (1948, page 158), who grew flowering-size bulbs, which are normally quite large, in just a nail keg, wrote, "This bulb (one to start with, now five) has never missed a single season for bloom, and is quite happy in the container. The soil has never been changed, and I must admit, I've forgotten to fertilize."

For propagating, the offsets can be removed from the mother bulb and planted with the neck at the soil surface or deeper in colder areas. The soft, fleshy seeds should be planted when fresh and just on the soil surface, which must be kept moist for their germination. Germination can occur in two weeks, but seedlings of *Amaryllis belladonna* require from three to six years or even longer to flower.

There are some fascinating intergeneric crosses that use *Amaryllis belladonna* as one of the parents. The first such record is by Cowlishaw (1935) who reported that in 1870 Mr. Bidwell, a horticulturist in Australia, crossed *A. belladonna* with a *Brunsvigia*. It is now believed the species was *B. orientalis* (Hannibal, 1980). These hybrids were variously named by Cowlishaw "*B. multiflora,*" "*B. multiflora alba,*" and "*B. multiflora rosea.*" They produced seed but, as expected, their offspring did not come true. They had spectacular heads of 30 to 40 flowers, with "*B. rosea*" having the largest heads and "*B. alba*" the smallest (see Figure 3-4). Another Australian, H. B. Bradley, raised fine seedlings of these Multifloras, including one he called 'Haythor', which was pure white with an orange-yellow eye. These grew well at Sydney, which receives annually about 46 inches (1168 mm) of rainfall, and flourished in any sort of soil in either sun or partial shade. A brown spotting is characteristic of seeds of 'Haythor' (Welch, 1982).

Les Hannibal (1980) believed that the important intergeneric cross was *Brunsvigia orientalis* × *Amaryllis belladonna* to produce what was known as *Brunsdonna bidwellii*. Hannibal (1980) criticized the use by *Hortus Third* of the bigeneric name *Amarygia* instead of *Brunsdonna* for this hybrid. When it was backcrossed with *Amaryllis belladonna*, the hybrid became known as *A.* 'Multiflora'. The flowers had a beautiful radial umbel and tended to bloom slightly later than the flowers of *A. belladonna*. One particularly lovely white form with a yellow throat was mentioned, and that must have been the cultivar 'Haythor' that Cowlishaw (1935) wrote about (see Plate 10). A sibling backcross of *Brunsdonna bidwellii* onto *Amaryllis belladonna* was done by Lady Parker under Bidwell's instruction, and this is listed in *Hortus Third* as *Amarygia parkeri*. Hannibal intercrossed the Bidwell hybrids, Bradley's 'Haythor', and *A. parkeri* and got nothing distinctive, only the typical Multifloras.

When *Amaryllis belladonna* pollen was put on *Brunsvigia josephinae,* there was a different floral change. The segments were narrower, much more fragile, and pigmented a near butter yellow. The hybrids of

FIGURE 3-4.
Amaryllis 'Multiflora'.

this cross were also more tender and difficult to grow. Hannibal (1980) reported that when backcrossed onto *A. belladonna*, the flowers had long slender trumpets, usually creamy pink in color, and set only a few seeds that were small and almost impossible to grow.

Crinum species and hybrids also will strike on *Amaryllis belladonna* to produce the intergeneric ×*Amacrinum*. These have also been called ×*Crinodonna*. Hannibal (1980) reported success using a tetraploid *Crinum* hybrid onto *Amaryllis belladonna* and onto *Amaryllis* 'Multiflora'. Hannibal called these the "Amar-Bruns-Crinum" to reflect the three genera in their parentage. All the ×*Amacrinum* are sterile. The crosses only take when using *Crinum* pollen while temperatures are around 65°F (18°C). So far it has not been possible to make the reciprocal cross of *Amaryllis belladonna* pollen on *Crinum* (Traub, 1963).

A comment by Hannibal (1983, page 5) is important here:

[L]ike *Nerine* and *Crinum* the plants prefer to produce maternal parthenogenetic seed in view of sexual. I found that out 40 years ago. But in cool weather you can get a few sexual crosses, possibly two or three out of a pod of 40 maternal seed.

What Hannibal described here is the phenomenon of apomixis, in which a plant may go through pollination and the motions of sexual reproduction, but the embryo that develops in the seed is derived from maternal tissue alone and thus has the same genetic composition as the mother plant. This phenomenon must complicate the work of hybridizers if only about 5 percent of the seeds are from their attempted crosses and then only if the temperature is right.

Hannibal (1952a) described the apomitic and sexual seeds in the cross of *Amaryllis belladonna* var. *rubra* with *Crinum moorei* as the pollen parent. Two seed types resulted from this initial cross. The most prevalent seeds in the pods were the relatively small, coral-red, fleshy type so typical of *A. belladonna*. The seeds, as Hannibal verified in subsequent crosses, were strictly parthenogenetic, but about 15 large, opalescent, green seeds were found in several pods. They were relatively distinct from

A. belladonna seeds and were germinating in the pod. Such behavior is typical of *Crinum*.

In Holland, T. M. Hoog (1935) crossed *Amaryllis belladonna* with *Brunsvigia josephinae* and *B. orientalis* (syn. *B. gigantea*) to produce *A. belladonna* 'Parkeri', which was a tall *A. belladonna* type of plant with up to 20 flowers. (There may be some confusion here with *Amarygia parkeri*; I find no explanation of Hoog's use of the epithet *parkeri*.) *Amaryllis belladonna* 'Parkeri' was then crossed with *A. belladonna* var. *purpurea major*, which resulted in a strain of free blooming *A. belladonna* types with numerous and large flowers of a very beautiful coloring, deep pink and white with yellowish throat, on strong stems. In Europe in the fall there are very few if any bulbous plants with long stems and large beautifully colored blooms of long endurance in flower. Hoog (1935, page 114) added, "Here is one of great beauty."

I have grown the *Amaryllis* 'Multiflora' hybrids from Les Hannibal's garden and find them to be very impressive flowers that range in color from white through all shades of pink to nearly red. The umbels often have over 25 flowers that bloom from late summer through early fall. They are as tough and hardy as their *A. belladonna* parent, make good cut flowers, and come highly recommended.

Loubser (1981) reported flowering a cross between *Amaryllis belladona* and *Nerine angustifolia* but doubted that it would have horticultural value. He mentioned that *Amnerine tubergenii* 'Zwanenburg' is a cross between *Amaryllis belladonna* and *Nerine bowdenii* produced in the Zwanenburg Nursery in Haarlem, Holland, in 1940.

Excessive heat, as may occur in the interior Sacramento and San Joaquin valleys of California, will wash out the color of *Amaryllis* flowers. Hannibal (1952b) found that two weeks of temperatures above 100°F (38°C) caused flowers to be a dirty, bleached-out white, while along the coast, foggy 60–70°F (16–21°C) temperatures chill the flowers to a near coral red. He concluded (page 142) that "the daytime temperatures at the opening period of the indvidual blossoms of the floral umbel definitely establish the amount of red pigmentation that is present in the blossom."

A customer once wrote me that her life would not be complete until she could once again have *Amaryllis belladonna* in her garden. Her enthusiasm is understandable. Everything about these plants is positive. The naked ladies are good cut flowers, and the Multiflora hybrids are truly spectacular.

Lockwood and Elizabeth de Forest (1942, page 2), who were renowned landscapers, gardeners, and writers in Santa Barbara, wrote,

> Those who want a pink flower in August and September, one that will bloom without fail year after year and that will bloom regardless of rainfall or heat can do no better than to plant that ubiquitous bulb often called naked ladies, *Amaryllis belladonna*. . . . it is a disease-proof bulb that will flourish under any conditions, one that is not common in other parts of the country, and is very highly prized in most parts of the world.

Ammocharis (Amaryllidaceae)

Ammocharis is an appropriate and charming name derived from the Greek *ammos,* "sand," and *charis,* "beauty," to reflect the habitat of these pretty flowers.

In 1936 Sara Coombs wrote that this fine Amaryllid is practically unknown in America; this is still the case a half-century later. The rose-pink or crimson flowers are fragrant and borne in an umbel 8 inches (20 cm) across. The plants grow best in sandy soil and full exposure to the sun where they can benefit from the heat. They are summer-growing, deciduous plants that are dormant in the winter.

In Basutoland the Southern Sotho use a thick paste of the cooked bulb of *Ammocharis* to repair cracks in clay pots (Watt and Breyer-Brandwijk, 1962).

Ammocharis coranica is a widespread species, the sole member of the genus in the Cape flora, but it does not grow in the southwestern Cape south of Stellenbosch. In that area it is replaced by a closely related plant, *Cybistetes longifolia* (formerly named *A. falcata*). The flowers of *A.*

coranica are a much deeper pink than those of *C. longifolia*. The eight or nine strap-shaped leaves of *A. coranica* lie flat on the ground like a split rosette and are capable of growing quite long. They arise from dormant leaf bases initiated in a previous season. The stalk, which carries the umbel of strongly scented flowers, is only about 10 inches (25 cm) high. *Ammocharis coranica* blooms in midsummer. The mature bulbs grow to be quite large, even reaching 8 inches (20 cm) across (Eliovson, 1967).

This summer-growing plant needs a long dormant and distinctly dry period in winter. The seedlings take six to seven years to flower. The bulbs are planted with the neck at the soil surface. Offsets are slow to form and the plants are best left undisturbed. These plants are not good horticultural subjects because of their frost tenderness and slowness to propagate. I have only three *Ammocharis coranica* plants in my garden, and the coastal summers may be too cool; the Cape receives more radiation than northern areas of the same latitude, and my plants may need to be moved to a warm sunny greenhouse.

Anapalina (Iridaceae)

According to John Bryan (1989), *Anapalina* comes from the Greek *anapalin,* "reversed order," referring to the bracteoles being longer than the bracts. Today *Anapalina* is sometimes included in *Tritoniopsis*. Seven species are in the Cape flora (Bond and Goldblatt, 1984), but the only one I have found available is *A. caffra* (see Plate 11).

The brick red flowers of *Anapalina caffra,* which appear in spring, are borne on either side of a slender 12 to 24 inch (30 to 61 cm) stalk, an arrangement that botanists call *distichous*. The flowers open from the bottom upward. The base of a flower is tubular, then outwardly the segments become reflexed except for the uppermost segment, which is quite extended and concave. The linear leaves have two or three veins.

Propagation is from seeds or corms that in nature are deep-seated, so they should be planted at least 3 inches (8 cm) deep. A sunny site is preferable.

Anapalina caffra is a good container plant, and the flowers are fine for cutting.

Androcymbium (Colchicaceae)

Gardening is even more interesting when the derivation of the scientific names of the plants is known. What does the name mean and how does it describe a dominant characteristic of the species? What does it reveal about the botanist who thought it up? John Bryan (1989) took pains to interpret the names in his authoritative, two-volume treatise on the world's bulbs, so I find myself relying frequently on the fruits of his etymological research. Such is the case with *Androcymbium,* which he said comes from the Greek *aner,* "man," and *kumbion,* "cup." I presume that combination is based on the observation that the tiny flowers are in a small umbel that sits in a cuplike structure surrounded by large bracts, giving them the common name of little men in a boat. Nine species are listed in the Cape flora by Bond and Goldblatt (1984).

My first glimpse of this plant was in the mountainous area of Liliefontain in Namaqualand. The species I saw there exactly fits Barbara Jeppe's illustration of *Androcymbium ciliolatum* in her splendid book on the spring- and winter-flowering bulbs of the Cape (Jeppe, 1989). The numerous small plants had two leaves that lay prostrate on the surface of the damp ground. The large and conspicuous white bracts looked as though someone had strewn about clumps of white crepe paper. This sounds untidy, but it was an interesting, arresting, eye-catching effect.

The two leaves of *Androcymbium ciliolatum* have minutely fringed margins. The cluster of small white flowers is surrounded by the large, white bracts, which are the major attractive feature. A related species, *A. pulchrum,* which I missed seeing at Nieuwoudtville, has pink flowers and purplish red bracts. I have *A. ciliolatum* growing from fresh seed, but it can also be propagated from offsets. The corms have a fibrous covering and may be planted about 3 inches (8 cm) deep. From seeing the plants in the wild I suspect they prefer damp ground while in foliage. John Bryan

(1989) claimed these plants can provide a great deal of interest in a rock garden in a sunny spot where there is no winter frost. They are small plants reaching just over 4 inches (10 cm) in height. Sima Eliovson (1980) considered them to be splendid container plants.

Anomalesia (Iridaceae)

The name *Anomalesia* is from the Greek *anomales,* meaning "unequal," but it could just have easily come from the Latin adjective *anomalos,* meaning "diverging from the usual," in reference to the interesting shape of the flowers. In *A. cunonia,* for example, the middle segment of the upper three is long and decurved like an inverted spoon, but the other two upper segments flare out like wings.

There are only three species in this genus. I offered the species *Anomalesia cunonia* to the trade in 1990, which may be the first time it was available in the United States. There is no reference to *Anomalesia* in *Hortus Third,* and I do not find it mentioned in most standard references or the better-known bulb catalogs. Sometimes it is included in *Gladiolus.*

Anomalesia cunonia (Figure 3-5, Plate 12) is a Linnaean species, although the genus in which it now belongs was not erected until 1937. One day I stopped at the beach a few miles north of Cape Town to photograph the spectacular view of Table Mountain with the city at its base. I was surprised and thrilled to see the branched inflorescence of *A. cunonia* thrusting up through the ice plant, *Carpobrotus edulis,* on the first small sand dunes or hummocks just above the high tide level. *Anomalesia cunonia* also grows on the lower mountain slopes near the coast. The flowers are red or bright crimson. Una Van Der Spuy (1976) described them as showy, luminous, and coral red. The flower color makes a nice contrast with the 12–18 inch (30–46 cm) stalk, which has a distinctly gray or glaucous sheen. The long narrow leaves are green or gray green.

Anomalesia cunonia is easy to grow and propagates readily from seeds and cormels. Seed germination required 37 days in my garden. The first flowers are produced in the second season. The corms do well if planted 3 inches (8 cm) deep in sandy soil or mix. It flowers in early

FIGURE 3-5.
Anomalesia cunonia
with distichous
flower arrangement.

spring. Una Van Der Spuy (1976) considered *Anomalesia* to be a fine container plant and effective if massed in the garden or rockery. I find the plants catch the eye of visitors.

Anomalesia cunonia tends to be a coastal species while the other two *Anomalesia* species grow in somewhat hotter and more arid locations. *Anomalesia saccata* grows in the rocky hills of Namaqualand. It has red flowers with a conspicuous sac (from which it derives its name) at the base of the upper segment. Seeds germinate in 33 days. The third Cape species is *A. splendens*, which may be just a variety of *A. cunonia* according to John Bryan (1989), and is not included by Bond and Goldblatt (1984) in their catalog of Cape Province flora. However, Clive Innes (1985) listed it as a valid species, and Du Plessis and Duncan (1989) considered it to be distinct. I grow *A. splendens*, which simply disregards the taxonomic uncertainty and performs beautifully regardless of what it is. Its seeds germinate in 19–22 days. These *Anomalesia* species are showy plants that deserve greater recognition.

Anomatheca (Iridaceae)

The derivation of the name *Anomatheca* is either from the Latin *anomalous*, meaning "abnormal or irregular," or from the Greek *anomos*, meaning "singular or irregular," and *theca*, meaning "case or capsule." The name refers to the papillae covering the fruiting seed capsule, once thought to be unusual.

The species of *Anomatheca* are often listed in the genus *Lapeirousia*, but in 1972 Peter Goldblatt clarified their separation. He found that species of *Anomatheca* have corms surrounded by tunics of fine, netted fibers and always have $n = 11$ chromosomes, whereas *Lapeirousia* species have woody, flat-based corms and variable numbers of chromosomes but never eleven.

There are six species of *Anomatheca;* of the three that occur in the winter-rainfall area of the Cape, I have grown only *A. viridis*, which is so aggressively weedy that I had to eradicate it from my garden. A very desirable species is *A. laxa* (*laxa* meaning "loose or distant"), which occurs

FIGURE 3-6.
Anomatheca laxa.

as a woodland plant in the summer-rainfall area (see Figure 3-6). However, it has a winter-growing cycle and is dormant in the summer, as are most Cape bulbs. Its range extends northward from the eastern Cape area.

Anomatheca laxa (sometimes listed as *Lapeirousia cruenta)* has red, white, and blue flower forms. The blue and red varieties have a striking dark spot of the same color at the base of the lower segments. The third form is pure white. The plants grow to 18 inches (46 cm) with long-tubed flowers one inch (2.5 cm) in diameter. The flowers may appear in late fall or early winter and bloom well into spring.

Anomatheca grandiflora is not a Cape species, but it can be grown compatibly with *A. laxa.* It has larger flowers that are a carmine red, and it blooms later than *A. laxa.*

Anomatheca is a good container plant, an easy grower that prefers partial shade in warmer gardens. It is readily propagated from seeds or offsets.

Antholyza (Iridaceae)

The name *Antholyza* is derived from the Greek *anthos,* meaning "flower," and *eyssa,* meaning "rage." The author of this scientific name may have had a vivid imagination. The gaping flower segments are said to resemble the open mouth of a raging animal or roaring lion ready to bite, hence "flower in rage." The plants are much more endearingly called Aunt Elizas.

Antholyza is endemic to the Cape Province and has two species. The genus is sometimes included in *Babiana* because of the ribbed leaves, which look much like those of *Babiana.* The leaves appear after the first autumn rains and remain green until late spring or early summer. The zygomorphic flowers have a pronounced, hoodlike, upper segment. The flowers bloom from midwinter well into spring. The corms are deep in sandy soil. In cold areas *Antholyza* needs frost protection.

Antholyza plicata (Plate 13) is named for its heavily pleated leaves. The plants grow in sandy coastal areas with low rainfall. The sturdy flower stalks range in height from 16 to 28 inches (41 to 71 cm) and under especially favorable conditions can reach 3 feet (1 m) according to Duncan (1980). Attractive crimson-red flowers are borne on a number of short branches along the stalk. The lower segments are marked green and black. I have had this species for years, but it is a very reluctant bloomer, which is both puzzling and disappointing; this species, although confined to certain coastal locations, can sometimes be found in abundance in large colonies, creating a magnificent sight when in full bloom.

Antholyza sets seeds very easily if cross-pollinated by hand. Graham Duncan (1980) recommended that the black seeds, which resemble those of *Babiana*, be sown in the fall in deep pots where they will germinate in about a month if kept moist. The soil should be sandy. The seedlings need watering until early summer, and then should be allowed to die back before being stored in a dry place. Inspection of the soil will reveal small, elongated, white corms that should flower in their third or fourth season.

Antholyza ringens has the common name of rat's tail because it grows a curious sterile gray or brownish spike. African sunbirds are said to perch on the spikes to reach the nectar in the bright red flowers, which are on a side branch at an angle to the ground. My plants are small, growing only to about 8 inches (20 cm) high. These odd flowers are more widely distributed along the Cape coast than are those of a sister species, *A. plicata*, and there are several ecotypes. I frequently encountered them in sandy ground in the coastal area just north of Cape Town.

Propagation is best from seeds, some of which will flower in their third season. The corms, which are slow to form offsets, should be planted 6 inches (15 cm) deep and are capable of pulling themselves down to 9 inches (23 cm) by their contractile roots. I have not been able to keep *Antholyza ringens* very long and occasionally need to replace it.

In England, *Antholyza ringens* has been grown as a novel container plant. Graham Duncan (1980) hoped that *Antholyza* species would be seen more often in cultivation; they are excellent subjects for the collector of wild flowers, and they add an interesting touch to any garden.

Aristea (Iridaceae)

Clive Innes (1985) believed the name *Aristea* is from the Latin *arista,* meaning a "point," in reference to the sharp apex of the irislike leaves. Of 30 species listed in the Cape flora by Bond and Goldblatt (1984), two, possibly three, have been cultivated by gardeners. Other species with garden value occur outside the Cape. The plants are evergreen, and the rootstock is a rhizome. The ephemeral flowers are in shades of blue.

Aristea ecklonii has irislike leaves and blue flowers on stalks 16–30 inches (41–76 cm) high (see Plate 14). In the wild *A. ecklonii* flourishes in a permanently wet situation (Du Plessis and Duncan, 1989), as does *A. major*. *Aristea major* is the better of the two, for it has long, dense inflorescences of satiny, royal blue flowers and is an attractive plant growing to 4 feet (122 cm) high.

Aristea grows in full sun or partial shade and prefers a soil rich in organic matter. It is propagated by division of the rhizome in the fall, or from seeds. Germination of *A. major* seeds occurs in 25 days, but seedlings require three years to flower. They like more water than my xeric garden can readily afford, so while my own enthusiasm is somewhat diminished, they are welcome flowers elsewhere.

Sima Eliovson (1980) thought the stately *Aristea major* would be outstanding if the flowers did not close after midday. Sarah Coombs (1936, page 89) considered them great favorites and wrote:

> [A] sight to be remembered is a mountain pass where the slopes were covered with masses of tall deep-blue *Aristea*, each plant with 3 or 4 foot [1 m or more] stalks of flowers and growing with them quantities of a big pink *Watsonia,* the stalks of the pink flowers equaling the *Aristeas'* blue ones.

Una Van Der Spuy (1976) agreed that the statuesque *Aristea major* should be planted with pink *Watsonia*.

Babiana (Iridaceae)

Other than *Babiana*, I am hard pressed to think of any plant genus that is named for its major herbivore. The pioneer Afrikaaners observed baboons relishing the corms, so they commonly called them baboon flowers, *babiaantje* (pronounced bab-eon´-ky).

The plant collector Carl Thunberg in 1772 used the anglicized name babianer in connection with a plant called *Gladiolus plicatus*. According to Smith (1966) the plant grew on the slopes of Lion's Head at Cape Town and was therefore easily accessible to the early botanists such as Thunberg. The plant was designated in 1802 as the genotype of *Babiana*. It is now known as *Babiana disticha*. Bond and Goldblatt (1984) list 36 Cape species.

Bright colors and pleated, ribbed leaves are characteristic of *Babiana*. The flowers are of two types: actinomorphic and zygomorphic. *Babiana* is among the hardiest of Cape bulbs. It thrives in impoverished soils, is floriferous, and multiplies rapidly. In Santa Barbara it naturalizes easily and grows in all sorts of improbable places, crowding up through cracks between stones or appearing in a bed of annuals.

As its name indicates, *Babiana pygmaea* is a small, ground-hugging plant but it has a surprisingly large (3 inch, 8 cm) yellow flower with a purple throat. It is ideal for small pots, as is *B. ambigua,* which is a small, prolific plant reaching 4 inches (10 cm) high. The flowers are blue with basal white areas on the lower segments. The species closely resembles *B. nana,* which has a pinkish tinge to the flowers, and both species are sweetly scented (Duncan, 1982).

A very striking member of the genus is *Babiana rubrocyanea,* usually called the wine cup babiana because the cup-shaped flowers are dark blue with a red center. It grows to about 8 inches (20 cm) high and is a fast-growing species, sometimes blooming in its first season. Another attractive, medium-size species is *B. tubulosa* var. *tubulosa,* which has cream-colored flowers with red markings.

The taller species ideally suited for many gardens include *Babiana villosa* (Figure 3-7), which has crimson flowers with black anthers (see

FIGURE 3-7.
Babiana villosa.

Plate 16). This eye-catcher grows up to 12 inches (30 cm) tall and naturalizes in my Santa Barbara garden. Other good garden subjects are *B. disticha*, with blue flowers and broad leaves; *B. pulchra*, with dark blue flowers; and *B. stricta*, with different shades of mauve. I also recommend *B. cedarbergensis*, *B. ecklonii*, *B. leipoldtii*, *B. patersoniae,* and *B. scariosa.*

Babiana grows readily from its hard black seeds sown in autumn in deep pots in a sandy medium. My garden records show germination of *B. ecklonii* in 33 days, *B. pulchra* in 21 days, *B. rubrocyanea* in 30–35 days, *B. sinuata* in 18 days, *B. stricta* in 29–35 days, *B. tabularis* in 24 days, and *B. villosa* in 23 days. Contractile roots may pull the corms to a surprising depth. The young seedlings should be kept somewhat shaded. Most flower in their second season. While *Babiana* species are dormant during the summer when watering should be withheld, they will survive some watering in well-drained soil. Certain species produce bulbils in the leaf axils, and all *Babiana* species can be propagated from offsets from the corms, which should be planted at least 4 inches (10 cm) deep. Although tolerant of poor soil, *Babiana* needs good drainage in a sunny situation and flourishes with liberal watering during the growing period from fall through spring flowering.

The taller species, such as *Babiana villosa, B. stricta,* and *B. disticha* are good garden plants and well suited for rock gardens. The low-growing species, such as *B. pygmaea, B. ambigua,* and *B. nana,* are fine container plants and can be left undisturbed for years. This group of Cape bulbs is undemanding.

Baeometra (Colchicaceae)

Baeometra uniflora is the only species in this monotypic genus. The illustration by Jeppe (1989) showed it to have several golden yellow flowers that are reddish underneath. This dwarf plant, growing to only 9 inches (23 cm) tall, may merit attention. I have just started seedlings because it has only recently become readily available.

Bobartia (Iridaceae)

I have had no experience with this Irid genus and know it only from the literature. It was named for Jacob Bobart, keeper of the Oxford Botanic Garden in the early 18th century (Bryan, 1989). It has a woody, creeping rhizome. I mention its existence simply because it is a Cape geophyte in the Iridaceae, which includes a great number of worthy garden flowers. Someday it may be discovered as deserving attention by gardeners.

Boophane (Amaryllidaceae)

Each vowel in *Boophane* is pronounced separately, making it a four-syllable word. It is incorrectly spelled *Boophone* in *Hortus Third* and *Buphane* by others. John Bryan (1989) said that *Boophane* is derived from the Greek *bous*, "ox," and *phonos*, "slaughter." Perhaps the name reflects the poisonous character of the plant, which is fatal if eaten by cattle or sheep. Bushmen poisoned their arrows with a *Boophane* bulb extract. The bulbs of these plants are enormous. Guy Wrinkle (1984) found many with a diameter of 12 inches (30 cm). I saw my first *Boophane* during a walk on a spring morning in the sandveld of Namaqualand. It was an impressive sight and a splendid photo opportunity. I can readily believe that the enormous bulbs found in the wild, like those of *Brunsvigia*, may be over a century old.

The genus *Boophane* is related to the genus *Brunsvigia*, and the umbels of the former can have up to 100 flowers each. *Boophane* is hysteranthous. When the flower head dries, the infructescence breaks off and is blown about by the wind, tumbling over the ground just as tumbleweeds do in the American West. Species of *Brunsvigia* have the same method of seed dispersal.

Most of the literature attributes five species to *Boophane*, but Willi Olivier (1981) suggested the genus is still imperfectly known and may well need a careful revision. All the currently recognized species except *B. disticha* occur in the winter-rainfall area of the western Cape as far north as Namaqualand and southern Namibia (Wrinkle, 1984).

Boophane guttata has small maroon flowers. The leaves lie flat on the ground and have maroon margins. On the other hand, *B. haemanthoides* has interestingly twisted, upright leaves that spread out from the huge bulb like an 18 inch (46 cm) fan. Most of the immense bulb is above ground. This species forms large clumps. The flowers are yellow but turn pink with age.

Boophane pulchra grows near Garies in Namaqualand. The flowers are wine red and the prostrate leaves have red to white marginal bristles.

Boophane flava is a yellow-flowered species that also grows in Namaqualand.

Boophane disticha is a variable and widespread species ranging from the summer-rainfall area of South Africa as far north as Kenya and Uganda. The Xhosa use the dry scale of the bulb as a dressing after circumcision and as an application for boils. The Manyika apply the scale for burns and grow the plant outside their huts as a charm to ward off evil dreams, to bring good luck, and to bring rain. The Europeans moistened the dry scale and applied it as a dressing on boils, sores, and septic cuts. In the Karoo near Touws River, a European remedy for the relief of hysteria and sleeplessness is to sleep on a mattress filled with the bulb. The Hottentots and Bushmen used the bulb to poison their arrows (Watt and Breyer-Brandwijk, 1962). The flowers of *B. disticha* are a pinkish brick color and the leaves are upright. Harold Koopowitz (1986) found an unusual color form with white flowers turning pinkish. *Boophane disticha* is self-sterile, but cross-pollinated clones set seed.

Boophane propagation is best from seeds because offsets are very slow to form. Seed is sown fresh in a very sandy mix that must be kept moist. Willi Olivier (1981) grew *Boophane* in his South African garden with the greatest of ease from seeds that flowered in six years. Koopowitz (1986) reported his seedlings in California flowered after eight years. Seedlings can be moved in their second or third year into their permanent containers where they should not be disturbed. The plants prefer sun and are frost tender. Olivier (1981) stressed that since *Boophane* comes from semi-arid regions it will not survive even one season of rainfall during the dormant period unless very well-drained soil is provided. Wrinkle (1984) found *Boophane* easy to grow in his California garden as long as its dormancy requirements were met.

A mature *Boophane* plant in the garden of an avid collector of Amaryllidaceae is truly an absolute treasure.

Brunsvigia (Amaryllidaceae)

John Bryan (1989) explained the derivation of the name *Brunsvigia* thus. In the 18th century the great houses of Europe vied in the collection of unusual plants. Ryk Tulbagh, then governor of the Cape Province, sent bulbs to the Duke of Braunschweig in Germany, who flowered the plants. The name accordingly honors the House of Brunswick.

The Zulu use a decoction of *Brunsvigia* for coughs and colds and as an enema in renal and hepatic conditions. The Southern Sotho use the decoction as an enema for relief of pains in the back and also as a remedy for barrenness (Watt and Breyer-Brandwijk, 1962).

There are ten species in the Cape flora. It is unfortunate that the literature was fouled by the misguided effort of some authors to rename *Amaryllis belladonna* as *Brunsvigia rosea*. The genera are now properly considered distinct. These deciduous plants of *Brunsvigia* are hysteranthous (as are many other Amaryllids); the flower stalk emerges and blooms in early fall. The *Brunsvigia* inflorescence is an umbel that enlarges enormously after the flowers mature. It then dries, breaks off, and is tumbled along the ground by the wind, dispersing its seeds in the same fashion as *Boophane* and tumbleweeds of the American West. Most of the species I know have several broad, flat leaves that lie prostrate on the ground, but *Brunsvigia josephinae* has erect leaves.

Brunsvigia gregaria has four short, flat, and prostrate leaves on the soil surface. The flower stalk is about 8 inches (20 cm) in height and the flowers are dark pink to crimson.

A more glamorous and sought after species is *Brunsvigia marginata* (Figure 3-8). It is confined to the mountainous regions of the southwestern Cape and is such an outstanding species that Willi Olivier (1983)

FIGURE 3-8.
Brunsvigia marginata.

believed every effort should be made to ensure its future. The compact umbel of scarlet flowers is on an 8 inch (20 cm) stalk that blooms in the fall. Johan Loubser (1981) called it his favorite Amaryllid and described its large umbel of glistening red as an oversize *Nerine sarniensis*. He noted that while mountain species are notoriously difficult to grow, this is not the case with *B. marginata*. The mountain rocks decompose into the sandy soil in which *B. marginata* naturally grows, but Loubser found that it also flourishes in the heavy clay soil of his garden. It is easy to grow from seed but the process is slow, for it requires five years to flower.

Brunsvigia orientalis, often called the candelabra flower, has brilliant red flowers in an enormous umbel sometimes reported to be 24 inches (61 cm) in diameter (hence the synonym *B. gigantea*). My flowers have been about 14 inches (36 cm) across. The flower stalk reaches about 15 inches (38 cm) in height. The broad leaves lie flat on the ground.

Brunsvigia josephinae is a striking plant with upright, straplike leaves. The crimson flowers are in large heads on stalks that can reach 25 inches (64 cm). The bulbs have many layers of papery scales. The bulb of an old plant can be enormous, and fully two-thirds of the bulb may be above ground. Pauline Perry (1991) measured bulbs that were 24 cm (9.5 inches) across at the Karoo National Botanic Gardens, Worcester. Although I have had my plants for some time, they have never bloomed, so I am inclined to think Roy Genders (1973) was entirely correct when he said that plants took 12 to 15 years to flower.

Brunsvigia litoralis is an endangered species that grows in coastal sands in the area toward Port Elizabeth (Plate 17). The leaves are gray-green, semi-erect, and have undulating margins. The flowers are dull red on tall stalks. Koopowitz (1986) found that while *B. litoralis* is self-sterile, seeds will set if pollinated by closely related *Brunsvigia* species or genera including *Amaryllis belladonna* and *Nerine* hybrids. The seedlings of *B. litoralis* bloom after six years.

The results from crossing *Brunsvigia* species with those in other genera are very interesting. *Brunsvigia* has been crossed with *Amaryllis belladonna* to produce hybrids called *Brunsdonna*. According to John

Bryan (1989), a cross between *Brunsvigia josephinae* and *Amaryllis belladonna* produced violet-pink flowers and was named *Brunsdonna tubergenii*. In 1983 Johan Loubser mentioned a cross between *Brunsvigia marginata* and *A. belladonna*, first done by Dr. J. P. van der Walt of Pretoria and repeated by Loubser. He called the plant *Amarygia marginata* and described it as "a glorious plant with a long stem and wine red flowers" (page 8).

Les Hannibal (1980) crossed *Nerine humilis* on *Brunsvigia appendiculata*. The foliage and flowers of the sterile hybrids resembled *Nerine*, but the umbels bore more blossoms. Loubser (1981, page 10) described his hybrids of *Brunsvigia marginata* × *Nerine sarniensis* as follows:

> The leaves are adpressed to the ground like those of *Brunsvigia* but longer and narrower. The flowers, being superficially similar in the two parents, resemble both parents in the hybrid. Unlike most *Brunsvigia* spp. the inflorescence of *B. marginata* is a compact head when the flowers open, which makes it look like an oversize *Nerine*. In the hybrid, however, the pedicels are extended when in flower, making it look more like a typical *Brunsvigia*. The bulbs divide up like those of *Nerine*.

Propagation of *Brunsvigia* is best from fresh seeds, which sometimes germinate while still on the plant. The ripe seeds should be sown on the surface of a very sandy medium and kept moist for germination. The radicle will start to grow after planting, but in some cases the leaf may not appear until the next year. The seedlings are put in larger pots at the end of their second season and can go into their permanent stations at the start of their third year. *Brunsvigia* plants prefer full sun and a sandy medium. Propagation by offsets is impractical, because they seldom form, but Du Plessis and Duncan (1989) claim that basal cuttage works.

Sima Eliovson (1980, page 79) cautioned that the bulbs resent disturbance and are brittle and must be lifted with great care: "If one tries to pull them out of even 1/2 inch [14 mm] of soil at the bottom, the soft and brittle bulb will break off and the precious root will be spoilt."

A few *Brunsvigia* plants are a must for any serious collector of Amaryllidaceae, but aside from their value as conversation pieces—the enormously enlarged mature umbels that tumble along the ground always surprise and fascinate visitors—they may not have a place in most gardens. However, Sara Coombs (1936) wrote that *Brunsvigia* is a splendid container plant for veranda or garden, and she felt that it should be better known.

Bulbine (Asphodelaceae)

Bulbine is from the Greek *bolbos*, "bulb," an inappropriate name, since few if any of the species have a definite bulb. Instead they have fleshy, tuberlike roots, leading Jackson and MacGregor (1989) to suggest that the name was a Linnaean mistake.

I first grew *Bulbine* plants a decade ago, but my plants turned out to be invasive weeds seeding themselves freely in the garden. I found their succulent-like growth in mystifying places. It took several seasons to eradicate them, and my initial impression soured me on the genus generally. My personal bias may be neither fair nor rational, for Sima Eliovson (1980) spoke well of several species, as did Una Van Der Spuy (1976). Lisabel Hall (1986) gave a review of some dwarf species and mentioned a division of other species into caulescent and asphodeloides groups. There are 19 species in the Cape flora, and several species are sold by South African nurseries. They are also available at a number of nurseries on the West Coast of the United States.

Bulbinella (Asphodelaceae)

Bulbinella is the diminutive of *Bulbine*. Botanists differentiate the genera by the condition of the filament (the stem that bears the anther). The filament is bearded or coated with fluff in *Bulbine*. To me as a gardener the two genera are entirely different, so different, in fact, that though I have eradicated all my *Bulbine* plants, I treasure my *Bulbinella* specimens.

Bulbinella is deciduous in summer. It has surprisingly large, fleshy roots that grow from a small, erect and hairy rhizome. The very numerous small flowers grow in a dense raceme. *Bulbinella* is winter growing and there are 16 species in the winter-rainfall area of the Cape. Pauline Perry (1987) provided a careful revision of the species of *Bulbinella*.

On Neil MacGregor's farm, Glenlyon, in Nieuwoudtville, a solid stand of several acres of *Bulbinella latifolia* var. *doleritica* in full bloom was a breath-taking sight in September 1987. These tall plants grow over 3 feet (1 m) in heavy, red, apparently doleritic soil but also do well in a much lighter, sandy medium in my garden. The numerous orange-colored, star-shaped, small flowers are in a dense raceme (Figure 3-9). The species also has the yellow flowered variety, *B. latifolia* var. *latifolia*. The specific name *B. floribunda* is frequently encountered in the literature, but it is considered to be invalid and is now a synonym of *B. latifolia* (see Plate 18).

Another yellow-flowered *Bulbinella* is *B. nutans,* which is smaller than *B. latifolia*. The genus also contains the white *B. cauda-felis* as well as *B. triquetra,* which may be either white or yellow. I have recently acquired *B. graminifolia,* which has grasslike leaves. Since it has not yet bloomed I know its white flowers only from their illustration by Barbara Jeppe (1989).

Propagation of *Bulbinella* is best from seeds, although the rhizomes can be carefully divided. Growing from the small, erect rhizome is a great mass of thick and swollen roots. These roots must be carefully handled if the mature plants are transplanted. I find they are more safely moved as young two-year-old seedlings than as older plants. The seedlings bloom in their fourth year. They flourish in a sandy medium and grow magnificently if kept watered during their growing season, but they must be allowed to dry out in summer. One objectionable feature is that they are prone to having aphids attack the flowers.

As tall background plants in front of shrubs they are strikingly effective. All *Bulbinella* are well worth having and make good cut flowers.

FIGURE 3-9.
Bulbinella latifolia
flowers in a raceme.

FIGURE 3-10.
Chasmanthe floribunda
var. *duckittii*.

Chasmanthe (Iridaceae)

The name is derived from the Greek *chasme*, "gaping," and *anthe*, "flower," but I fail to get the connection. In the species that I grow, the flowers are curved and hooded but not gaping as I construe the concept.

The genus has been revised by Miriam De Vos (1985) to include three species in the Cape flora. These are tall, deciduous, winter-growing plants with large corms. They are vigorous and easy to grow. In fact, they are too easy and can become weedy if not restrained. They readily naturalize in my garden.

I once sent corms of *Chasmanthe* to Monticello, the historic home of President Thomas Jefferson, but was puzzled by the request, since Peggy Newcomb, greenhouse manager at Monticello, stresses authenticity in her plants. Katherine Whiteside (1991) has explained the mystery, reporting that Jefferson in fact did order *Chasmanthe* for his cool greenhouse at Monticello.

Chasmanthe bicolor grows to 3 feet (1 m) or more. The flowers arise from both sides of the stalk to give a flattened appearance to the inflorescence. The flower stalk is often branched. The red or vermillion upper segments are long, hooded, and curved, with protruding black anthers. The lower segments are greenish yellow. Although this species has been grown in Europe for many years it is quite rare in the wild, and Miriam De Vos (1985) reported that an extensive search for it in 1984 was unsuccessful. It is a handsome plant that blooms in midwinter.

Chasmanthe floribunda also has the interesting flattened appearance to the inflorescence. The nominal species, *C. floribunda*, has orange flowers that I find rather dull, but the variety *C. floribunda* var. *duckittii* is a tall, stately, and rather elegant plant with yellow flowers that I much admire (Figure 3-10). It is named in honor of the Duckitt family of Darling who have created wildflower preserves and have been instrumental in the operation of the spring wildflower shows at Darling for most of the 20th century (see Plates 19, 20).

The third species is *Chasmanthe aethiopica*, which has orange-red flowers that tend to come from one side of the stalk. *Chasmanthe aethio-*

pica has naturalized in Santa Barbara (but not from my garden) and verges on being a pest. I remove all the volunteer seedlings I find and keep the parent confined to a container. If it weren't for the gorgeous rufous and Allen's hummingbirds that feed on its nectar as they migrate through here in February, I would put it into the compost heap.

No other genus of Cape bulbs is easier to propagate. *Chasmanthe* grows readily from seeds or offsets and is not particular about soils or garden location.

Aside from their bad relative, *Chasmanthe aethiopica*, the other species have merit. The rare *C. bicolor* is very attractive, and the tall, elegant *C. floribunda* var. *duckittii* has many uses. Graham Duncan (1985) suggested that a mixed planting of *C. floribunda* var. *duckittii* and *Agapanthus* can be very effective.

Clivia (Amaryllidaceae)

The name honors the Duchess of Northumberland, granddaughter of the Robert Clive of India fame. It is believed that *Clivia miniata* first bloomed in her conservatory in England about 1854. According to Coombes (1985) *Clivia* is pronounced klie´-vee-a. Sima Eliovson (1967, page 103) said that "some people pronounce the name with a long *i*, but most refer to it with a short *i*, since few people know the origin of plant names."

The root of *Clivia miniata* is used as a snakebite remedy by the Zulu, who also use the root in treating febrile conditions and the herb to facilitate delivery at childbirth or to initiate parturition when its onset is retarded (Watt and Breyer-Brandwijk, 1962).

There is no *Clivia* in the Cape flora, but four species grow in other parts of South Africa. Walters (1988) reported that it occurred naturally in Natal in light woodlands from near the coast to at least 3000 feet (1000 m) high in humus soil on top of a freely draining subsoil. Hannibal (1984) noted that in its native habitat, *Clivia* may grow over moss-covered rocky outcroppings, and that *C. caulescens,* the least common species, often grows in trees along with other epiphytes in the cloud-moistened areas.

Thus while *Clivia* is not truly a Cape bulb, it is so common and so useful in shady situations in southern California that I feel its inclusion in this encyclopedia is justified.

Clivia miniata (Figure 3-11) has been given the common names of kaffir lily, bush lily, and St. John's lily (see Plate 21). The species name, according to Zimmerman (1935), is derived from the Latin *minium*, "red oxide of lead," to describe the flower color. However, this flower color has variously been described as ranging from tawny orange to flaming apricot to cinnabar red to scarlet with a yellow throat. There is a much-sought-after yellow form, *C. miniata* var. *citrina*, that is rarely available and is coveted by gardeners (Plate 22). Graham Duncan (1985c) noted that naturally occurring plants of this variety were first found wild and collected in Zululand in the 1890s, but there is uncertainty about the origin of the variety *citrina* in cultivation today, for it may be a hybrid and not the wild type. Duncan (1985) described the cultivar 'Kirstenbosch yellow' as having light yellow flowers, well-reflexed petals, and deep yellow at the base of the segments. These flowers have a sweet fragrance, and their bright yellow fruits are small, containing no more than four seeds each. He also grew a second yellow form at Kirstenbosch, with unscented flowers of a different shade and large, bright-yellow fruits containing up to eight seeds. It also differs in leaf form and blooms later than 'Kirstenbosch yellow'.

The erect flower stalk of *Clivia miniata* can reach 18 inches (46 cm) or more. The umbel may have 12–20 trumpet-shaped flowers that bloom mostly from late winter well into spring. Although they may bloom into summer, sporadic blooms appear throughout the year. The leaves are evergreen, broad, and straplike. The fleshy seed capsules turn a brilliant red as they mature, which may take six to twelve months after flowering.

Clivia miniata plants do not grow from a true bulb or corm. Instead, a bulblike thickening of leaf bases develops with many strong, fleshy roots that have a food storage function. Daughter plants arise from laterally growing rootstock. Duncan (1985, page 85) wrote that they prefer a rich soil containing plenty of compost or leaf-mould and require regular watering during their growing period, which is in the summer months. During winter they can survive with very little water, but they are not adversely affected by heavy winter rainfall provided the soil is well drained.

Gardeners in the eastern states commonly grow *Clivia* in pots, and Kevin Walters (1988) pointed out that a sick-looking *Clivia* is probably suffering from the effects of bad drainage. It resents disturbance and should be allowed to remain in its container for years. Les Hannibal (1984) suggested the container be partly filled with a good loam over adequate drainage material. The root tips are then worked into the loam, and fine gravel is used to fill in under the root crown and around the roots so that the stalk is held upright. Normally a fine moss will form on the semi-exposed roots, and Hannibal suggested that symbiotic soil bacteria may be involved in growth.

Wally Lane (1976, page 8) reported that

when the plant is ready to be divided it should be carefully removed from the pot and all of the soil washed off by dunking in a bucket of water or by gently washing with spray from a garden hose. By doing this one can see where to cut the individual plants apart with the least harm to the roots.

Lane advised repotting in a small container, as did Gladys Blackbeard (1939, page 193) who cautioned, "Never 'over-pot' *Clivia* plants as they will not flower, but only increase in leaf and root system." She added that *Clivia* species flower well in 9 inch pots and that the secret to flowering is to starve the plants rather than to overfeed them.

From these experts it is clear that *Clivia* plants bloom well even when crowded and can be kept in a container for years if good drainage is maintained. An occasional feeding with a fertilizer high in potassium is desirable, but some gardeners feel *Clivia* should be fed generously. *Clivia* makes its growth of leaves immediately after the flowering season, and the time to transplant it is when the leaves are mature in summer.

FIGURE 3-11.
Clivia miniata.

Clivia can be propagated from the large seeds that are removed and placed on the soil surface or lightly covered with a mixture of sand and peat moss. If kept moist, seed germinates in about a month but will require four to six years to flower.

Walters (1988) reported that the yellow form, *Clivia miniata* var. *citrina*, was self-sterile but readily crossed with the wild type *C. miniata*. The resulting F_1 hybrids may yield a small percentage of yellow-flowered plants and when backcrossed with the parental variety *citrina*, about 50 percent of the progeny should be self-fertile, "thus breaking the existing breeding barrier for further yellow-flowered forms from seed" (page 30). This was confirmed in Australia, where Morris (1990) grew seeds received from Les Hannibal in California as a result of using pollen from ordinary orange *C. miniata* on a self-sterile yellow *Clivia*. He then found that by crossing the F_1 seedlings with themselves and, when possible, with F_2 yellow seedlings, the yellow factor acts as a simple recessive gene. This is shown as follows:

$$F_1 \text{ (orange)} \times F_1 \text{ (orange)} = 20 \text{ percent yellow}$$
$$F_1 \text{ (orange)} \times F_2 \text{ (yellow)} = 50 \text{ percent yellow}$$
$$F_2 \text{ (yellow)} \times F_2 \text{ (yellow)} = 100 \text{ percent yellow}$$

McNeil (1985) reported on hybrids of *Clivia miniata* with *Eucharis grandiflora* that are scented; no wild *C. miniata* are scented. Other interesting (almost incredible) crosses reported are *C. miniata* with *Narcissus tazetta*, and *C. miniata* with *Hippeastrum* species. Another species, *C. caulescens,* has been crossed with *Agapanthus* to produce very dark navy blue flowers. (Perhaps *Agapanthus* is an amaryllid after all; see the discussion of proper family placement in the section on *Agapanthus*.)

One occasionally sees the species *Clivia nobilis*, which has an umbel of many tubular but drooping reddish flowers with green tips. It has been hybridized with *C. miniata* to produce the hybrid *C.* ×*cyrtanthiflora*. As the name suggests, the plant has *Cyrtanthus* flowers. These were first grown by Van Houtte at Ghent, Belgium, and first shown in bloom at the Berlin flower show in 1859, according to Zimmerman (1935).

I find that *Clivia miniata* does well in the shade of coast live oaks in California and thrives there in spite of a disgraceful amount of neglect. Their success in this location is surprising in view of the much more moist situation of the Natal woodlands where they grow naturally, a tribute to the tough character of this versatile plant.

Crinum (Amaryllidaceae)

The Greek word for lily is *krinon*. There are many species of *Crinum* in the world, but the genus is barely represented in the Cape flora; only two species were listed by Bond and Goldblatt (1984).

The type locality of *Crinum variabile* is at Garies in Namaqualand, where I saw the plants in early spring growing in the running water of an ephemeral stream. I have never seen the species in cultivation, nor am I familiar with the other Cape species, *C. lineare,* which is reported to grow in the coastal hills near Port Elizabeth.

David Lehmiller (1987), a *Crinum* enthusiast from Texas, made a special trip to South Africa to observe and photograph indigenous *Crinum* in the wild. His article illustrated flowering *C. lineare* in a photograph taken near Port Elizabeth in February. He also published a February photograph of *C. variabile* in a dry stream bed south of Nieuwoudtville and described the plants as growing in full sun in the bone dry stream bed (Lehmiller, 1987, page 55):

> Although the leaves were brown and dried, several plants bore scapes in full bloom. The flowers had short tepal tubes, which was an important identifying criterion. Near Garies, there were hundreds of bulbs tightly wedged between the rocks in the stream bed. All the leaves were shriveled and brown. Several bulbs looked very large, perhaps 18–20 cm [7–8 in] in diameter, but a compressed air hammer would have been required to dislodge them from between the rocks.

While these Cape species of *Crinum* are apparently not available to gardeners, there are many spectacular species from other parts of the world that are highly valued by Amaryllid fanciers. From the standpoint of Cape bulbs it is of interest that *Amaryllis belladonna* has been crossed with *Crinum* to produce hybrids called either × *Amacrinum* or × *Crinodonna*. The hybrids are available in the trade, and I have found them sold in the fall at a nursery in my area. Les Hannibal (1980) spoke of such intergeneric crosses, and to reflect the parentage of the hybrids, which also involve *Brunsvigia*, has called them "Amar-Bruns-Crinum."

Crocosmia (Iridaceae)

The crushed flowers of *Crocosmia* infused in hot water are said to emit a strong odor reminiscent of saffron, and the name *Crocosmia* is understandably derived from the Greek *krokos* or the Latin *crocus*, meaning "saffron," and *osme*, meaning "smell." Miriam De Vos is clearly the authority on these plants and revised the genus in 1984.

Crocosmia does not occur in the Cape flora but is from the inland and eastern summer-rainfall areas of South Africa, where six species grow. I have included it because it is South African and is so compatible in a garden of Cape bulbs.

Crocosmia is distinct in having large, persistent, perennial, and tunicated corms. New corms are formed annually, but the older corms remain alive for two or more years and if separated will produce foliage and flowers. It is common to find long underground stolons produced from axillary buds on the corms. New plants develop from these stolon tips, so the tall, hip-high plants tend to form clumps. The corms sprout in winter or early spring and bloom in summer. The genus is closely related to the Cape *Tritonia* and *Chasmanthe*. The commercial plants were formerly called *Montbretia*.

The commonly encountered cultivar is a cross made by using *Crocosmia aurea* pollen on *C. pottsii*. This was done by the French horticulturist Victor Lemoine at Nancy. His plants flowered for the first time in August 1880, and he released them to the trade as *Montbretia crocosmiaeflora*. Miriam De Vos (1984) recognized this plant as *Crocosmia* × *crocosmiiflora* (Figure 3-12) and stated that it has characters intermediate

FIGURE 3-12.
Crocosmia ×*crocosmiiflora*.

between its two parent species. It has slightly zygomorphic, funnel-shaped flowers with a color range through the orange and yellows. Sometimes there are reddish marks in the throat of the perianth.

I also grow *Crocosmia paniculata*. As the name suggests, it has a panicle of flowers on a slender stalk 39 inches (100 cm) or more in height. It forms large clumps and is nearly evergreen if the watering season is extended. The flowers are strongly zygomorphic and narrowly funnel-shaped. They come in a variety of colors, including orange-red, rusty red, and brownish orange.

Crocosmia can be propagated from seeds or from corms that should be planted 3 inches (7 cm) deep and the same distance apart. It multiplies like mad and can grow waist high but is easily controlled. *Crocosmia* grows in full sun in my coastal garden but inland, where summers can get hot, it should have partial shade. It does well in pots and is a fine cut flower, blooming as early as June in Santa Barbara and later in the summer in the Pacific Northwest.

Cyanella (Tecophilaceae)

When Linnaeus described this genus he had in his hand the bluish flowered *Cyanella hyacinthoides*, so he used the name *Cyanella* derived from the Greek *kyanos,* "blue." The specific epithet *C. hyacinthoides* means "like a hyacinth." There are six species of *Cyanella* confined to the western Cape.

Cyanella has deep-seated, tunicated corms adapted to grow in the arid parts of the Cape Province. They are often found wedged between rocks and are difficult to dislodge. They are edible and are in fact a dietary staple of the indigenous people of Namaqualand, who dig them with a crowbar. They are roasted or boiled in milk and taste like a sweet potato according to Scott (1989b). The corms appear to lack toxins of any kind and have recently been investigated as a possible food crop. They have been compared nutritionally with potatoes.

Cyanella hyacinthoides (synonyms include *C. capensis* and *C. pentheri*) is widespread in the Cape region and grows in a variety of soils. It is often a pioneer in disturbed sites and can be a bit weedy. It blooms in late spring or early summer. It grows to about 15 inches (38 cm) and has a many-flowered inflorescence. The flowers are not really blue but are lilac or mauve with yellow stamens. The leaf margins may be wavy to very crisped.

According to Scott (1989), who has written a charming article on this genus, *Cyanella orchidiformis* grows in dry riverbeds, on riverbanks, or between rocks in fairly heavy clay soil. From a distance its flowers resemble a small orchid, hence the name. It is sweetly scented and blooms earlier in spring than does *C. hyacinthoides*. The flowers are pale lilac with a darker throat. The corms of this species are also edible.

Cyanella lutea (Figure 3-13) is the most widespread species of *Cyanella* (see Plate 23). It has a common name of five fingers, referring to the five upper stamens. The specific epithet, *C. lutea,* means "deep yellow," and my plants have starlike, appropriately yellow flowers with distinct greenish veins. Pink and highly scented forms are reported, but I have not had them. *Cyanella lutea* grows to about 15 inches (38 cm) high. The leaves are ribbed and have wavy margins.

The three species—*Cyanella hyacinthoides, C. lutea*, and *C. orchidiformis*—are the only ones I have found available from South African nurseries, but there are other *Cyanella* species that have horticultural merit. For example, the most gorgeous of the genus is *C. alba,* which has the largest, showiest flowers that may be yellow, white, or pale pink. The common name is lady's hand because the five large, upper stamens arch together over the lower one like the fingers of a tiny hand. This description by Scott (1989a) makes me eager to have them in my collection.

Other species are *Cyanella lineata*, a low-growing pink flower, and last but not least is *C. aquatica,* which grows in seasonally water-logged clay among large rocks in Nieuwoudtville's klipkoppies. *Cyanella aquatica* has the most limited distribution of the *Cyanella* but should make a good garden subject, with its tall, stately racemes of orange flowers. Scott (1989a) notes that in spite of its growing naturally in heavy wet clay it has flowered well in a sandy soil in cultivation.

FIGURE 3-13.
Cyanella lutea.

Cyanella can be propagated from corms but is quickest from seeds. In a sandy medium, germination of *C. lutea* is in 41 days and *C. orchidiformis* is in 26 days. Seedlings may flower in their second year. The corms should be planted at least 3 inches (8 cm) deep in a sunny spot. As is the case with all winter-growing Cape bulbs, they need good drainage and a dry summer.

Cyanella is just another example of the many very worthwhile Cape bulbs deserving gardeners' attention.

Cybistetes (Amaryllidaceae)

When the flowers of *Cybistetes* mature and dry up, the umbel becomes detached from the stalk and is tumbled over the ground by wind, so the genus name derived from the Greek *kubistetes*, "a tumbler," is certainly appropriate. This method of seed dispersal is also seen in *Brunsvigia* and *Boophane*.

Cybistetes is monotypic, *C. longifolia* being its single species. Les Hannibal (1986) reported that it holds the top record for the number of botanical names attached to it, and he cited at least 22. It has mistakenly been called *Ammocharis falcata*, which may be the case in the article by John Martley (1939), who described flowers from the Cape flats that are most likely *C. longifolia*.

The flowers of *Cybistetes longifolia*, which open white and then become pink-flushed, are about 3 inches (8 cm) long, almost as wide, and strongly reflexed. There may be 20 or more of these sweetly fragrant flowers in a single umbel, which is borne on a fleshy stalk less than 12 inches (31 cm) high. In the Cape they bloom during the summer months with the latest flowers appearing in the higher rainfall areas, according to Graham Duncan (1979). The bulbs are quite large. The leaves are prostrate on the soil surface and grow quite long, which accounts for its specific epithet. In the wild, *C. longifolia* favors sandy soil.

Propagation is from offsets or seeds. Many seeds are produced, but Duncan (1979) believed it could take seedlings ten years to flower. In planting offsets, the bulb neck should be at the soil surface. John Bryan (1989) considered *Cybistetes longifolia* to be a good container plant.

Cyrtanthus (Amaryllidaceae)

Cyrtanthus means "curved flower." The flowers characteristically tend to curve downward from the apex of the flower stalk. *Cyrtanthus* is entirely an African genus. It is the largest Amaryllid genus in Africa, with about 50 species, 19 of which at least grow in the Cape Province in areas of comparatively high precipitation. *Cyrtanthus* tends to grow in moist places, such as near streams, and at higher elevations, where Sarah Coombs (1948) noted they have cool, damp night air. Dyer (1939) reviewed the genus.

There are both evergreen and deciduous species, and the leaf form is quite variable. Certain deciduous species flower spectacularly after veld wildfires but bloom only sporadically otherwise. Understandably such species are commonly called fire lilies. According to Brown and Le Maitre (1990), a good example of such a fire lily is *Cyrtanthus ventricosus,* which produces few bulbils and seeds only once every 10–20 years.

At Kirstenbosch, Graham Duncan (1990a, 1990b, 1990c) is growing over 30 species of *Cyrtanthus* and many hybrids. While all species are suited to container cultivation, only certain species are suited to general garden culture. From Duncan's comments and those of other experienced growers, the following species would be welcome additions to any collection of Amaryllids.

Cyrtanthus brachyscyphus (syn. *C. parviflorus*) is a little evergreen species and one of the easiest to grow. The flowers in shades of red and orange are produced in spring and summer on 12-inch (31-cm) stalks. Reduced watering in winter is advisable. The bulbs are planted with the bulb neck at soil surface.

Cyrtanthus elatus is a new name for a particularly striking member of the genus that was first known to gardeners as *Vallota speciosa* and more recently as *C. purpureus*. No sooner did we learn that change than we were told by Hilliard and Burtt (1986) that the correct name for this widely grown and well-known species is *C. elatus*. This most famous of the *Cyrtanthus* species has also had several common names, including George lily, Knysna lily, and Scarborough lily. It is evergreen, can grow to 18 inches (45 cm) tall, and has singularly beautiful, trumpet-shaped, scarlet flowers in summer. There is also a lovely rare pink form. To the delight of gardeners, *C. elatus* generously produces offsets. David Verity (1976), who successfully grows *Cyrtanthus* in containers in California, claimed the best time to divide the clumps is when active growth begins in the late winter. The bulbs should be set so they are just covered.

Cyrtanthus mackenii, commonly called the Ifafa lily, is another ornamental, evergreen species and one of the easiest to grow (Figure 3-14). The flowers are scented and variable in color. Richfield (1984) mentioned apricot, yellow, pink, and cream colored flowers. The tubular flowers are borne on stalks that can reach 16 inches (40 cm). This species was used in several breeding programs, most recently in the one at the University of California at Irvine (Koopowitz, 1986). (See Plate 24.)

Cyrtanthus obrienii is another evergreen species. It produces red, pendulous flowers mainly in spring. Graham Duncan (1990b) says it is a fairly attractive and tough plant that does not like to be disturbed.

Propagation of *Cyrtanthus* is by seeds or by offsets. A technique discovered by Hendrik and Rhoda Van Zijl and reported by Willi Olivier (1980) is to place the fresh seeds in a container of water that is changed once a week to restore the oxygen. The seeds soon become plump, and a radicle is formed followed by young rootlets. Eventually a tiny, glasslike bulb is formed. When the leaf appears, the seedling is given a weak feeding of liquid fertilizer and then transferred to a seedling tray. The mix in the tray consists of sand, bonemeal, and peat moss to which a little seaweed fertilizer may be added. Regular feeding is important. The seedlings are kept shaded during their first season. Good drainage is of utmost importance.

Not everyone uses this water technique, but it is commonly known that seeds of *Cyrtanthus* have a limited period of viability and must be

FIGURE 3-14.
Cyrtanthus sp.

sown when very fresh. The black, flattened, slightly winged seeds should be sown just below the surface in a very well-drained and quite sandy medium according to Graham Duncan (1990a), who suggests that the seed containers be kept in a shaded situation. Some species may germinate in ten days; others may take several weeks.

Sarah Coombs (1948, page 103) had more advice:

Seeds need a large proportion of sand in their soil, probably two-thirds at the start. Drainage must be perfect. Later, a good garden soil will be right but always with good drainage. It is possible to overdo the sunlight with young plants. They must be watched. Once well grown, with care in drainage, much water when blooming and witholding it gradually as they stop growing, they will do well. When they reach mature growth, they will stand a good deal of indifferent treatment without resenting it, though thankful for extra kindness. . . . [*Cyrtanthus* is] an amiable lot, really, when a few necessities are looked after.

Good gardening is often the art of watering, and Graham Duncan (1990a) emphasizes that correct watering procedure is critical to successful cultivation of *Cyrtanthus*. Most deciduous species are dormant in winter, during which time they should be kept as dry as possible. The evergreen *Cyrtanthus* also require a rest period and should be watered far less frequently during winter. The roots of most species tend to rot if overwatered or if watered during dormancy. It has been Duncan's experience at Kirstenbosch with both the deciduous and evergreen species to permit the growing medium to dry out almost completely between waterings during summer, which is the growing season for most *Cyrtanthus*. While he admits there is no hard-and-fast rule, he strongly advises that when in doubt, "don't water!"

Willi Olivier (1980) cautioned that reserve food and nutrients are used in the production of flowers and seeds, so there is a need for feeding the plants regularly when they are under cultivation. Graham Duncan (1990a, page 20) pointed out that unlike *Nerine*, a genus in which feeding is not generally recommended, dilute feeding during the growing period is indicated for *Cyrtanthus*. The evergreen species benefit particularly from the application of liquid fertilizers with a high potash but relatively low nitrogen content. . . . the use of bonemeal mixed into the growing medium and granular slow-release fertilizers sprinkled on the soil surface have also proved beneficial.

Graham Duncan (1990a, 1990b, 1990c) published a series of three very informative papers to popularize *Cyrtanthus*, to provide a summary of the advances in horticultural knowledge of the genus, and to give explicit cultivation hints on various species. These articles clearly show that *Cyrtanthus* is highly ornamental, easy to maintain, and rapidly gaining popularity with Amaryllid enthusiasts. Koopowitz (1986) believed that *Cyrtanthus* has considerable potential as a cut flower for florists.

Dierama (Iridaceae)

Hilliard and Burtt (1991) recognized 44 African species of *Dierama* ranging from Knysna in the southern Cape, through a concentration of species in the Natal Drakensberg area, then northward to Ethiopia. The genus name is from the Greek *dierama*, meaning "funnel" or "like a bell." The evergreen plants are found in moist grassland habitats, which accounts for a common name, grassy bells (Coombs, 1936). They are also called wand flowers or harebells, although Hilliard and Burtt (1991) corrected this to hairbells because of the hairlike flower stalks. *Dierama* is especially lovely if grown to arch its flowers over a pool. The pendulous flowers, suspended by their delicate stems from the gracefully arching and remarkably slender stalk, appear to be constantly in motion, which has inspired the name fairy fishing rod (Scholtz, 1985) or angel's fishing rod.

Bond and Goldblatt (1984) listed a single species, *Dierama pendulum*, in the Cape flora (Plate 25). *Dierama pendulum* and *D. pulcherrimum* are two common species in horticulture. Their differences are not apparent in dried material, but the live flowers of *D. pendulum* are truly bell-shaped and flare out at the apex; the segments of *D. pulcherrimum* never spread widely from a conical base but tend to be parallel-sided. The tips are only scarcely spreading.

Both species have a range of pink flowers and have white forms. Everett (1981) reported that hybrids have occurred spontaneously at the Strybing Arboretum in San Francisco and probably elsewhere. They have been grouped as *Dierama hybridum*. While Hilliard and Burtt (1991) have little doubt that hybrids occur, they do not validate the names *D. hybridum* or *D. intermedium*.

Propagation is from the rootstock, which is a persistent corm that should be planted 2 inches (5 cm) deep and left undisturbed but kept watered. In England, replanting is done in the spring. Propagation is also from seeds (mine germinate in 24 days), and seedlings flower in their third season, although some may bloom in the second year. *Dierama* flourishes in a sunny site in well-drained, fertile soil that should be kept moist. Du Plessis and Duncan (1989) found that the plants do best on a north-facing slope in South Africa, which is a south-facing slope in North America. *Dierama pendulum* was killed to the ground in a Virginia winter by temperatures as low as 3°F (−16°C) but recovered to bear its graceful flowers in summer.

According to Hilliard and Burtt (1991) *Dierama pendulum* has escaped from cultivation and naturalized itself in New South Wales, southeastern Australia, as well as in the north and south islands of New Zealand. They also reported *D. pulcherrimum* as a garden escape in Tasmania.

Dietes (Iridaceae)

The name *Dietes* was first proposed in 1812. It is derived from the Greek *dis,* "twice," and *etes,* "an associate," to reflect the dual affinities with *Iris* and *Moraea*. In fact *Dietes* is often erroneously called *Moraea* by gardeners, but *Moraea* grows from corms and is deciduous while *Dietes* is evergreen and has a thick, tough, creeping rhizome. Peter Goldblatt (1981c) made a thorough analysis of *Dietes* and his fascinating paper is used extensively in this account.

There are six species of *Dietes*. Five are African, and one (*D. robinsoniana*) is a remarkably disjunct relict on Lord Howe Island in the Tasman sea between Australia and New Zealand. The species of *Dietes* grow in forest margins or along streams and other wet places. They are survivors of an ancient time when the African climate was far more equable than it is at present.

Dietes iridioides (syn. *D. vegeta*) is the most widespread and common species of the genus, extending from nearly the southern tip of Africa to Kenya. It has been in cultivation for over 200 years. A common name is fortnight lily. The species name means it is like an *Iris,* and any gardener that grows non-bearded *Iris* immediately sees the resemblance (Figure 3-15). The flowers are white with blue to violet style branches and a yellow nectar guide. The blossoms are ephemeral, lasting only a day, but are continually replaced with new flowers. The plants are about 2 feet (61 cm) in height. This is an undemanding species that seems to thrive in Santa Barbara with very little attention. A closely related species is *D. flavida,* which has cream to yellow flowers, but I have never found it available for testing in my garden. I have a cultivar of *D. iridioides* named 'Lemon Drop', which has yellowish flowers.

Dietes grandiflora is, as the name suggests, the largest flowered species of the genus. It is related to the more widespread *D. iridioides* but is easily differentiated by its height of 3 to 4 feet (91 to 122 cm) and its larger flowers, which last three days in contrast with those of *D. iridioides* that last a single day. The flowers are white with yellow nectar guides and a distinguishing and dense yellow beard on the three outer segments. The style branches are pale mauve. Once established, the plants are persistent even when neglected, though more and larger flowers and a longer flowering season reward gardeners who give the plants better care.

Dietes bicolor is considered a primitive species related to the Lord Howe Island relict, *D. robinsoniana*. It is confined to a limited area east of the Cape and is found in moist situations. The flowers are yellow with a dark brown nectar guide on the three outer segments. The plant is free flowering, and although each flower lasts only one day, new flowers

FIGURE 3-15.
Dietes iridioides.

are produced almost every day for several months. If well grown, the plant may reach 3 feet (92 cm). If not properly grown, it may produce only foliage and no flowers. The plant is attractive and its use in fire-resistant xeriscapes appears to be increasing. It is the only polyploid species of *Dietes*.

I have acquired seed of *Dietes robinsoniana* from the seed exchange program of the newly formed International Bulb Society to which all serious bulb growers should belong. It will be interesting to compare the performance of *D. robinsoniana* with its South African relatives from which it has apparently been separated since the break up of Gondwanaland millions of years ago.

Propagation of *Dietes* is by seed (*D. bicolor* seed germinated in 33 days) or by division of the rhizomes in late summer. Lateral buds on the rhizome produce side branches that grow into new plants forming a clumped group with the original parent. *Dietes* is not particular to soil type and will survive inattention but will flourish in the garden if given water and even a minimum of care. It is most successful in full sun and moist soil; it will grow in shade but flowers there erratically.

Drimia (Hyacinthaceae)

John Bryan (1989) wrote that the root sap of *Drimia* is acrid and may cause inflammation of the skin, and indeed, the name is from the Greek *drimys,* meaning "acrid." This negative introduction is not improved by any great horticultural merit, so I agree with John Bryan that *Drimia* may not be worthy of much attention. There are about 22 species in Africa with six listed in the Cape flora (Bond and Goldblatt, 1984). I have grown an eastern species, *D. angustifolia*, but I cannot imagine it being of interest other than to bulb collectors.

Empodium (Hypoxidaceae)

Empodium has about ten species, four of which are listed in the Cape flora. These winter-growing plants are deciduous and have a cormous rootstock. The leaves are distinctly pleated. The flowers open in the morning and close in midafternoon. The flowers of all the Cape species are yellow.

Empodium is a dwarf plant that I have not grown. Du Plessis and Duncan (1989) found it attractive in a rock garden or in containers where it can be left undisturbed. Offsets are slow to form, so plants are multiplied more quickly by seeds. Seedlings flower in the third year.

Engysiphon (Iridaceae)

The name *Engysiphon* is derived from the Greek *enguos*, "narrow," and *siphon*, "tube," referring to the characteristically narrow perianth tube (Innes, 1985). Bond and Goldblatt (1984) included *Engysiphon* with the *Geissorhiza* of the Cape flora to which *Engysiphon* is related but differs in the arrangement of the stamens and styles and the length of the filaments and flowers. Most species have a single, erect leaf with a raised margin and midrib. All plants are deciduous. The rootstock is a corm with a tunic of woody, shiny fibers completely fused together. The eight species of *Engysiphon* grow in the Cape Province in sandy and stony locations.

The best horticultural account is given by Jim Holmes (1981), who found all species to produce a single stalk with three to eight pink or white flowers distinctly veined pink with dark pink or red on the underside. The actinomorphic flowers can be more than 2 inches (5 cm) wide with 2-inch (5-cm) long perianth tubes. The plants grow from 6 to 10 inches (15 to 25 cm) in height.

From seed the flowers appear in the third year. Results are best when seedlings are planted *en masse* in clean sand in full winter sun. Give plants a dry rest in summer.

Jim Holmes (1981, page 3) concluded: "This genus is seldom found in cultivation—a pity, as most species are attractive and would surely add interest to any bulb collection."

Eucomis (Hyacinthaceae)

The word *Eucomis* may be derived from the Greek *eu*, "good," and *kome*, "hair," or from the Greek *eukomes*, translated roughly as "beautifully headed." In either case, the name clearly refers to the interesting tuft of leaflike bracts at the apex of the inflorescence. The resulting resemblance to a miniature pineapple gives these plants their common name, pineapple flowers.

The ten species in the genus range from the Cape to south tropical Africa; three belong to the Cape flora (Bond and Goldblatt, 1984). All are deciduous, summer-growing, and dormant in the winter except for *Eucomis regia*, a winter-growing Cape species. The inflorescence is a dense raceme or spike of many small white or pale green or yellowish green flowers. In some species the flowers are quite heavily margined with dark purple. The large bulbs of *Eucomis* produce a rosette of smooth, shiny leaves that can grow to 24 inches (61 cm) long.

Eucomis autumnalis is a Cape species that has the synonym *E. undulata*, which is appropriately descriptive because the leaf margins are in fact undulated; a subspecies is *E. autumnalis* subsp. *clavata*. These sturdy, attractive plants can grow to about 3 feet (91 cm) high under good care. The flowers, which appear in summer, are yellowish green.

Eucomis comosa (syn. *E. punctata*) is another Cape species. The sweetly scented flowers are variable but may be white tinged with pink or wine-purple, the ovaries are wine colored and the flower stalks are spotted purple. These are particularly attractive cut flowers.

Eucomis bicolor has cream flowers with purple margins. The flowers are handsome but may have an unpleasant scent.

The smallest species that I grow is *Eucomis zambesiaca* (Figure 3-16), with its wonderfully African name. It grows to about 12 inches (30 cm). It is quite prolific, an easy grower, has white flowers, and is the first *Eucomis* to bloom, starting in late spring.

Propagation of *Eucomis* is from offsets or seeds (*E. autumnalis* seed germinated in 34 days). Seedlings flower in three or four years. The bulbs are large and should be planted 4 inches (10 cm) deep in rich soil and in full sun near the coast or in bright shade inland. The clumps should be lifted and thinned every three years. *Eucomis* is dormant in winter and blooms during the summer; if protected with mulch it can take moderate

FIGURE 3-16.
Eucomis zambesiaca.

frosts. It should be watered regularly from the time it starts growth in early spring until fall. After foliage dies back in fall or winter, it can go almost dry, although moisture will not hurt it if drainage is good.

Eucomis has many plus factors. It is a useful garden plant, good container subject, and the interesting cut flower is truly a conversation piece.

Ferraria (Iridaceae)

The genus *Ferraria* is named for Professor Giovanni Battista Ferrari, who first described and illustrated it in 1633. He was unaware of its South African origin and instead thought it was from Batavia. There are about ten species of *Ferraria*, and six of them are listed in the Cape flora (Bond and Goldblatt, 1984). The most authoritative taxonomic work on *Ferraria* was published in 1979 by Miriam De Vos. The greatest concentration of Cape species is in the western coastal districts of the Cape Province.

Ferraria has continually attracted attention from the time it was first introduced in Europe. The very unusual flowers have remarkable color combinations and erect tufts of hairlike processes on the styles. The corms of *Ferraria*, which are persistent and without tunics, are completely different from those of any other genus in the Iridaceae. The annual development of a new corm with the perennial nature of the older corms results in a string of corms (Figure 1-4) weakly connected by a thin neck. The row of corms may be arranged vertically, obliquely, or almost horizontally in the soil. If one of the older corms is separated and replanted, it will form a new plant. It is interesting that some roots emerge from the upper part of a corm. Even under favorable conditions a corm may rest for more than a year without sprouting, an observation that has been made under horticultural conditions and probably also occurs in the wild as an adaptation to ensure survival underground during periods when some catastrophic event might decimate the exposed plant parts above ground.

The flowers of many *Ferraria* species emit a scent that may be unpleasant. The odor and copious amounts of nectar attract pollinators,

FIGURE 3-17.
Ferraria crispa.

short-tongued insects such as flies and small beetles. Soon after the flowers open, the perianth segments become strongly reflexed, and the resulting effect has given the plant the popular name of spider flowers. The flower segments have crisped or undulate margins. The fugacious flowers last from one to three days, depending upon the species. With age, the flower tips curl inward over the style and anthers to close the flower. After closing, some autolysis occurs in the perianth, and a drop of liquid forms inside the closed perianth.

The best known species is *Ferraria crispa* (Figure 3-17), which grows in coastal sand in some very arid areas. The plants reach 12 to 18 inches (30 to 46 cm) in height. The 2-inch (5-cm) flowers last one day and have an unpleasant odor. The perianth segments can be dark brown to maroon to almost black with cream to pale yellow lines and blotches. The anthers have bright orange pollen. Professor De Vos (1979) described a new, geographically separated subspecies, *F. crispa* subsp. *nortierii*, with flowers of pale yellow and margins of brown.

Ferraria densepunctulata is a rare and probably endangered species known from only three small locations (Plate 26). It was first found by Johan Loubser (1981b) in the spring of 1963 at Elandsbaai, where it grows in coastal sand. Propagation by Loubser progressed slowly, for the species is not self-compatible with its pollen. Unfortunately, a virus required the destruction of a number of corms. In 1979 Professor De Vos recognized it as a very distinct new species. Johan Loubser was finally able to distribute seeds to other gardeners in 1980.

Ferraria densepunctulata is the earliest flowering of the Cape species. The flowers appear in midwinter, about a month after the first leaves, and develop before the formation of the new corm. The almost odorless flowers have pale gray or grayish green segments with crisped margins. The three outer segments are densely spotted with small maroon or purple dots. The inner segments have a large maroon or purple blotch. The pollen is orange to deep yellow. The very attractive flowers are more beautiful than those of most other *Ferraria* species. It is a desirable species to cultivate, although it is not as easy as some others. Loubser (1981) reported a hybrid with *F. ferrariola* that is interesting but not as attractive as *F. densepunctulata.*

Ferraria uncinata has pale yellow, blue, or purplish blue flowers. The segment margins are greenish or yellowish. The flowers are faintly and pleasantly scented and remain open for two to three days. The plants grow in sandy shale or ground with some clay content. The species is readily distinguished by its leaves, which have finely crisped, irregularly toothed, or somewhat wavy margins.

Ferraria divaricata has four subspecies and flower color can vary widely between yellow, green, blue, brown, and mixtures of these shades. *Ferraria divaricata* subsp. *aurea* has golden yellow flowers.

Ferraria ferrariola occurs in Namaqualand. The flowers are mostly green and have a sweet scent.

Propagation of *Ferraria* is easiest from division of the corms. The plants, which grow from 12 to 18 inches (30 to 46 cm) tall, prefer a sunny site in sandy, well-drained soil in a location that promises winter rains and a dry summer.

Species of *Ferraria* are seldom found in cultivation and probably deserve far more attention. The flowers, while not showy, are delightfully complex and thoroughly fascinating.

Freesia (Iridaceae)

Other than *Gladiolus*, no other South African genus of bulbs has been so thoroughly cultivated and selected as *Freesia*. The genus was named in 1866 for the horticulturally minded German physician Friedrich Heinrich Theodor Freese of Keil. When Klatt (1866) published the name *Freesia,* he presumably found it as a manuscript name on Christian Ecklon's collection of *F. corymbosa*. Ecklon was an ardent plant collector, and Freese had been his student.

Freesia is endemic to southern Africa and restricted almost entirely to the Cape Province. Peter Goldblatt (1982) recognized 11 species of which only *F. andersoniae* occurs outside the southern Cape Province. *Freesia* is a typical Cape bulb that grows during the winter and is deciduous during the dry summer. The rootstock is a corm with tunics of net-ted fibers. The foliage is lance shaped and usually erect. The inflorescence is a spike of usually strongly scented flowers that are white, yellow, and in some species, pink.

The published horticultural history of *Freesia* seems confused and contradictory because of the misapplication of specific names, and we are indebted to Peter Goldblatt (1982) for carefully sorting them out. Briefly, the species now recognized as *F. leichtleinii* was the first to be a popular ornamental container plant and available in the nursery trade. The next important introduction was *F. alba* and not *F. refracta,* as the literature often suggests.

The breeding of *Freesia* began after *F. alba* came on the market in 1878, but the important step forward was the 1897 introduction of the rose-pink *F. corymbosa,* which was then named *F. armstrongii.* This pink flower provided the real stimulus to *Freesia* breeding and resulted in a fine display at Kew Gardens in 1901, where a hybrid between *F. leichtleinii* and *F. corymbosa* was included. The Dutch firm of Van Tubergen crossed *F. alba* with *F. corymbosa* about 1905 and through continuing efforts produced tall freesias with colors ranging from blue, mauve, rose, and yellow to white. These were the progenitors of the modern cultivars.

The subsequent history of *Freesia* breeding, according to Peter Goldblatt (1982), does not involve the wild species but is a complex story of new varieties, polyploid cultivars, and double-flowered types that bear less and less resemblance to the wild species. It is generally believed that in this breeding program much of the fragrance of the wild species has been lost, but as Goemans (1980, page 162) pointed out, "one person in nine is quite unable to smell Freesias."

Freesia alba has open, almost actinomorphic, upright flowers with subequal, spreading segments. This is considered a somewhat primitive character, so *F. alba* is regarded as the most generalized and least specialized species in the genus. The flowers are pure white or have a pale purple flush on the outer segments, which intensifies as the flowers age. Plants are generally about 12 inches (30 cm) tall with upright narrow leaves, but occasionally the stalk is inclined to fall toward the ground. A small bulbil is produced in some of the leaf axils, which is characteristic of other species that grow in sandy locations.

When first offered for sale in 1878, *Freesia alba,* with its white, richly scented flowers, created a sensation in the horticultural circles of Europe and North America. Botanists then treated it as a variety of the very different and horticulturally less attractive *F. refracta,* which has led to erroneous statements that *F. refracta* was important in the early breeding of *Freesia.* Most horticultural forms have *F. alba* in their pedigree and even today many bear a strong resemblance to it in the form of the flower. The superb scent, however, has been diluted or sometimes lost in some cultivars through breeding for other characteristics.

I find that *Freesia alba* is very easy to grow and is the most prolific of all the *Freesia* species in my collection.

Freesia leichtleinii is named for Max Leichtlin, horticulturist and plant collector, who found the plants in a neglected part of the Botanical Gardens at Padua in 1872. How these South African plants were obtained by the Botanical Gardens is a mystery. The species was not known in its native South Africa until a new species, *F. muirii,* was described in 1932. It is now recognized as the long lost, true wild form of *F. leichtleinii.*

Freesia leichtleinii is an attractive, vigorous plant with strongly scented, pale yellow flowers and bright yellow markings on the three lower segments. The reverse side of the segments and perianth tube are lightly flushed with purple, which, as is common with other *Freesia* species, intensifies as the flowers age. *Freesia leichtleinii* always grows near the coast in sandy soils. It produces a small bulbil in some of the leaf axils.

Freesia corymbosa, described in 1768, was one of the first two species of *Freesia* known to science. It is related to both *F. refracta* and to *F. occidentalis.* Typically the flowers are pale yellow, with the lower segments bright yellow to orange, occasionally pink, with a yellow throat. The flowers are often without scent. The pink-flowered form, formerly called *F. armstrongii,* was important in the breeding of the modern commercial cultivars.

Freesia occidentalis grows largely in inaccessible and remote areas of the very arid eastern foothills of the western Cape mountains. It is closely related to *F. refracta,* but the flowers are much more attractive (see Plate 27). They are pure creamy-white with yellow lower tepals and lower tube. They may be lightly sweet-scented or odorless. I find *F. occidentalis* easy to grow and am quite fond of it.

Freesia refracta is a tough species that I have seen in the arid Karoo growing in rock crevices, although it grows generally on clayey soils in dry conditions and often under shrubs or low bushes. The flowers are dull yellowish brown with orange markings on the lower segments and purple veins in the throat. To me the colors are a bit muddy. The flowers can have a spicy scent.

Freesia fergusoniae (Figure 3-18) is an attractive species with a flower stalk that may have one or two branches, each bearing several flowers. The flowers are creamy-yellow with deep yellow or almost orange markings on the three lower segments. They are typically scented but less so than *F. alba.* The species was named in 1927 for a Mrs. Ferguson who collected it and sent specimens to the attention of the noted South African botanist Louisa Bolus. It grows in clay soil in open or burned areas, not at all in dense bush.

Freesia sparrmannii was named by Carl Thunberg for Anders Sparrman who collected it in the 1770s. It is a low-growing species with a local distribution along forest margins. The unscented flowers are white inside and purple-flushed outside, with a small yellow mark on the lowermost segment.

Freesia elimensis has scented white flowers flushed light purple on the reverse side of the segments and a yellow-orange mark on the lower segment. It has a very restricted distribution, being found only in sandy soil in a limestone ridge on the Elim road south of Bredasdorp. It is closely related to *F. caryophyllacea,* a species that I have not grown.

Propagation of *Freesia* is from the daughter corms or from seeds. *Freesia corymbosa* germinates in 32 days and *F. fergusoniae* in 27–37 days. Some species of *Freesia* have flowered in eight months, but most take

FIGURE 3-18.
Freesia fergusoniae.

much longer. The pointed corms should be planted point up and close together at a depth of 2 to 3 inches (5 to 8 cm). Close planting helps to support the seedlings, which have an irritating habit of falling over. Deep planting also makes the stalks more secure. As with all the winter-growing Cape bulbs, the soil should be well drained, and the bulbs should be given water when growing and a dry rest in summer. A sunny site is preferable along the coast, but partial shade may be better inland. There is nothing difficult in the cultivation of *Freesia*.

Freesia is a good cut flower and is such an easy, rewarding, bright, and often scented flower that no garden or patio should be without it.

Galaxia (Iridaceae)

Carl Thunberg, who authored this genus in 1782, was reminded of a galaxy of stars by a carpet of these small flowers covering the ground. The name is derived from the Greek *galaxias*, referring to the starlike flower cluster.

For our technical knowledge of *Galaxia* we are indebted to the works of Peter Goldblatt (1979a, 1984a). There are about 14 species of *Galaxia*, all restricted to the southwest Cape or Namaqualand, truly Cape bulbs. The corms are tiny, and the leaves form a cluster or rosette that hugs the ground and is seldom more than 2 inches (5 cm) in any direction. The star-shaped flowers are about one inch (2.5 cm) in diameter and are yellow, white and yellow, or pink.

Galaxia ovata is presently the species easiest to obtain and most common in cultivation. The name means "egg shaped," and I am not sure how it applies. The flowers are bright yellow and have a long perianth tube that puts them above the rosette of channeled leaves that are less than 2 inches (5 cm) long.

Galaxia barnardii, named for the plant collector Professor T. T. Barnard, has the most striking flowers of the genus. They are pink with a dark center, as are the flowers of *G. versicolor*. Seeds of *G. barnardii* germinate in 113 days, *G. versicolor* in 61 days.

The name of *Galaxia fugacissima* reflects the fugacious nature of *Galaxia* flowers that last only a day. This species has yellow flowers.

Galaxia luteo-alba has flower segments that are yellow at the base and white in the apical half, as the name suggests.

Propagation of *Galaxia* is from division of the corms or from seeds. The clumps should be disturbed as little as possible and the corms planted only 0.5 inch (1 cm) deep. The seeds are extremely small and should barely be covered. Flowers may first bloom in the second year. *Galaxia* needs a sunny site, perfect drainage, and a long, dry summer. It is a bit tender to frost.

Galaxia is a dwarf and makes a nice container plant that could also be used in a rock garden. While individual flowers do not last more than a day, the flowering season is extended. Some species of *Galaxia* are now offered by South African dealers, so they may be seen more often in bulb collections.

Galtonia (Hyacinthaceae)

Galtonia, named for Francis Galton, is a small genus of summer-flowering plants restricted entirely to South Africa. It does not occur in the Cape Province, but it is so attractive and easy to grow that I include it in my collection.

Galtonia candicans is a summer-growing species that is dormant in winter (Plate 28). The common name is summer hyacinth. It reaches about 4 feet (122 cm) high. The flowers look like white bells. *Galtonia candicans* has been grown in English and American gardens for many years. According to Margaret Lawder (1978), these Berg lilies from the cold of the Drakensberg mountains flower well in warmer areas if refrigerated from autumn until spring.

Sarah Coombs (1936, page39) wrote,

[They] are not nearly as well known as they deserve to be for they are beautiful flowers of the very easiest culture. They grow on long stalks with a cluster of white drooping bells. They are among the best summer bulbs and planted in groups are always a charming sight. It is one of the queer things about gardens, which are full of surprising happenings, that flowers so lovely and easy to grow should be so seldom seen.

Propagation to achieve the maximum increase in *Galtonia* is probably best from seeds that are abundantly produced and will flower in their third season. The plants produce offsets, and the bulbs, which become quite large, are planted just below the soil surface. *Galtonia candicans* is reasonably cold hardy. Sima Eliovson (1980) believed this species combines particularly well in the garden with *Crocosmia*, which flowers at the same time.

Geissorhiza (Iridaceae)

The name *Geissorhiza* is from the Greek *geisson*, "tile," and *rhiza*, "root," in reference to the tunic that covers the corm like tile on a roof.

This is a large genus of about 80 species of small plants restricted entirely to the winter-rainfall region of the Cape Province (more species if *Engysiphon* is included). The latest and finest work on *Geissorhiza* is by Peter Goldblatt (1985), who found that the genus is closely related to the genus *Hesperantha*. One difference between them particularly interests entomologists. The *Geissorhiza* species are always day-blooming, typically scentless, brightly colored, and believed to be bee-pollinated, whereas the unspecialized *Hesperantha* is evening-blooming, strongly sweet-scented, and basically moth-pollinated.

Species of *Geissorhiza* have radiated extensively in the southwestern Cape and have come to occupy a greater variety of environmental niches than most other genera of Iridaceae, both in the Cape and elsewhere. Peter Goldblatt (1985) attributed this to edaphic factors; soil type is particularly significant in the distribution of various geophytes.

In the predominant flower form the flowers are radially symmetric, typically short tubed, open during the day, and brightly colored. Their common name is sequins, but some species are called wine cups.

Geissorhiza ornithogaloides is a dwarf, slender species with bright yellow flowers. I confess to having had trouble sustaining it in my collection and have not yet discovered its needs.

Geissorhiza darlingensis has a large, pale yellow flower with a purple center reminiscent of the flower of *Babiana pygmaea*, a case of floral mimicry that is a common phenomenon in *Geissorhiza*.

Geissorhiza mathewsii is a rare local endemic of the Darling area, where it grows in wet, low-lying situations. It has the distinctive coloring found in *G. radians* and *G. monanthos*. These species all grow in the same area but have distinct habitat preferences. *Geissorhiza radians* (Figure 3-19) grows in the wettest places, even in standing water. *Geissorhia mathewsii* prefers slightly higher ground but still grows in almost waterlogged soil, and *Geissorhiza monanthos* occurs only in well-drained areas surrounding wet depressions. It should be remembered that these are the winter conditions only; in the summer the habitat of these three species is dry.

Geissorhiza radians (formerly known as *G. rochensis*) is certainly one of the most striking species in the genus and has been known since the 1770s (Plate 29).

Charles Hardman (1985) had difficulty with *Geissorhiza radians,* which developed chlorosis when he grew it in granite sand. He found this was remedied by applying aluminum sulphate to make the granite-sand mix more acidic. I have had trouble maintaining a population and keep supplementing it with new seedlings, but the effort is rewarded by the wonderful flowers. The large, deep blue, goblet-shaped flowers have a contrasting white band around the red center. This combination gives the species the common name of wine cup geissorhiza. It has peculiar pitted markings in the midline of its segments that are lacking in the related *G. mathewsii*, which has similar wine-cup coloring. *Geissorhiza radians* is a very popular flower with the visitors to my garden.

Geissorhiza purpureolutea has a cream to yellow flower with a dark brown to purple center. It grows on wet, sandy gravel flats on the coastal plain of the Cape region, which suggests that a sandy mix is its optimum-growth medium.

FIGURE 3-19.
Geissorhiza radians.

Geissorhiza aspera is a common Cape species with deep glistening blue flowers. One of the easiest to cultivate, it is related to *G. inaequalis,* which has larger and pale lilac flowers and grows in rather heavy soils unlike the generally sandy situations in which *G. aspera* is found. Both of these species grow to about 10 inches (25 cm) tall. Most other species are a bit shorter.

Geissorhiza splendidissima is endemic to the extremely flower-rich area of Nieuwoudtville, where it grows in light clay soil. It is a stand-out species with large, glossy, deep blue-violet flowers that are yellowish in the throat and zygomorphic (Plate 30). It is reasonably easy to grow, and I think it has real merit.

Geissorhiza tulbaghensis has a large white or cream flower with a maroon or brown center. It is another distinctive species that is well worth having. Natural hybrids with *G. aspera* have been reported, suggesting that the potential for developing splendid flowers by hybridizing the species of *Geissorhiza* is enormous. To my knowledge it is an unexplored field.

The last but certainly not least species I grow is *Geissorhiza inflexa* var. *erosa*. It has stunning flowers of brilliant carmine with yellow anthers.

Propagation of *Geissorhiza* is by seeds or offsets. Germination of *G. imbricata* takes 53 days; *G. inaequalis,* 33 days; *G. inflexa,* 36 days; *G. monanthos,* 58 days; *G. radians,* 42–50 days; and *G. tulbaghensis,* 41 days. Most species flower in their third season.

The species described above are just a fraction of the *Geissorhiza* species that grow in the Cape region. The genus needs to be discovered and thoroughly explored by horticulturists. *Geissorhiza* species make terrific container plants. Jim Holmes (1983) believed they enhance natural areas, wildflower gardens, and rockeries. He suggested they be allowed to grow in the lawn, which is not mowed until the growth cycle is finished.

Gethyllis (Amaryllidaceae)

Gethyllis surely must rank among the most fascinating plants of the Cape flora. There are about 12 species that range through the Cape northward into Namibia. The name is derived from the Greek *gethullis*, a diminutive of *gethuon*, meaning "leek." The botanist who named them must have thought that they looked like little leeks.

The annual cycle of *Gethyllis* has three distinct phases (*Gethyllis*, 1983). In Phase I, the leaves appear in autumn, grow through the winter, and die down completely in late spring or early summer. The leaves are spirally twisted and are sometimes corkscrew shaped. The leaf sheath is attractively spotted or mottled.

In Phase II, the delicate, strongly scented, starlike flowers appear out of the bare earth in the heat of the dry midsummer and wither in a day or so. A rare summer rain will suddenly stimulate their appearance. The flowers are pure white or flushed with pink, are about 3 inches (8 cm) across, and smell like jasmine. There is no flower stalk, just a long perianth tube that emerges from the bulb. Only one flower is produced by a bulb. December is midsummer in the Cape and since these flowers appear around Christmas time a common name in South Africa is Christmas star.

Months later in Phase III the ground is pierced by the tip of a long, club-shaped fruit (botanically it is actually a berry), usually orange-colored, with a semi-transparent skin through which can be seen numerous seeds imbedded in pulp. The fruit has been described as an orange-colored finger poking straight up from the ground or as a slender semi-transparent carrot (the broad end at the top) 3 to 5 inches (8 to 13 cm) long. They are strongly and sweetly scented with a scent richer than the scent of wild strawberries or like custard-apple with a dash of port wine. They taste, according to Edith Stephens (1939), like a mixture of banana and pineapple. The common name for them in South Africa is *kukumakranka*, a name given them by the Hottentots who found them an important addition to their seasonal food supply.

Edith Stephens (1939, page 114) wrote that before half of its length has emerged the fruit has probably been collected by country children (and grown-ups) who scour the veld for kukumakranka in the autumn:

They hunt them both by sight and by scent, and far-seeing young-sters will have taken the precaution of surrounding each flower in December [summer] with a ring of stones. . . . They eat them, or press and dry them as a present for their mothers, to use like laven-der to scent handkerchiefs or the linen cupboard; or sell them to men to put into brandy, for several left in a bottle for a few months give it a delicate liqueur-like flavour and aroma. This, or a draught made by steeping kukumakrankas in boiling water, is considered a very good remedy for stomach-ache.

Gethyllis are now rare around Cape Town and its suburbs because of the urban spread, imported acacia and pines, and the depredations of bulb-hunters.

Propagation of *Gethyllis* is from seeds. In South Africa the mature fruit is soaked in water for two days, and then the skin is ruptured. The pulp is kept in the water for another two days to soften, after which the seeds are removed and cleaned. The seeds are sown in a mixture of seven parts pure sand and one part peat moss. They must be shaded and kept well watered.

It is recommended by an anonymous author (*Gethyllis*, 1983) in the bulletin of the Indigenous Bulb Growers of South Africa that the bulbs be planted about 2 inches (5 cm) deep in pots and then left undisturbed for years. The container should have a layer of rocks at the bottom and then be filled with coarse sand and a little peat with a tablespoon of bone meal added. While growing, the pot should be watered well every two weeks but the soil can dry out with no ill effects. No matter how green and lush the foliage appears, watering should stop in spring and the pot kept dry during the summer in a sunny position, though it should not bake in the sun. No water should be given when the flowers appear or the bulbs will rot. The flowers from all the bulbs appear almost simultane-ously and must be cross-pollinated.

Gethyllis afra, G. ciliaris, G. spiralis, and *G. villosa* are species that have been introduced from the Cape. These are odd flowers and many gardeners may not wish to spend the effort to cultivate a plant that produces only one flower a year and then quickly withers. But I do, for their life cycle fascinates me, and I love the Hottentot name, *kukumakranka*!

Gladiolus (Iridaceae)

All gardeners are familiar with the stiff spikes of the common *Gladiolus* cultivars, but very few gardeners are aware of the 85 winter-growing *Gladiolus* from the Cape Province of South Africa. The latter have a delicacy of color, a gracefulness of form, and fineness of texture not seen in the ordinary garden *Gladiolus*. In addition, as Sarah Coombs (1936) reminded us, the Cape *Gladiolus* is frequently fragrant. It deserves particular attention in Mediterranean gardens for it is adapted to such conditions and grows naturally in areas with winter rainfall and summer drought. There is a wide variation in color, size, and form and a collection of species will provide almost a year-long sucession of bloom. In fact, Delpierre and Du Plessis (1973, page 9), in a remarkable project to photograph each species in the wild, found that there is "not a moment in the year when there is not a *Gladiolus* in flower somewhere within 400 kilometres [248 miles] of Cape Town, and it is possible to find a different *Gladiolus* every weekend from January to December."

Du Plessis and Duncan (1989, page 139) wrote,

Gladioli have been cultivated for longer than two hundred years and there can be very little doubt that the genus has been Southern Africa's most important contribution to the world of horticulture. . . . the number of species in Southern Africa is in excess of a hundred and four, and it is very likely that there still are undiscovered species, especially in the mountains of the Western and Southern Cape. The Southern African kinds occur in a wide variety of shapes, sizes and colours, and because they have succeded in occupying virtually every ecological niche offered, there is not a time of the year when there is not at least one of them in flower. About seventy-two species of *Gladiolus*, often referred to as Cape species, are endemic to the winter rainfall region of the Cape Province.

According to McLean et al. (1927, page 5),

The South African *Gladiolus* are the parents of all of our modern garden forms, for the European sorts were found not to intercross readily with the South African ones, and they are so inferior to the South African species that they have been largely discarded.

In an interesting piece titled "On Hybrids and Hybridization," Barnard (1972) attributed the origin of the *Gladiolus* now in world horticulture to hybrids of a few South African summer-flowering species and three or four of the Cape winter growers through crosses originally made more than a century ago. Even so, "the scope for further hybridization within the group seems limitless" (page 304). Barnard further noted that there are hybrids with the closely related genera *Homoglossum* and *Anomalesia*, and the tropical *Acidanthera*. Of these intergeneric crosses the best known are Collingwood Ingram's "Homoglads."

Although I tend to be a purist and maintain a collection of true *Gladiolus* species, there is an enormous temptation to try crosses among them. It is an exciting, rewarding, and inexpensive hobby in which any patient gardener can indulge. The possibilities for developing an outstanding cultivar are endless. Harold Koopowitz (1986) reported that at the arboretum and gene bank of the University of California at Irvine, scientists are actively exploring this vast potential and are creating garden hybrids quite unlike anything else ever produced. Charles Hardman (1985a) noted that in hybridizing *Gladiolus* the female (seed) parent seems to give the seedlings their physical characteristics such as height, form, and flower texture. The male *Gladiolus,* or pollen parent, transmits its color range to the progeny.

Since the Cape species of *Gladiolus* grow in a wide variety of habitats a gardener can select species for special garden situations. Not all are easy but some seem almost indestructible and naturalize readily in Santa Barbara. A few species have very limited distributions in South Africa, and other species, once common, have been greatly reduced in numbers.

These threatened or endangered flowers may be conserved through cultivation by dedicated gardeners.

The wild species of *Gladiolus* usually have zygomorphic flowers with some interesting hooded forms (Figure 3-20), but a few species, thought to be primitive types, have open or star-shaped blossoms (Figure 3-21). The *Gladiolus* species normally require cross-fertilization to produce seed. In nature, various insects carry the pollen from flower to flower. To assist in pollination, the flowers of some species produce scent at certain times in the day to attract specific pollinators, and most *Gladiolus* flowers have markings or nectar guides to which the insects react. Noted author and superb photographer Freeman Patterson (1984, page 71) has delightfully described this pollination by insects:

> Plants lure insects with flowers. By the shape, color, and markings of the blossoms, a plant identifies a landing strip for the appropriate insect, tells it where to touch down, and how far to taxi. If the insect follows instructions, it receives a load of nectar as a reward—but it also gets a cargo of pollen. The insect transports these male cells directly to the female cells of another flower of the same species (since it uses the same lures).

A discussion of the winter-growing Cape species can well start with *Gladiolus alatus*, whose spunky little flowers bloom in early spring (Plate 31). The common name in Afrikaans is *kalkoentjie* (pronounced kal-koon´-ky), meaning "little turkey." Perhaps the flower segments remind folks of the wattles on a turkey.

The flower stem, which is about 9 inches (23 cm) long and often branched, may bear as many as six blossoms, although a single flower is not uncommon. The foliage is slender, and the flowers are comparatively large. The upper three segments are various shades of salmon, brick red, terra cotta, or orange-red. The central or dorsal upper segment is hooded, arched, and fairly wide. The three lower segments are narrower, mostly greenish yellow or lime green with orange-red tips. The flowers are

FIGURE 3-20.
Hooded, zygomorphic
flowers of *Gladiolus
orchidiflorus*.

FIGURE 3-21.
Open, actinomorphic
flowers of *Gladiolus
quadrangulus*.

scented and this has been described as "sweet briar" or the perfume of early apples.

The flowers of *Gladiolus alatus* were first painted in water color by Heinrich Claudius, an artist who accompanied Simon van der Stel on an important expedition to Namaqualand in 1685. Linnaeus described the species in 1760.

Initially *Gladiolus alatus* is rather easy to grow. However, over a period of time, the population slowly declines, and must be restocked with new seedlings. I do not understand why this happens, since the plant reproduces vegetatively by corm division, by sessile cormels, or by cormels at the end of short stolons, and it may even develop bulbils in the axils of the sheathing bases of the lower leaves. At the Cape, *G. alatus* grows in both heavy soils and sandy locations. It is widespread, and several varieties are recognized. I grow *G. alatus* var. *meliusculus*, which is from the Darling area and is quite attractive. Its flowers are softer in texture than the typical species and are more pink, old-rose, or rose-orange with a small lime-green area edged with dark red at the base of the three lower segments. For me, this variety does better in cultivation than typical *G. alatus*. A rare albino form reportedly was once exhibited at the Darling Wildflower Show. I do hope someone may rediscover that gem. Naturally occuring hybrids reported are *G. alatus* × *G. virescens* and *G. alatus* × *G. carinatus* (yellow form).

Related to *Gladiolus alatus* are several other species also in the kalkoentjie group: *G. equitans, G. orchidiflorus, G. uysiae, G. virescens,* and *G. watermeyeri.*

Gladiolus equitans grows in the rocky hills of Namaqualand. It has four leaves about one inch (2.5 cm) wide and up to 12 inches (30 cm) in length with thickened reddish margins and spiny tips. The large red flowers are scented.

Gladiolus virescens is widespread. It is found in sandy soil and grows to about 10 inches (25 cm) tall. Three varieties are recognized: *G. virescens* var. *virescens* has scented, yellow flowers blooming in early spring; *G. virescens* var. *lepidus* has distinctly veined, dull mauve, scented flowers and may have 11 flowers on a stalk; I am not familiar with the third variety *G. virescens* var. *roseo-venosus*.

Gladiolus uysiae (pronounced ace´-ee-ee) is a small, rare species best grown as a container plant (Plate 32).

Gladiolus watermeyeri is another small, rare, scented species with heavy veining in the two outer segments. I found it growing in the shade of shrubs along a paved road in Nieuwoudtville and was able to get seeds from the arboretum of the University of California at Irvine.

Another species of the kalkoentjie group found growing in sand is *Gladiolus orchidiflorus*. The central upper segment curves forward, giving it a hooded appearance and giving rise to the synonym *G. viperatus* "like a snake," perhaps a hooded cobra. Una Van Der Spuy (1976) described the flowers as amber, suffused with palest green with a maroon stripe on the two side petals and maroon and lime-green on the lower segments. I find it difficult to describe, and at first, like Sima Eliovson (1980), I thought it dull, greenish yellow. In the northern part of its range the corms are deep seated in the sand, forming a long neck; according to Lewis et al. (1972) this is a well-known adaptation to a hot, dry habitat. Although I did not care for it at first, I would not be without this exquisitely scented flower.

Gladiolus tristis was named by Linnaeus in 1762. The word *tristis* means "dull colored" or "sad," though why Linnaeus should describe the flowers in this way is puzzling. Gardeners who grow *G. tristis* are certainly not likely to call this elegant species the "sad glad." It is sometimes termed the marsh Afrikaner because it is common in seasonally marshy areas, called *vleis* in Afrikaans. South Africans also call these flowers white, evening-scented *aandbloome*, meaning "evening flowers" in Afrikaans. Cut flowers give off a delicious perfume, which has been variously described as strong carnation, clove pink, almond, violet, night-scented stock, honeysuckle, magnolia, and sweet rocket. While the flowers in nature are fragrant only at night, they will also become fragrant in midday if placed in a dark closet (Poindexter, 1931). The scent of *G. tristis* attracts moths for pollination.

Gladiolus tristis was one of the first South African species of *Gladiolus* to be cultivated in England, where it was grown at the Chelsea Botanic Garden as early as 1745. It was used in early hybridization work by both Dutch and English hybridizers during the 19th century. In 1928, Dearing reported that it had already been in Santa Barbara gardens for many years. It is an elegant species that normally has three large, tubular, bell-shaped flowers 2.5 to 3 inches (6 to 8 cm) across at the top of a slender 2 foot (62 cm) stalk. The flowers vary from white to cream to pale yellow tinged with greens. There is a pencilled gray to purplish brown median stripe on the inside of the three upper segments. According to de Forest and de Forest (1937, page 2),

> There is no more lovely flower for using in arrangements. . . . The leaves are as high as the flower stalk and are cylindrical with prominent ribs, somewhat rush-like. Its very narrow leaves do not make an ugly spot in the garden when the plants are through blooming.

Emily Brown (1976) described a variety *G. tristis* var. *concolor* as having pale yellow, unspotted, and exceedingly fragrant flowers.

Gladiolus tristis is comparatively hardy, growing outdoors in southern England and in the Pacific Northwest. It grows well in my Santa Barbara garden but probably would do best with some partial shade if grown in the hotter inland valleys. Since it grows naturally in somewhat marshy areas, I give it ample water in winter, particularly during years with light rainfall.

Gladiolus carneus is one of the showy species called painted ladies. It was historically one of the first species to be used in the early (1819) hybridization efforts in England. The plants are very floriferous and the eight to ten flowers are distichous. After a good rainy season or after a wildfire in the Cape, *G. carneus* flowers profusely. The species is rather widely distributed in the Cape. The many varieties are ecotypes that regularly flower every year in different localities at different times. The forms of *G. carneus* flower collectively over a period of six months. According to Barnard (1972), each isolated population of *G. carneus* flowers for two to three weeks on approximately the same dates every year. The flowering times of the different ecotypes are not only constant in the wild from year to year but remain relatively constant in cultivation, and when plants have adapted themselves to the seasons in the Northern Hemisphere they continue to flower earlier or later, according to their inherited timing. Barnard further points out that hybrids between plants with different flower seasons may approximate to one or other parent but are usually intermediate.

The natural variation between localized populations of *Gladiolus carneus* has resulted in a swarm of synonyms for the species, including *G. blandus, G. macowianus,* and *G. pappei.* The nomenclature rule of priority prevents the use of these names, which in the case of *G. blandus* is unfortunate, since *blandus* means "delightful"—certainly a proper description of the flowers.

I grow a white variety of *Gladiolus carneus* (Plate 33) and also a lovely strawberry-ice-cream pink one from near Kleinmond. This latter clone has its velvety pink color highlighted by a crimson V-shaped mark on each of the three lower segments. It is an attention getter and should be very useful to any hybridizer. *Gladiolus carneus* is not difficult to grow, but Charles Hardman (1985) found it was enhanced by the application of some aluminum sulphate to make a granite-sand mix more acidic.

Another species name that has been confused in the literature is *Gladiolus carinatus.* It has been mixed up with the species *G. recurvus.* The flowers of *G. carinatus* are in shades of mauve with yellow markings on the lower segments. Their delicate scent is much like that of violets. *Gladiolus carinatus* has three to five flowers at the tip of a slender 2-foot (62-cm) tall stalk. The species is found growing in sandy places in the Cape.

Gladiolus recurvus has somewhat tubular flowers with spreading segments tapering to slender recurved tips. The color is a dull greenish gray with some fine purplish dots on the lower segments. It will never be a horticultural favorite, but it does have a pleasant fragrance. It begins flowering in winter.

Gladiolus liliaceus is a most remarkable species because it undergoes a diurnal color change. In the daytime it is yellowish or pale dull yellow densely flecked with brown dots or streaks, accounting for its common name of large brown Afrikaner; at night the color changes to a dark mauve or blue! This species with large flowers was named *G. grandis* by Carl Thunberg in 1800. It also becomes very fragrant at night, exhibiting the same phenomenon described for *G. tristis*. It is easy to grow and is widespread in the Cape, though it is not prevalent in any particular area.

Although it has no fragrance, *Gladiolus gracilis* is a very graceful species with flowers on a slender 18-inch (46-cm) tall stalk. Some flowers are almost gray-blue while others are whitish with a definite blue tinge. The lower three segments have a touch of yellow and are speckled with many purple dots. I find it a welcome early bloomer and easy to maintain.

Another species with heavily spotted lower segments is *Gladiolus tenellus*. The flowers are pale to sulphur yellow or yellowish white with dark purple markings. It is an early species and delightfully scented with flowers on 18-inch (46-cm) tall stalks.

Gladiolus aureus was first described in 1896, and the name *aureus* means "golden yellow," an apt description of the richly colored flowers. Botanists have had difficulty deciding whether this species belongs in the genus *Gladiolus* or the genus *Homoglossum*. These genera are very closely related, and the single distinguishing characteristic is the shape of the perianth. As a gardener I see no valid reason for their being given separate generic status. Their growth habits are identical and they readily hybridize to form Homoglads.

Gladiolus aureus is endemic to the southern Cape Peninsula. To Koopowitz and Kaye (1983), it is a prime example of an endangered species. Always rare, it once occurred along 4 miles (10 km) of the Atlantic coast side of the Cape Peninsula. It declined from 70 plants in 1975 to only 18 in 1977, and these were growing between a picnic area and a children's playground, an unlikely place to survive for long!

Gladiolus aureus ranks among the most beautiful of the winter-growing *Gladiolus* (Plate 34). Koopowitz and Kaye (1983, page 130) described it as "a slender wand of four or five drops of molten gold, wafted in the breeze, mimicking the African sun above." The rich golden yellow flowers are unscented and bloom over a protracted period. The mature plant stands up to 22 inches (57 cm) high and has two to three thin, hairy, gray-green leaves. There may be three to seven flowers on the stalk, which is thin and wiry and withstands wind amazingly well. The individual flower spike is long lasting and often blooms for over two weeks.

Graham Duncan (1981a, page 18) described the successful cultivation of the rare *Gladiolus aureus* at Kirstenbosch as follows:

> It thrives in a slightly moist, sandy soil, preferring partial shade and needs a completely dry period during the summer months. Although pollen is not produced as liberally as in most other indigenous *Gladiolus* species, seed sets fairly easily, especially after hand pollination, and large seed pods are quickly formed, which ripen within about eight weeks. This species also reproduces by cormlet formation, but does not seem to reproduce by division of the mature corm. Fresh seed germinates easily, provided it is kept constantly moist and best germination results have been obtained at Kirstenbosch by sowing rather late.

Seeds have been disseminated to gardeners thoughout the world by Kirstenbosch so that this splendid plant may be conserved through cultivation.

Another rare species, *Gladiolus citrinus*, could not be found by Delpierre and Du Plessis (1973) during their project to photograph all the Cape species in their native habitats, but they were able to include a photograph for their book through the courtesy of Dr. Maurice Boussard, who grows this plant at his garden in Verdun, France. This is a very good example of the value of conservation through cultivation. A rare flower that scientists could not find in its native habitat was located under cultivation in a private garden.

Gladiolus citrinus is considered to be a primitive *Gladiolus* (Plate 35). It has actinomorphic flowers that are funnel shaped, and yellow with a dark maroon stain in the throat. They are small, 6- to 8-inch (15- to 20-cm) plants.

I have grown two other primitive species, *Gladiolus stellatus* and *G. quadrangulus*. For some unknown reason *G. stellatus* died out. *Gladiolus quadrangulus*, with its open pink flowers, persists without difficulty.

Gladiolus caryophyllaceus has a rich pink color and sweet scent (Plate 36). As a robust plant it can grow to 29 inches (74 cm) tall. Rourke (1985) thought it restricted to only a few isolated sites in the Cape veld, where its future survival is bleak. While this rarity is carefully nurtured in pots at Kirstenbosch, in western Australia it is a weed and difficult to eradicate from cultivated areas. There it flourishes in the well-defined Mediterranean climate and the deep sandy soils. Its unchecked spread in western Australia is attributed to the absence of predatory moles.

Several *Gladiolus* species are hysteranthous. Of these I grow *G. brevifolius,* which is a rather delicate pink-flowered species, and *G. carmineus*, which is far more robust and rewarding. *Gladiolus carmineus* grows to about 12 inches.(30 cm). Its almost-watermelon-pink flowers have a white central mark in each of the three lower segments. It is commonly called the cliff *Gladiolus* for, as Delpierre and Du Plessis (1973) pointed out, it is found on the coast near Hermanus where it favors damp, shaded cliffs and grows so close to the sea that at times it is within reach of the sea spray.

Propagation of the winter-growing *Gladiolus* can be by seeds sown in autumn. Seed germination time varies considerably. Loubser (1982) found that germination of *G. aureus* ranged from 49–112 days with an average of 74 or 75. In my garden it germinated in 38 days. My other records show that *G. carneus* 'Albidus' germinates in 29 days, *G. dalenii* in 28 days, *G. garnieri* in 25 days, *G. involutus* in 36 days, *G. maculatus* in 74 days, *G. ochroleucus* in 25–31 days, *G. orchidiflorus* in 36 days, *G. vaginatus* in 21 days, and *G. virescens* in 40 days. Loubser (1982) gave some germination times in ten-day ranges: *G. carmineus* and *G. tristis,* 20–30 days; *G. longicollis,* 30–40 days; *G. citrinus, G. odoratus,* and *G. sempervirens,* 40–50 days; *G. maculatus,* 50–60 days; and *G. undulatus* (Plate 37), 60–80 days.

At Kirstenbosch, Graham Duncan sows *Gladiolus* seeds in a well-drained sandy medium to which fine compost has been added, and he keeps them constantly moist by regular watering with a fine mist. The seeds should be sown thinly in large pots to prevent overcrowding. The pots are kept in the shade until the seedlings are established; they are then moved into full sun. Germination takes about a month, and if the seedlings are well grown some will flower in the second year. The plants respond well to regular applications of a liquid fertilizer and should be well watered during their growing season. Besides reproducing from seeds, the *Gladiolus* species reproduce vegetatively by corm division and production of tiny cormlets. In some species I have grown, the cormlet production of a single plant had a gross mass weight greater than the new corm itself. Cormlets may be produced when the seedlings are quite young and well before they first flower. The pots should be kept dry when the corms are dormant in the summer. Every third summer the old thick clumps can be divided and the soil mix renewed.

Gladiolus is the favorite genus of Cape bulbs among the members of the Indigenous Bulb Growers of South Africa. Gardeners who have not before tried these winter-growing *Gladiolus* from the Cape will soon understand their popularity among bulb specialists.

Gloriosa (Colchicaceae)

As the name indicates, *Gloriosa* is a really glorious flower and is variously called flame lily, glory lily, cat's claw, or climbing lily. The present consensus is that the genus is monotypic with *Gloriosa superba* being its single, very widespread, and extremely variable species (Field, 1971). Others count two African species. This view is not shared by Narain (1988), who identified nine natural species and 40 cultivars. The chromosome numbers in this species range from diploids to octoploids. *Gloriosa superba* does not grow wild in the Cape but occurs naturally from Natal northward into Zimbabwe, tropical Africa, and into Asia. I am content to consider it horticulturally one species with an octoploid variety named *Gloriosa superba* var. *rothschildiana*.

The flowers of *Gloriosa superba* live up to their name, for they are truly outstanding. The flower architecture is unique (Figure 3-22). The long segments are separate and completely reflexed, so the superior ovary

FIGURE 3-22.
Gloriosa superba.

and the six very long stamens are nakedly exserted. The style is long and peculiarly rises at a sharp right angle to the ovary. The flowers vary in color from pure yellow to scarlet with rather dramatic combinations of the two colors. The plants can climb surrounding vegetation by means of tenacious leaf tendrils and if well grown can reportedly reach 6 feet (nearly 2 m) tall. Mine reach a little over 3 feet (1 m) tall. The rootstock is neither a tuber nor a rhizome, as most literature states. It is a stoloniferous corm (Du Plessis and Duncan, 1989) consisting usually of two swollen, joined lobes that form a V and tend to grow horizontally (Figure 1-7). The plants are summer growers with a pronounced dormancy period in the winter when they die back.

It is believed that red color predominates in the flowers of octoploid plants, which seems to be the case with *Gloriosa superba* var. *rothschildiana* in my garden. It is supposed to have larger flowers than the diploid *G. superba,* but that is not evident in my plants.

Propagation is by seeds or by division of the rootstocks at the joint of the two lobes. The bud at the tip of the corm will produce a new plant. Experts say the seeds should be planted in the spring. Germination may be slow, so Sima Eliovson (1980) warned not to give up for four months. Three to four years are required for maturity. The corms are rather brittle and need to be handled carefully. Some gardeners say to plant them 2 inches (5 cm) deep, but I think 3 or 4 inches (8 to 10 cm) is better. If left undisturbed, they gradually pull themselves quite deep, even to the bottom of a container. I plant them horizontally. The plants are not cold hardy and need frost protection in cold situations. They like a rather rich soil and ample water during their spring and summer growth, although in nature they can be found growing in poor soils along South African roads. Most experts suggest light feedings every two weeks and some support for the climbing plants.

Gloriosa superba is a long-lasting cut flower that can be used with dramatic effect in floral arrangements. A word of warning: Every part of this plant—leaf, flower, stem, rootstock—is extremely poisonous, so do not decorate salads with this plant and keep it away from pets and kids.

Gynandriris (Iridaceae)

I presume the name *Gynandriris* indicates that this is a "gynandrous Irid," since the species in the genus have gynandrous flowers; each of the three stamens (male) is appressed to a style branch (female).

Gynandriris is a small genus with seven species in South Africa and two in the Mediterranean (Goldblatt, 1980). These are small plants with fugacious flowers that are of more interest to the collector of Iridaceae than to the general gardener. *Gynandriris* is a relative of *Moraea* and *Homeria*, two groups with much more striking flowers.

Propagation is from division of the corms or from seeds, and the only problem is that some species are too easy and can be weedy.

Gynandriris setifolia is very adaptive and often occurs in seemingly unfavorable habitats such as along roadsides, in cracks in paving, and where soil has been disturbed. It is a lawn weed in South Africa and it tends to be a weed in South Australia where it was introduced. Its tendency to be a weed is encouraged by its ability to set seed from its own pollen. The flowers are small, pale blue-purple, and very ephemeral. They bloom in the afternoon and fade toward sunset. I grow this species simply as an item in my collection. It is a cinch to grow, and grow it does. One of these days I will probably give it up.

Gynandriris cedarmontana is much better behaved than *G. setifolia* and is the only member of the genus with white flowers. While it comes from the dry interior valleys of the southwestern Cape, it is localized and apparently grows in moist sites only, either in seeps or along ditches or stream banks. Although it is self-compatible like *G. setifolia*, it seems that self-fertilization does not normally occur. I think this plant is worth growing.

I have planted seed of *Gynandriris pritzeliana*, but it is not far enough along for me to comment on its performance. The species is distinctive in having strongly coiled leaves and large, very dark blue to violet flowers. For some time it was thought to be a *Moraea*. Unlike *G. setifolia*, it is strongly self-incompatible and so will probably not have weedy tendencies.

The other species I have grown is *Gynandriris simulans*. The flowers are small, pale blue-lilac with dark speckles and yellow nectar guides. With this polyploid species, the flowers are so ephemeral that one has to set an alarm clock to catch them before they fade. Some have given the time of flowering as between 4 and 5 P.M., but Peter Goldblatt (1980), who grew them in St. Louis, Missouri, found that they regularly opened around 3:30 P.M. and faded by about 7 P.M. *Gynandriris simulans* is strictly a curiosity for the collector.

Haemanthus (Amaryllidaceae)

The genus name *Haemanthus* is derived from the Greek *haema*, "blood," and *anthos*, "flower," and a common name is blood lily.

Some spectacular flowers formerly placed in *Haemanthus* have now been separated into the genus *Scadoxus* (Friis and Nordal, 1976). The gardening world has not yet completely caught up with this taxonomic shift, so considerable confusion exists. The greatest identification problem is with the blood lily, formerly called *H. katherinae* but now called *S. multiflorus* subsp. *katherinae*.

At times it may seem that taxonomists are splitting hairs, but in the case of *Haemanthus* and *Scadoxus*, the separation has a justifiable basis. As now recognized, species of *Haemanthus* have true bulbs, usually two fleshy leaves, and 16 chromosomes. Their geographic concentration is mainly in arid areas such as Namaqualand. By contrast, *Scadoxus* is rhizomatous, the foliage is thin textured with a distinct midrib, there are 10 chromosomes, and its distribution is in less arid regions (Du Plessis and Duncan, 1989). *Haemanthus* has 22 African species.

Haemanthus albiflos is an evergreen species. The flowers are white, and it prefers partial shade. Its range is from the eastern Cape into Zululand. Terry Hatch (1987b) reported successful propagation from leaf cuttings. *Haemanthus* typically produces two leaves each year, and several sets of these may persist in this evergreen species.

William Drysdale (1987, page 43) wrote,

The most common form of *Haemanthus albiflos* in California is an easy-to-grow, shade- and moisture-loving plant. Soil, so long as it is well drained, seems to be unimportant as they thrive in my garden in a sandy mix, one with humus, and equally well in plain garden soil. The plant is something of a chameleon in that it appears to be a totally different plant under coastal conditions from those grown in interior valleys.

At Riverside, California, where Mr. Drysdale has his garden, the plants have leaves 3 inches (7 cm) wide, 18 inches (46 cm) long, and conspicuously hirsute. Under coastal conditions at Laguna Beach, the same clone has leaves 6 inches (15 cm) wide, that are a deeper shade of green and are held half erect. Drysdale (1987) crossed the evergreen *H. albiflos* with the deciduous *H. coccineus* and got a variety of flower colors ranging through shades of peach, apricot, and terra cotta. They were briefly deciduous and not cross-fertile.

Haemanthus coccineus is widespread in the Cape and was one of the first plants collected there by Europeans. It was illustrated as early as 1605 (Snijman, 1981). It is deciduous, winter growing, autumn blooming, and should be kept dry in summer. The top of the bulb should be at or just below the ground surface. It is a variable species that has been grown in California for many years, but it is not common. It is the species that gave the genus the common name of blood lily although its flowers can be pale salmon or even white. Usually it ranges from coral pink to scarlet.

William Drysdale (1987, page 44) gave this description:

The flowerhead is about two inches [5 cm] across and is principally made up of colorful filaments of scores of otherwise inconspicuous flowers tightly compressed within six large flower bracts. These are bright red, very conspicuous, and make for the red appearance of the inflorescence. Actually, the filaments of the flowers are a coral color. The generous amount of pollen on the filaments creates a red and gold combination that is striking.

The bractlike appendages that surround the flowers are technically called *spathe valves*. The flowers of *Haemanthus sanguineus* (syn. *H. rotundifolius*), which vary from pink to bright red, are borne on a stout wine-red stalk. *Haemanthus sanguineus* is from the winter-rainfall area and its two large, nearly prostrate leaves are deciduous.

Propagation of *Haemanthus* is from offsets, leaf cuttings, or seeds. The offsets are removed just after flowering and replanted immediately. The seeds are sown as soon as they are ripe. They are removed from the pulp and planted just below the surface or pressed into the soil flush with the surface. They bloom in their third or fourth year.

Pests reported in South Africa are the amaryllis lily borer, snails, and nematodes. Mealybugs have infested bulbs in California.

Haemanthus is best grown as a container plant.

Hesperantha (Iridaceae)

The Greek name *Hesperantha* means "evening flower." Many of the species have flowers that open all too briefly in the late afternoon. Some of them are sweet scented and probably moth pollinated. Flowers of *Hesperantha* (Figure 3-23) have a characteristic stigma divided into three long branches seen at the the mouth of a relatively long perianth tube. The corms are tunicated. *Hesperantha* is a rather large genus with about 60 species in Africa, of which at least 22 occur in the Cape region.

Hesperantha bachmannii has white, fragrant flowers on 12 inch (30 cm) stalks. It is widespread and fairly common in the Cape. The flowers become recurved when they open in the late afternoon.

The flowers of *Hesperantha cucullata* and *H. falcata* are also white but with red to brown on the reverse. *Hesperantha falcata* is a common species in the Cape, and its flowers open in the late afternoon and close at dawn. *Hesperantha erecta*, which particularly likes sandy soil, is more stingy with its white flowers, which open around noon and close in late afternoon.

Pink flowers are characteristic of *Hesperantha pauciflora* and the

FIGURE 3-23.
Hesperantha angusta.

dwarf species *H. pumila*. The flowers of *H. pauciflora* open at midday and close by evening.

The most striking species is *Hesperantha vaginata*, with large flowers that are yellow with black markings (Plate 38). I have seen a large colony of this species growing in heavy clay soil at Nieuwoudtville, but the plants grow well for me in a sandy medium. They are not propagated as easily as the other species. Seed germinated in 57 days. The flowers open for only a few hours late in the day, but I think they are worthwhile.

Propagation of *Hesperantha* is from seeds or corms. *Hesperantha* is a typically deciduous, winter-growing Cape bulb that is dormant in the dry summer. I grow it in a well-drained, sandy mix in a sunny site, although it also does well in partial shade. Its size makes it suitable as a container plant.

Hessea (Amaryllidaceae)

Hessea, a genus of about a dozen species, is endemic to the winter-rainfall area from Namibia southward. The inflorescence is an attractive, hysteranthous umbel of star-shaped, pink flowers. A cataphyll arises from the bulb and forms a collar around the basis of the true leaves.

Hessea cinnamonea (syn. *H. crispa*) is a small plant about 6 inches (15 cm) in height. The hysteranthous flowers are soft pink. This species has an extended growing period through the winter into summer.

Hessea is related to *Strumaria* and is treated in the same manner horticulturally. Propagation is quicker from seeds than from the slow-to-form offsets. Seedlings begin to flower in their third season. For these dwarf plants, container culture is best, with the bulbs shallowly planted 0.5 inch (1–2 cm) deep. The mix should be sandy and well drained. As with *Strumaria*, closely grouped and crowded bulbs make a nice display.

Hexaglottis (Iridaceae)

The name *Hexaglottis* is from the Greek *hex*, "six," and *glottis*, "tongue," referring to the style branches, which are a distinguishing feature. The style branches are deeply divided and again divide into two slender arms. According to Peter Goldblatt (1987b), *Hexaglottis* is a small genus of six Cape species entirely restricted to the winter-rainfall area.

I grow only the species *Hexaglottis longifolia*, which has yellow flowers with a greenish median line on the outer surface of the segments. The flower stalks can reach over 3 feet (1 m) tall.

Hexaglottis virgata is edible and has a delicious nutty flavor. According to Metelerkamp and Sealy (1983), in pre-European times the hunting and gathering Bushmen and the nomadic pastoralist Hottentots, now collectively known as the Khoisan, ate many of the irids, including corms of *Babiana*, *Gladiolus*, *Hexaglottis*, *Ixia*, *Moraea*, and *Watsonia*.

Hexaglottis is propagated from corms or seeds. Its seedlings will bloom in their third season. It likes a sunny site in well-drained soil. It is winter growing and summer dormant. The flowers are ephemeral, and not many gardeners will get excited about *Hexaglottis*. It is related to *Homeria*, which is more useful horticulturally.

Homeria (Iridaceae)

The genus *Homeria* does not commemorate Homer, as some think, but is derived from the Greek *omero*, "to meet together," referring to the filaments being united in a sheath around the style. *Homeria* is an entirely South African genus of about 31 species concentrated in the Cape region (Goldblatt, 1981). The flowers are quite bright and colorful, but they are poisonous to cattle and some are very weedy; gardeners must be cautious because some *Homeria* can become noxious and can be extremely difficult to exterminate. Johan Loubser once warned me against ever growing the weedy *H. miniata* because of his experiences with it. I have heeded his advice.

Homeria species are winter-growing, deciduous, summer-dormant geophytes. They are propagated by seeds or by corms, which have a distinctive, tough, brown tunic.

Homeria collina (*collina* means "growing on low hills") is a common species formerly known as *H. breyniana* (Figure 3-24). A common name is Cape tulip. (See Plate 39.) The flowers are scented and have a

FIGURE 3-24.
Homeria collina.

salmon color, but there are yellow varieties. *Homeria collina* grows to about 2 feet (61 cm) tall or more. It is poisonous to cattle and has weedy tendencies. I have difficulty finding any difference horticulturally between *H. collina* and *H. flaccida*.

Homeria comptonii is a very colorful species (Plate 40). The variety I grow is orange to salmon pink with a yellow center. It grows to about 18 inches (45 cm) tall.

Homeria ochroleuca, as the name indicates, is yellow. Its growth form is similar to *H. collina.*

Homeria framesii is a dwarf species less than a foot tall (30 cm) with orange-pink flowers.

One species formerly called *Homeria lilacina* is now recognized as *Moraea polyanthos*, and I grow it under that name.

Homeria should be planted in a sunny location in well-drained soil. It can be planted about 3 inches (8 cm) deep and about 2 inches (5 cm) apart for a nice display. The species of *Homeria* can brighten the spring garden with their 2-inch (5-cm) wide orange or yellow flowers.

Homoglossum (Iridaceae)

According to Clive Innes (1985) the name *Homoglossum* is derived from the Greek *omoios*, "similar," and *glossa*, "tongue," presumably in reference to the shape and color of the perianth segments. There are ten species in the Cape flora. Miriam De Vos (1976) concluded that the only difference between *Homoglossum* and the very closely related *Gladiolus* (*Homoglossum* is often included in *Gladiolus*) is in the shape of the perianth.

In the Cape the common name for *Homoglossum priorii* is flames or the red Afrikaner (Plate 41). It was named for Alexander Prior, a plant collector of the 19th century. It is the first species of this genus to bloom in my garden. The bright red flower has a yellow throat and appears in Santa Barbara at the end of October, continuing to be a very bright spot in the garden in November. It is certainly welcome around Thanksgiving time when days begin to feel wintry and the garden otherwise does not have a riot of color. I always look forward to its flowering, along with the remarkable *Lachenalia viridiflora,* which also first appears in November.

Homoglossum huttonii, named for Henry Hutton, is the easiest species of *Homoglossum* to cultivate (Figure 3-25). It is from the eastern Cape and opens its bright scarlet flowers in early spring. The flowers are borne on a slender 18-inch (46-cm) tall stalk, as are also those of *H. priorii.* I have hybridized it with a number of *Gladiolus* species.

Professional botanists have not agreed on the proper placement of the rare and beautiful *Gladiolus aureus.* Joyce Lewis et al. (1972) placed it in *Homoglossum,* but Miriam De Vos (1976) and others placed it in *Gladiolus,* and I have accepted the latter view.

I grow two other species, *Homoglossum quadrangulare* and *H. watsonium* but have had less experience with them. They have red or coral red flowers.

Collingwood Ingram (1977) grew hybrids of *Homoglossum watsonium* and *Gladiolus tristis* that he termed "Homoglads." He expressed amazement at the diversity in color and patterns of the flowers. Some were pure scarlet, and others were soft pinky-mauve, but most were striped or bicolored, red and cream. He seemed particularly intrigued by one with bluish gray lateral segments because there is not the slightest hint of blue in the flowers of either parent.

Ingram believed that his "Homoglads" would thrive not only along the Pacific Coast where the climate is similar to the natural habitat of their parents, but also, based on his experience in his Kentish garden in England, in the cooler places of the Pacific Northwest.

Johan Loubser (1985) crossed *Gladiolus odoratus* with *Homoglossum priori.* This hybrid was a very pleasing plant with the hardiness of the *Homoglossum,* a bright red color, and the strong scent of the *Gladiolus.*

Propagation of *Homoglossum* is by seeds or corms. Germination time for *H. abbreviatum* is 40 days, and for *H. quadrangulare,* 38 days. *Homoglossum* is cultivated just like the Cape's winter-growing *Gladiolus.* It is content in Mediterranean climates and does very well if given a sunny site in well-drained soil with no water during the summer rest period.

FIGURE 3-25.
Homoglossum huttonii.

Species of *Homoglossum* are just waiting to be discovered by Pacific Coast gardeners (Doutt, 1988). They make colorful splashes in the garden and are good cut flowers. They are splendid subjects for hyridizers, as Collingwood Ingram has demonstrated.

Hypoxis (Hypoxidaceae)

Hypoxis is a large genus that is pantropical, including seven Cape species, but it is not considered of any great worth horticulturally. The plants have fibrous rhizomes, hairy leaves, and yellow star-shaped flowers in a raceme.

The one species recommended for cultivation is *Hypoxis rooperi,* which does not occur in the Cape (Du Plessis and Duncan, 1989). It was used medicinally by the early, indigenous South Africans. A preparation was given to children by the Tswana and Kwena to produce purgation. The juice from the rootstock was used as an application to burns. To cure a headache in Basutoland, the rootstock is shaped into a small hollow receptacle in which some blood from the afflicted person's forehead is collected. The receptacle is then buried, and the headache is supposedly cured. Rope made from the leaf is used in the building of huts and reed enclosures and for sewing grain baskets (Watt and Breyer-Brandwijk, 1962).

In winter, *Hypoxis rooperi* is naturally deciduous if it is grown in a summer-rainfall area, but it remains evergreen if grown in a winter-rainfall area.

I have only recently started some seedlings and rely on Du Plessis and Duncan (1989) for information on *Hypoxis rooperi*. They suggested the corms be planted about 3 cm (1 in) deep in full sun. Because the clumps multiply rapidly, those authors cautioned that *H. rooperi* may become invasive.

Ixia (Iridaceae)

There are two interpretations of the derivation of the genus name *Ixia*. John Bryan (1989) claimed it is from the Greek *ixos*, meaning "bird lime," used by the philosopher and botanist Theophrastus in reference to the clammy sap of the plants. Clive Innes (1985) wrote that it is from a Greek name *Ixia*, a plant noted for its color variability. South African writers tend to favor the latter view and believe that Linnaeus chose the name on account of the color variability of flowers when he described four species in 1726.

There are now about 50 species of *Ixia* all indigenous to the Cape Province and adapted to winter rainfall followed by a dry summer. The corm is small with a fibrous covering. The leaves are long and linear. The plants range from 8 inches (20 cm) tall to over 2 feet (61 cm) tall. The flowers are regular and borne in spikes on long slender erect stalks. *Ixia* has a fine color range, and the flowers are bright, often with a dark center. They are commonly called wand flowers, and there are many very decorative species.

Ixia rapunculoides is the first *Ixia* species to bloom in my garden, starting in late fall. It has pale blue flowers on a branched stalk about 18 inches (46 cm) high. The perianth tube is greenish. It is an easy grower, and I have always been fond of it because it gives me a preview of the spring-flowering Cape bulbs.

Ixia dubia (Figure 3-26) has bright golden yellow to orange flowers with a dark center on a slender 20-inch (52-cm) tall stalk. *Ixia dubia* forms colorful clumps and is very reliable and undemanding. I saw it growing in a seasonally wet site in the wild, which suggests it may benefit from ample water during its growing period. (See Plate 42.)

I grow three *Ixia* species that have pink flowers. Two of these, *I. scillaris* and *I. flexuosa,* have graceful 18-inch (46-cm) long flower stalks. *Ixia trifolia* has bright pink flowers with yellow centers on plants about 8 inches (20 cm) high.

Ixia conferta is a charming dwarf species. It has large, bright yellow flowers with chocolate brown centers. The flower stalk seldom exceeds 20 cm (8 inches) in height (Plate 43).

Ixia maculata has very handsome yellow to orange flowers with purplish black blotches in the throat. The stalks will reach 2 feet (61 cm) in height.

FIGURE 3-26.
Ixia dubia.

Ixia monadelpha generally has blue flowers with a darker center, but there are other color forms. It grows to about 12 inches (30 cm) tall.

Ixia viridiflora has numerous turquoise-green flowers with dark centers on tall, wiry stems (Plate 44). This is a very striking species, but I find it difficult to maintain in cultivation and must frequently replace it.

Propagation of *Ixia* is by seeds and corms. Seeds germinate in about a month (*I. paniculata* in 36 days) and flower in their third season. *Ixia* is typical of many other bulbous plants of the Cape, needing water during the winter and a dry rest in summer. The corms should be planted about 2 inches (5 cm) deep in well-drained soil in a sunny location.

Ixia is graceful and colorful in the garden and is a useful cut flower.

Lachenalia (Hyacinthaceae)

Lachenalia (pronounced lah-shen-ahl´-ee-a) was named in 1784 for Werner de La Chenal, a professor of botany in Basel, Switzerland. The popularity of this genus among members of the Indigenous Bulb Growers of South Africa is second only to *Gladiolus*. The flowers may be tubular, bell-shaped, or urn-shaped (Figure 3-27). They may be sessile on the flower stalk or may have very short pedicels. The three inner perianth segments usually protrude beyond the outer three segments that surround them at their base. The tips of the outer segments often have a gibbosity, or swelling, at their apex, a distinguishing feature that often appears as a differently colored spot. *Lachenalia* is a large genus comprised of approximately 110 species (Du Plessis and Duncan, 1989).

The finest book on growing *Lachenalia* is *The* Lachenalia *Handbook* by Graham Duncan, the absolute authority on propagation of South African bulbs and the resident expert at Kirstenbosch. It was published in 1988 as volume 17 of the *Annals of Kirstenbosch Botanic Gardens* and is the bible for any *Lachenalia* enthusiast.

Of the estimated 100 Cape species, I grow the following outdoors in Santa Barbara. From correspondence I know that there are *Lachenalia* enthusiasts in the eastern states who grow these fascinating flowers in greenhouses.

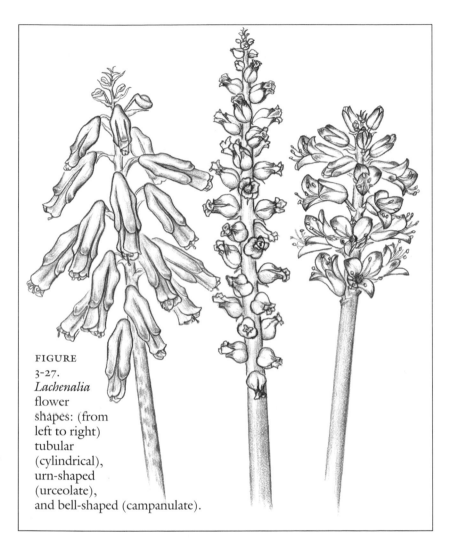

FIGURE 3-27. *Lachenalia* flower shapes: (from left to right) tubular (cylindrical), urn-shaped (urceolate), and bell-shaped (campanulate).

Lachenalia rubida, meaning ruby red, is the first species to bloom for me, starting in the fall. After that beginning, the *Lachenalia* plants in my garden bloom species after species until summer. For some reason *L. rubida* has been slow to reproduce vegetatively for me and often does not set seed. It is reportedly more prolific in the Cape. I found, however, that it readily produces bulbs from leaf cuttings, and that is the method I use to increase its numbers.

Of all the Cape bulbs I grow, none is more stunning than *Lachena-lia viridiflora* (Plate 45). It begins to bloom later in the fall, following the brilliant display of *L. rubida*, and continues to flower through the holidays. It was first found in humus-rich crevices in granite outcrops. In nature it is a dwarf species but it reaches 12 inches (30 cm) high or more in my garden. The color is truly unique and has variously been described as viridian green, blue-green, or even turquoise. When the flowers are back lighted by the sun, they are particularly gorgeous. It is my favorite *Lachenalia* because of its remarkable color and ease of cultivation.

One very reliable and predictable species is *Lachenalia bulbifera* (formerly *L. pendula*), which blooms for Christmas each year (Figure 3-28). Its red and green colors make it a splendid addition to holiday decor both in and out of northern gardens. (See Plate 46.) The name *L. bulbifera* reflects its tendency to form small bulbils on the leaf-base margins, and in general it is a very productive species. The flower stalks grow to almost 16 inches (40 cm). The individual flowers are red and cylindrical like firecrackers. The slightly protruding inner segments have green tips flanked with two purple zones.

A somewhat frost-tender plant for me is *Lachenalia pustulata*. D'Ewes (1978) considered the name disgusting in reference to the warty excrescences on the fleshy all-green leaves. Actually I think the plants are quite attractive.

Lachenalia peersii is named for Victor Stanley Peers, a remarkable botanical collector and cultivator of South African plants. He was also an archaeological explorer of "Peers Cave" in Fish Hoek Valley. He collected *L. peersii* at Hermanus in 1912. It was given the manuscript name *L. peersii* in 1917 by Dr. Rudolph Marloth and the name was validated by W. F. Barker in 1978, who published a charming biography of Victor Peers in 1980. The plants of *L. peersii* have one or two leaves, are 7 to 12 inches (18 to 30 cm) high, and are quite floriferous. The scented, urn-shaped white flowers fade to pinkish as they age. The aroma is reportedly reminiscent of carnations. The plants bloom in midspring.

FIGURE 3-28.
Lachenalia bulbifera.

Many species of *Lachenalia* have an extremely limited distribution, and some are even confined to a single wild locality. For example, *L. mathewsii* is known only from a restricted area of the Cape's west coast. It was first collected in 1923 and was described in 1931. Collections were made in 1938 and again in 1943, but after that there were no more collections; the species was thought to be extinct as a result of plowing the veld for agriculture. Nearly 40 years later it was rediscovered in a seasonally wet area unsuitable for agriculture (Duncan, 1986). *Lachenalia mathewsii* is a desirable species, being both attractive and hardy. The bulbs flower over a three-week period, making it a good candidate for container plantings. *Lachenalia mathewsii* ranges from 5 to 8 inches (12 to 20 cm) in height. The flowers are oblong, bell shaped, and bright yellow with conspicuous green gibbosities. The flowers appear in early spring.

Lachenalia purpureo-caerulea is another endangered species on the west coast of the Cape. It occurs only in the Darling area and survives in the Tinie Versfeld Reserve. The species name describes the color of the heavily scented, bell-shaped flowers. The outer segments are blue at the base and shade to purple or magenta with greenish brown gibbosities apically. The slightly protruding inner segments are widened and colored magenta with darker tips. These are very desirable plants, flowering in spring. The height ranges from 4 to 11 inches (10 to 28 cm).

While the flowers of *Lachenalia zebrina* do not match those of many other species, the leaf is certainly distinctive, and its resemblance to the hind leg of a zebra inspired Barker (1983) to create the name. The height ranges from 6 to 12 inches (15 to 30 cm). The flowers are cream colored and begin appearing in early spring.

Lachenalia giessii is a dwarf species that grows 3 to 6 inches (7 to 15 cm) high. It is a localized species discovered in 1941 in the southwestern corner of South West Africa and Namibia and has not been found south of the Orange River. The species is named for W. Giess, retired curator of the Windhoek Herbarium and a prolific collector of plants in South West Africa and Namibia.

The bulb of *Lachenalia namibiensis* is covered with rigid brown tunics that form a neck. Though its function is unknown, this type of dark brown or black corm is characteristic of certain species of Cape bulbs in several different genera found in arid locations and may help ensure survival in the desert. The flowers of *L. namibiensis* are white and bell shaped. Each of the outer segments has a green to purple gibbosity. The inner segments are slightly exserted and have a green to purple marking apically.

I grow several varieties of the widespread species *Lachenalia aloides*, which is named for its *Aloe*-like flowers. It tends to be a coastal species that grows in rocky habitats but also extends inland on rocky outcrops in the mountain ranges. A varied and colorful species, it is widely cultivated, very popular, and has been used extensively in hybridization.

Lachenalia aloides var. *aurea,* named for its striking golden-yellow flowers, is a fairly vigorous plant reaching 10 inches (26 cm) high. It is restricted to the Bainskloof mountains.

Growing closer to the coast in crevices in the Precambrian granite outcrops is *Lachenalia aloides* var. *quadricolor*, so named because each flower has four colors (Plate 47). The outer segments are reddish orange at the base shading to yellow and terminating in green gibbosities. The inner segments are yellow with maroon tips. This is the showiest and also the most prolific of the varieties I grow.

Lachenalia aloides var. *luteola* is yellowish green, and often has several reddish orange, sterile flowers at the tip of the inflorescence. It grows on the Cape Peninsula, is quite floriferous, and tends to bloom later than the other varieties.

In 1984, Barker described *Lachenalia aloides* var. *vanzyliae*. It was named for Mrs. L. Van Zyl, who first introduced it to Kirstenbosch in 1927, and it flowered there in 1929. It is another mountain inhabitant. The delicately shaded flowers differ from all the other color varieties of *L. aloides* in being pale viridian or pale blue at the base shading to white with green gibbosities. The protruding inner segments are pale yellow-green shading to white on the margins.

In my garden all the color varieties of *Lachenalia aloides* have been easy to grow, though the hybrid cultivar 'Nelsonii' has given me some difficulty.

Lachenalia mutabilis (Plate 48) is an especially interesting and long-lasting species. It grows to 14 inches (36 cm) high and blooms from late winter to midspring. The name refers to the remarkable color changes of the inflorescence. The tip of the inflorescence is electric blue, and below it is a zone of dense, urn-shaped flowers with outer segments pale blue shading to white with dark brown tips. The protruding inner segments are dark yellow with brown tips, and the yellow color predominates as the flowers mature. At the base of the inflorescence, the mature flowers become brownish red. *Lachenalia carnosa* is named for its fleshy leaves. It grows in Namaqualand and is a very showy species requiring good drainage. The outer segments are white with maroon gibbosities. The inner segments protrude and are white with striking broad magenta tips.

Lachenalia contaminata is called the wild hyacinth. The scientific name refers to the maroon floral markings, which in fact enhance rather than "contaminate" the flower. The inflorescence is quite dense with many broadly campanulate flowers. The outer segments are white with a maroon dot at the apex, the white inner segments have a maroon central stripe, and the foliage is grasslike for a pleasing overall effect.

The other *Lachenalia* species I grow include *L. algoense*, *L. arbuthnotii*, *L. capensis*, *L. elegans*, *L. framesii* (Plate 49), *L. latifolia*, *L. latimerae*, *L. liliflora*, *L. longibracteata*, *L. muirii*, *L. namaquensis* (Plate 50), *L. orchioides* var. *glaucina*, *L. pallida*, *L. pusilla*, *L. reflexa*, *L. rosea* (Plate 51), *L. salteri*, *L. splendida*, *L. trichophylla*, *L. unicolor*, *L. unifolia*, *L. variegata*, *L. violacea*, and *L. zeyheri*. Space limitations preclude comments on all of them, but I would not give any of them up and highly recommend all *Lachenalia* to gardeners.

Crosby (1978) found no published records of naturally occurring hybrids among *Lachenalia* species in the wild, but he reported deliberate hybridization starting with *L. aloides* 'Nelsonii', a cross between *L. aloides* var. *luteola* and *L. aloides* var. *aurea*, produced by John G. Nelson in England in 1877. Crosby also reported a successful cross of *L. aloides* × *L. reflexa* in 1891. From his own experimental work at the University of Leeds, he succeeded in crossing *L. aloides* with *L. bulbifera*, *L. glaucina*, *L. reflexa*, and *L. viridiflora*. He also crossed *L. bulbifera* with *L. glaucina*, *L. rubida*, and *L. viridiflora*, while *L. reflexa* was further crossed with *L. glaucina* and *L. viridiflora*. Crosby (1978, page 90) concluded, "while several of these are of merely scientific interest others have produced novel plants with horticultural potential."

In the bulb nursery at Kirstenbosch, Graham Duncan (1988) grows many species of *Lachenalia* in 8-inch plastic pots on raised benches under a fiberglass roof. The growing medium consists of coarse sand mixed with a little fine compost. Bulbs multiply rapidly by division. *Lachenalia* species are readily propagated by seeds, which should be sown in the fall. *Lachenalia carnosa* germinates in 17 days, *L. elegans* in 31–38 days, *L. fistulosa* in 39 days, *L. framesii* in 12 days, *L. hirta* in 36 days, *L. mutabilis* in 34 days, *L. namibiensis* in 13 days, *L. splendida* in 14–25 days, and *L. trichophylla* in 22–34 days. The seedlings bloom in their second season if grown well and bloom much better in their third year.

Lachenalia species are good container plants but are also effective in a rock garden. As container plants they can be brought indoors for short periods during peak bloom. The potted plants are most effective if seen at eye level. They are also good cut flowers. Every gardener should try one or two species of this superb genus of Cape bulbs.

Lapeirousia (Iridaceae)

Lapeirousia species are beautiful little gems and exquisite container plants. Though sometimes in the literature the genus has the obsolete spelling of *Lapeyrousia*, *Lapeirousia* is named for the botanist Baron Philippe de la Peirouse, not for the circumnavigator de la Peyrouse. There are about 11 species in the Cape flora and over 35 African species. In the literature there is some confusion with *Anomatheca*, but the genera are clearly separated by the shape of the corms.

FIGURE 3-29.
Lapeirousia oreogena.

Lapeirousia species are rather dwarf plants with small corms that are bell-shaped with a flat base and a hard, woody tunic. Many of the flowers have long perianth tubes and are arranged in a spike or corymbose panicle. In the wild I have seen some species growing in rocky situations, even in crevices in granite outcrops.

Lapeirousia corymbosa subsp. *fastigiata* has dark, blue-violet flowers marked with black. The flowers are arranged in a corymbose panicle as the name indicates. The corm is cone shaped with a very broad base.

Lapeirousia jacquinii has very dark purple flowers with cream markings. Like all the other species of *Lapeirousia,* it is a charming small plant. Its bracts have crisped margins.

Lapeirousia oreogena (Figure 3-29) also has purple flowers with white markings. The perianth tubes are very long, arising at soil level and exceeding the leaflike bracts, which have crisped edges. This is a most attractive plant but I have found it difficult to maintain. It grows naturally in clay soil, which may be the clue to its successful cultivation. I have only had it in a sandy medium, though other Cape bulbs from the same locality of heavy clay do well when grown in the sandy medium

Lapeirousia silenoides is a striking reddish pink with darker markings and could be a delightful container plant. I first saw it growing in crevices in a granite outcropping at Kamieskroon in Namaqualand. The corms were quite deep in the crevice, where they were protected from the summer heat.

Propagation of *Lapeirousia* is from the corms or from seeds. *Lapeirousia fabrici* germinates in 58 days, *L. jacquinii* in 19 days, *L. montana* in 20 days, *L. oreogena* in 34 days, and *L. rosea* in 35 days.

Massonia (Hyacinthaceae)

Massonia is named for Francis Masson, an early plant explorer in the Cape Province. It was a manuscript name suggested by Thunberg and used by Maarten Houttuyn in describing this genus in 1780 (Jessop, 1976). There are about five species in the Cape, and all are curiosities for ardent collectors.

Massonia characteristically has two large leaves that lie flat on the soil surface. The flowers are in a sessile umbel that arises between the two leaves. The stamens are longer than the perianth. *Massonia* is found in areas that are hot and dry during the summer. As is typical of Cape bulbs adapted to a Mediterranean climate, it is winter-growing and summer dormant. Common names given to *Massonia* include Abraham's book, pincushions, and, most charmingly, Dutch footprints.

Massonia depressa grows in Namaqualand in sandy flat areas with poor soil. The flowers are cream colored. The leaves are very smooth and broad. Although the ground may be very dry, when a *Massonia* leaf is lifted, the area underneath is quite moist. The bulb is reportedly edible.

Massonia pustulata (Figure 3-30) is more widespread than *M. depressa* and is more interesting, for its leaves have a roughened surface and the flowers may be white or pinkish. The leaves have linear ridges of pustules.

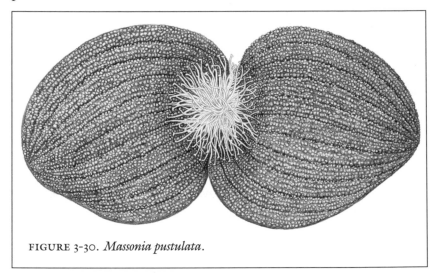

FIGURE 3-30. *Massonia pustulata*.

Massonia angustifolia is now a synonym for *Neobakeria angustifolia* (Plate 52). This species has shiny leaves with linear veins or ridges. The flowers are yellow with very conspicuous and extruded orange-red stamens.

Although *Massonia* can be propagated from offsets, I have had better success with their seeds grown in sandy medium and a sunny site.

Melasphaerula (Iridaceae)

The corm of *Melasphaerula* is black and round with a flattened base, and the name is descriptive coming from the Greek *melas,* "black," and *sphaira,* "a sphere," or *sphaerula,* "little ball." A common name is fairy bells.

This is a monotypic genus; *Melasphaerula ramosa* (formerly called *M. graminea*) is the only species (Plate 53). It is endemic to the Cape and is perhaps the most unusual species in the Iridaceae. The leaves are erect and swordlike. The word *ramosa* means "branched," and certainly the flower spike is many branched with the numerous small, half-inch flowers on threadlike pedicels. The branching and the numerous delicate pedicels give the flower spike an airy appearance. The zygomorphic flowers are greenish white with a fine purple median line on each of the pointed segments. The flowers are long lasting.

The plants, which grow in brushy areas in some shade in the Cape, do best if given partial shade. I find that *Melasphaerula ramosa* naturalizes readily in Santa Barbara. I do not yet consider it weedy, although it probably bears watching. Dr. Boussard (1985, page 62) very succinctly comments, "*Melasphaerula*: a weed!"

Melasphaerula ramosa is a plant of only modest horticultural value. Although the flowers are long lasting and give an airy effect they are a bit on the dull side. However, Sima Eliovson (1980, page 126) wrote, "This dainty member of the Iris family is well worth introducing into cultivation, for its delicate flowers are delightful in the vase and would make good florists' flowers of the same type as *Gypsophila*." Katherine Whiteside (1991) extolled its virtues as an indoor windowsill plant for gardeners in eastern states. She suggested planting as many as twenty-five corms in a 7-inch pot and placing it in a light window that does not get direct sun.

Propagation is from offsets, cormels, or seeds, which will bloom in the second year. The plants need water during their winter growth phase and should be kept dry in summer.

Moraea (Iridaceae)

In 1762 Linnaeus changed the spelling of *Morea* to *Moraea* to commemorate his father-in-law and his wife's family name, Moraeus. *Moraea* is a large genus of over 100 species in Africa, many of which are localized in the western Cape. Peter Goldblatt published a series of revisions that culminated in his splendid monograph on the *Moraea* of Southern Africa (1986).

Moraea aristata was grown in Holland as early as 1750. Today, it is one of the most critically endangered geophytes in South Africa, with a total wild population of no more than a few dozen plants. At present it is known only from a single locality near the Liesbeek River. This flower is one of the strikingly beautiful peacock *Moraea* group. It is closely related to *M. villosa* but has different flower color and markings as well as a completely hairless leaf and flower stalk. The large white flowers are attractively marked with black, blue, or green (Plate 54). The flower stalk, which may reach the height of 14 inches (35 cm), is often branched and floriferous, and the faintly scented flowers last three days.

Moraea loubseri is a rare flower named after Johan Loubser, a friend who helped me start my collection of Cape bulbs. He discovered the species in 1973 near Saldanha Bay on the granite Olifantskop, which was being blasted to supply ballast for the building of the Sishen-Saldanha railway. In subsequent years visiting botanists came away from the koppie without finding the colony and regretfully reported the species to be extinct in the wild. However, at that time *M. loubseri* was being saved at Kirstenbosch through its policy of conservation through cultivation, and a large stock of over 1000 plants was established there. It was first made available to members of the Botanical Society of South Africa in 1980 when Graham Duncan dispatched 135 packets of seed. In the spring of 1982, Loubser revisited Olifantskop and found some 200 plants alive and well and in flower. Now that the railway is completed and quarrying has ceased, it is hoped that *M. loubseri,* once considered extinct, will continue to survive in its own tiny piece of the veld. The large flowers of *M. loubseri* are deep violet with a black beard. They grow on a single or branched stalk about 14 inches (35 cm) high. The corms, typical of all *Moraea* species, are tunicated.

Both of these rare and localized species of *Moraea* (*M. aristata* and *M. loubseri*) flourish in my Santa Barbara garden and present excellent examples of conservation through cultivation.

Moraea atropunctata was first discovered in 1978 when a specimen was brought to the Caledon wildflower show. It was described by Peter Goldblatt in 1982 and then made available to gardeners through the Kirstenbosch program. It is a local endemic limited to a single farm, Vleitjes, on the slopes of the Eseljacht mountains where it grows in clay soil on the edges of farm tracks and margins of wheat fields. The cream flowers are red-brown on the reverse and the bases of the outer segments are thickly speckled with attractive black dots. It grows to about 8 inches (20 cm) high.

Moraea barnardii has small white flowers with blue-purple veins and nectar guides. It is a rare species, as is *M. calcicola*, a local endemic on the west coast near Saldanha Bay that was first described in 1982. *Moraea calcicola* is clear blue with blackish nectar guides, and it is one of the beautiful peacock species of *Moraea* that has a large spot on each segment, reminiscent of the gorgeous eye on a peacock feather. *Moraea calcicola* grows to about 16 inches (41 cm) high. Other flowers in the peacock group include *M. gigandra* (Plate 55), possibly the largest flowered *Moraea*, and *M. villosa*. I grow these strikingly beautiful *Moraea* in pots and believe it best to leave the corms undisturbed as long as posible.

The earliest *Moraea* species to bloom in my garden is *M. polystachya* (Figure 3-31), which starts flowering in early fall and blooms through early winter. It is many branched and grows to 32 inches (81 cm) high. The strap-shaped leaves are 14 inches (36 cm) long. The flowers are blue-violet with yellow nectar guides, and from a distance the plants look like a swarm of blue butterflies. The species naturalizes from seed dispersed in the garden but is not weedy. Peter Goldblatt (1986, page 120) reported that "in years of good rainfall it may extend over thousands of hectares, colouring the veld with a blue haze and making a glorious display." Unfortunately *M. polystachya* is poisonous to cattle. *Moraea bipartita* is similar to *M. polystachya* in branching and flower color but blooms in early spring.

Moraea polyanthos has blue flowers of the shape commonly seen in *Homeria* and in the past was recorded in that genus as *Homeria lilacina*. All attempted crosses of *M. polyanthos* with species of *Homeria* have failed. On the other hand, *M. polyanthos* and *M. bipartita* are closely related and readily cross.

There are two large, yellow-flowered *Moraea*. *Moraea ramossisima* is many branched, as the name indicates, and has peculiar spiny roots. It

FIGURE 3-31.
Moraea polystachya.

grows over 3 feet (1 m) tall. Even taller is *M. spathulata* with robust plants that form clumps. It grows in the summer-rainfall area from the coast of the eastern Cape northward to Zimbabwe. It therefore needs water in the summer and autumn.

By contrast, *Moraea serpentina* and *M. tricolor* (Plate 56) are dwarf species growing to about 6 inches (15 cm) high. The flowers of *M. serpentina* are white with large, deep-yellow nectar guides. The name refers to its coiled basal leaves. It is found in arid Namaqualand.

Another dwarf species is *Moraea vegeta*, which is the type species of the genus. The flowers are a yellow-brown flushed with purple on the reverse. The nectar guides are yellow. The species has neither the charm nor the elegance of many other *Moraea* and it has a tendency to become weedy, in part because it is self-compatible and does not require cross-fertilization.

Moraea neopavonia has unusual orange flowers with dark blue markings at the base of the outer segments (Plate 57). It is a very striking member of the peacock group and is closely related to the large-flowered, blue *M. gigandra*. Graham Duncan (1985) considers *M. neopavonia* to be his favorite *Moraea*, and since it is nearly extinct in the wild, he is making every effort to cultivate it extensively at Kirstenbosch.

Moraea fugax is a variable species with yellow, blue, mauve, or white flowers that are strongly scented. The fugacious flowers are indeed ephemeral but are glorious for those few afternoon hours in the sun. The corms are edible, pleasant tasting, and were an important food source for the first humans inhabiting the caves of the western Cape region.

Moraea gracilenta has small, pale blue flowers on graceful plants with panicle-like branching of the flower stalks. The sweetly scented flowers open in the late afternoon and are pollinated in South Africa by moths.

Other species in my garden that are easy to grow include *Moraea tricuspidata*. It has white or cream flowers with brown-speckled nectar guides and grows to about 15 inches (39 cm) high. *Moraea tripetala* also grows to 15 inches (39 cm) high and has pale blue flowers with white nectar guides and red pollen. It is named for the flower, which appears to have only three petals because the inner segments are extremely reduced.

Moraea unquiculata is an 8-inch (20 cm) tall species with small cream or dull white flowers that have yellow nectar guides. Another small species is *M. macrocarpa,* which has scented blue-mauve flowers and yellow nectar guides.

Graham Duncan (1983) has written authoritative instructions on the propagation of *Moraea*. The species respond favorably to cultivation in 12-inch plastic pots. The corms do best in a well-drained sandy medium to which fine compost has been added. Liberal watering is required during the winter months. The situation should be sunny. *Moraea* responds well to regular applications of liquid fertilizer. During the summer when the corms are dormant, the pots should be placed in a cool, dry area.

Seeds should be sown in autumn in deep seed trays in a sandy medium and placed in semi-shade until seedlings are well established. Afterward the amount of light can be increased. Deep seed trays are always preferable to shallow ones, allowing space for good root development and a faster maturity of corms. I prefer to plant the seeds in deep pots where they can be allowed to mature without being disturbed. Seeds germinate in about five weeks if the medium is kept constantly moist. Records show that *Moraea atropunctata* germinates in 42 days, *M. bipartita* in 37 days, *M. bituminosa* in 34–41 days, *M. gawleri* in 38 days, *M. inconspicua* in 32 days, *M. neopavonia* in 38 days, and *M. polyanthos* in 30 days. The seedlings should remain in the seed trays for their second season and can be planted into large pots at the beginning of their third season, during which time a number should produce their first flowers.

Moraea is one of the loveliest wildflowers of the Cape and should have a place in the garden of any bulb enthusiast.

Nerine (Amaryllidaceae)

Nerine is a water nymph in Greek mythology. Though the correct pronunciation is nay-ree´-nay most folks call the flower neh-reens´.

The genus *Nerine* is endemic to southern Africa. Bond and Goldblatt (1984) listed six species in the Cape flora. These bulbous plants have very showy flowers in multiflowered umbels. One common name is diamond lily.

Tony Norris (1980) amassed a *Nerine* collection of 80,000 bulbs including 900 named cultivars and most of the species. Unquestionably an authority on the genus, Norris pointed out that *Nerine* is found in a wide variety of habitats ranging from severe frost to intense heat. It grows from the 4000-meter (13,120-ft) heights of the Drakensberg, where it flowers with the first winter snows, to the coastal marshes; it grows in near-desert conditions and in running water.

Nerine sarniensis is commonly called the Guernsey lily because it was once believed to come from the Channel Islands. William Herbert, a distinguished botanist living in Spofforth, England, derived the epithet from Sarnia, the Latin name for the Channel Islands.

As one version of the story states, a Dutch ship bound for home from the Far East via the Cape in 1659 was wrecked off the Guernsey shore. *Nerine* bulbs that washed ashore took root and flourished. The details of this story conflict with evidence of a Dutch ship having taken bulbs from the Cape to France, where they were cultivated and, in due time, found their way to Guernsey.

Francis Masson put the botanical world right about the native home of *Nerine sarniensis*. While at the Cape, he found the species growing on Table Mountain and other heights within 40 miles (64 km) of Cape Town, and he was in no doubt that this lovely scarlet, gold-dusted flower belonged to the Cape. It is still found in the more remote and inaccessible parts of the southwest Cape.

Tony Norris (1980) gave an entertaining account of his search for species of *Nerine* in South Africa. He found that *N. sarniensis* on Table Mountain and on many mountains in the extreme southwest Cape grows in some of the poorest soil in the world. A soil analysis showed the available nitrogen at between 3 and 7 parts per million, while Norris's soil in England contained some 350 parts per million. This information revolutionized *Nerine* cultivation. To successfully grow *N. sarniensis*, Norris found that three parts acid sand, one part peat, and no fertilizer was ideal and resulted in 60 to 100 percent flowering.

Nerine sarniensis, a summer dormant species, has been in cultivation in Europe since 1630, so Norris was puzzled by how unreasonable techniques for cultivation came into vogue and was particularly critical of the statement "ripen the bulbs in full sun," repeated in book after book. He found in South Africa that at least a dozen species of *Nerine*, and certainly *N. sarniensis*, grow in the mist-covered mountains, in south-facing cracks, and in many places that never see the sun from one year to the next.

Graham Duncan (1984, page 55) gave an interesting account of a pure white sport of *Nerine sarniensis* that originally was found on Table Mountain (white forms are also known from three other *Nerine* species: *N. bowdenii*, *N. filifolia*, and *N. flexuosa*) and provided the following notes for the cultivation of *N. sarniensis* in pots or in the garden:

> The bulbs, which do best in a sandy well-drained medium can be grown in full sun or semi-shade and should be planted with the "necks" of the bulbs just above ground level. Liberal watering is required during the winter months but during summer watering must be withheld. . . . Bulbs do not like being disturbed, and should be left in the same position for a number of years until they become overcrowded, when dividing is necessary.

Nerine sarniensis is a good cut flower, and when grown in pots can be brought indoors for the flowering period. It produces seed easily and is important for breeding. Two of its well-known derivatives are 'Corusca Major' and 'Fothergillii Major'. These are the superlative diamond lilies.

Nerine sarniensis has been involved in crosses with other genera. The intergeneric cross of *Brunsvigia marginata* × *Nerine sarniensis* is described in the section on the genus *Brunsvigia*.

Nerine humilis is a charming small flower that grows in many of the valleys of the southwest Cape and is one of the summer-dormant species. Throughout the range of the species there is considerable variation in the size and color of the flower. The more usual form has a stalk of 8 to 12 inches (20 to 30 cm) high with an umbel of 6 to 16 or more florets. The segments are not crinkled for about two-thirds of their length and sweep sideways and upward. The color is pink with a strong central darker line for the full length of the segment. The species blooms in early fall.

Norris (1980) described the favorite habitat of *Nerine humilis* as a rocky riverbank with a shaded crack or south-facing crevice. Charles Hardman (1985), an expert on growing *Nerine* in the Los Angeles basin, reported that *N. humilis* must indeed have shade to develop properly.

Nerine masonorum is a dwarf winter-dormant species. The flower stalk is about 8 inches (20 cm) in height with a head of up to 12 rose-pink florets. The individual segments are crinkled along their entire length.

Nerine umtata is a new species with a provisional name. It was found by Norris near Umtata in the Transkei and is nearest to *N. masonorum* in habit. The individual segments are slightly waved, recurved, and pink with a darker pink central rib. The species differs from *N. masonorum* in that the perianth segments are not crisped in the basal half.

Nerine pudica is a useful species in breeding because each pure white floret has a streak of crimson down the center of the segment. The stalk is about 12 to 18 inches (30 to 45 cm) tall with a flower consisting of 5 to 8 florets. It, too, is a summer-dormant species.

Nerine undulata (Figure 3-32), *N. bowdenii*, and *N. alta* are summer growers with a brief period of winter dormancy. They are somewhat more hardy than the summer-dormant species. *Nerine bowdenii* is a popular species in the Pacific Northwest. *Nerine alta* (Plate 58) has slender 26 inch (66 cm) stalks and flowers in the fall. Butterflies love it.

Charles Hardman (1985b) gave an interesting account of the ways *Nerine* breeders in California have raised their bulbs. In the early 1900s a commercial nursery at Palos Verdes grew 40,000 bulbs in open acreage a short distance from the ocean; ocean breezes tempered hot summer days and cold winter nights. There were no frosts and no baking sunlight. The bulbs thrived.

A famous collection was once grown by Mr. and Mrs. Elmore Menninger in Southern California's San Gabriel Valley, 30 miles (48 km) inland from the ocean. Here the summer days are often blazingly hot and light to moderate frosts are common during the three-month period extending from mid-December to mid-February. The San Gabriel climate also includes cool late-summer nights, wet winters, and dry summers. Occasionally the leaves and a few bulbs were killed by frost. Also the intense summer heat killed some bulbs. The Menningers grew their bulbs outside, in pots, in a soil mix consisting of about equal parts of coarse granite sand and oak leaf mold. The bulbs that grew and muiltiplied with abandon were fed with a commercial fertilizer.

Fred Meyer in Escondido, California, a frost-free coastal area of San Diego County, has experimented with growing media. He has been very successful in raising *Nerine* and *Nerine-Brunsvigia* hybrids outside in a pre-mix of 50 percent gravel and 50 percent lava chunks. To this he adds 5 percent by volume of peat. Mild fertilizing with each watering results in almost hydroponic growing conditions. Charles Hardman (1985, page 82) reported that "the bulbs produced by this growing method are gargantuan, with root systems from three to five times larger than those produced by the standard cultural techniques recommended for *Nerine*."

Charles Hardman considers an ideal *Nerine* potting mix to be oak leaf mold combined with about one-third sand and a bit of composted sludge. To these potted *Nerine* he provides one or two trace element feedings during the growing season. In years when the bulbs are not repotted he gives the plants three or four weak feedings of phosphorus and potassium with a little nitrogen during the early growth stages.

Sir Peter Smithers (1984) in Switzerland changed his cultural methods in keeping with Norris's findings that *Nerine* shuns rich soil and heavy feeding. He now uses a mixture of sand and peat moss in equal parts without any fertilizer, reporting excellent results with no loss of bulbs. He further modified the mixture with the addition of about 10 percent poor garden soil and enough vermiculite to penetrate the compost and suspects this is the optimum mix. Smithers grows his specimen bulbs in 3.5-inch square plastic pots 5 inches (13 cm) deep. His 4-foot (122-cm) square

FIGURE 3-32.
Nerine undulata.

bench space thus accommodates about 180 plants, which are greenhouse grown to prevent freezing.

Charles Hardman (1976, page 34) wrote in a vivid way about these flowers, calling them the ballerinas of the plant world to which the words *flare*, *dash*, *elegance*, *charm*, and *flamboyance* can be applied. He claimed the similarities to ballerinas went beyond mere appearance:

> For all their grace and charming elegance, real ballerinas have to be tough, resilient, and durable. As their floral counterparts, *Nerine* also demonstrate these qualities. They are easy to accommodate, ignore most pests, and have few problems. Yet, year after year, the bulbs grow, multiply, and continue to produce flowers that are dazzlingly spectacular.

Onixotis (Colchicaceae)

Onixotis, formerly named *Dipidax*, has two species listed in the Cape flora. I grow only *Onixotis triquetra* (Figure 3-33). The inflorescence is a pretty, 18-inch (46-cm) spike of star-shaped flowers that are white and pink or white and maroon. The species grows naturally in very wet habitats such as marshes and seasonal pools. The bulbs are found rather deep. (See Plate 59.)

Onixotis triquetra can be propagated from corms or seed that will flower in the third season. Du Plessis and Duncan (1989) suggested that *O. triquetra* be grown in parts of the garden that are very wet in winter but dry in summer, or they may be grown in pots that can be submerged in a sunny pond in autumn. After flowering, the pots should be removed and allowed to dry out completely until the following autumn. Clearly, to grow this species well some supplemental water is appropriate even when most Cape bulbs thrive on the naturally occurring winter rains. The charm of these unusual flowers deserves the extra attention they require.

Ornithogalum (Hyacinthaceae)

The generic name *Ornithogalum* is derived from the Greek phrase "bird's milk," which seems nonsensical. According to Obermeyer (1978),

FIGURE 3-33.
Onixotis triquetra.

FIGURE 3-34.
Ornithogalum thyrsoides.

the name stresses the whiteness of some flowers. *Ornithogalum umbellatum*, a species common in Israel, was referred to in the Bible as dove's dung because the scattered white flowers, when seen from a distance resemble bird droppings.

Worldwide this is a large genus of between 150 to 200 species distributed in Europe, western Asia, and Africa. There is a concentration of 30 or more species in the Cape flora.

The common name for many species is star of Bethlehem, which is also applied to *Ornithogalum thyrsoides*, although it is better known as chincherinchee (sometimes spelled chinkerinchee). The name was originally given by Thunberg in 1772 as tinkerintees, an anomatopoeic word describing the sound of the South African wind blowing through a profusion of dry flower stalks as they grow wild on the Cape. In the nursery trade, flowers of *O. thyrsoides* are simply called chinks. (See Plate 60.)

Ornithogalum thyrsoides (Figure 3-34) is one of my favorite Cape bulbs. It is very easy to grow and is an absolutely superb cut flower, lasting for three weeks in a vase. In South Africa it is cut in the bud and shipped to Europe, where its long shelf life makes it desirable to florists. I sell large quantities to our local farmers' market and to wholesale florists. The flowers are white with a greenish brown center. They are in a dense pyramidal raceme on stalks 18 inches (46 cm) high. Unfortunately the peduncle, leaves, and flowers are toxic to stock. Domestic animals in South Africa have been poisoned by baled forage in which entire plants or plant portions were accidentally included.

Since all flowers of *Ornithogalum thyrsoides* are white, Meyer et al. (1990) wanted to get color into the commercial cut flowers and to develop container plant cultivars and novel cut-flower types. There are genes for yellow and orange in species (or species complexes) such as *O. dubium* (Plate 61) and *O. maculatum*. There are difficulties with conventional methods of hybridizing *Ornithogalum* because of ovary senescence in pollinated flowers prior to full development of an ovule into a viable seed. In a very high-tech project, Meyer et al. (1990) employed the embryo/ovule rescue (EOR) technique on ovaries harvested ten to fourteen days after pollination (DAP). The excised (aseptically removed) ovules were cultured in a special medium for two or three months and then transferred to a sterilized, soil-free mix. Flowering occurred after six to nine months. Using this system they achieved a generation in less than one year compared to the normal time of three to four years to flower from seed.

Meyer et al. (1990) found that crosses between highly colored species in the *Ornithogalum dubium*–complex and *O. maculatum*–complex with the *O. thyrsoides*–complex resulted in hybrids with an array of pastel-colored flowers from orange-sherbet to lemon-custard. They accomplished their original goals—to produce both cut and pot *Ornithogalum* in a wide range of colors and forms—in the first two generations. They made about 100 crosses in the third generation, mostly to fine-tune some aspects of productivity and cropping times, and embarked on the creation of true white-flowered types. Commercially available white types are either gray or greenish white, so they are striving for clean white types with an everblooming habit.

I have none of the plants produced by this remarkable and impressive project but grow the species that have been used in earlier experiments. I grow both yellow and orange forms of *Ornithogalum dubium*, but they are slow to increase. They are small 8- to 10-inch (20- to 25-cm) plants quite suitable for pot culture. So are the small plants of *O. pruinosum*, which have white and scented flowers.

Ornithogalum fimbrimarginatum has considerable merit as a garden flower (Plate 62). The white flowers, sometimes with dark centers, are on elegant 2-foot (61-cm) high stalks. They bloom late in summer and have a very brief period of dormancy.

The tallest species in my collection is *Ornithogalum saundersae*, which grows to 4 feet (over 1 m) high or more and is commonly called the giant chincherinchee. It is a winter-dormant, summer-blooming flower that grows in areas of summer rainfall outside the Cape Province. This robust, striking plant multiplies rapidly and is a good cut flower.

I also grow several species producing narrow yellow flowers with green keels, including *Ornithogalum secundum* and *O. suaveolens,* which are of little horticultural interest.

From my experience I can recommend growing *Ornithogalum dubium, O. fimbrimarginatum, O. pruinosum, O. saundersae,* and *O. thyrsoides.* The recent projects on hybridization of *Ornithogalum* give promise of exciting new and colorful cultivars.

Pauridia (Hypoxidaceae)

The name *Pauridia* is from the Greek *pauridios,* meaning "very small," which is most appropriate since these are among the smallest of South African bulbs. There are two species endemic to the Cape flora. Thompson (1979) reported that the snow-white flowers have been observed covering the ground like showers of brilliant little stars.

Rhoda van Zijl (1984) wrote a delightful account of accidentally acquiring *Pauridia longituba.* She had collected some bulbs of *Lachenalia viridiflora* at St. Helena Bay that were growing in a depression in granite that was filled with sand and debris. After she cleaned the *Lachenalia* bulbs the removed soil was mixed with sand for an indoor foliage plant. Later, to her great surprise, little white, star-shaped flowers of *P. longituba* were found blooming under the leaves of the potted foliage plant. Further investigation disclosed tiny, shallow corms that looked like dark little stones.

The habitat from which van Zijl inadvertently acquired *Pauridia longituba* is exactly that described by Thompson (1979), who reported that the species was confined to shallow pockets of soil in granite outcroppings and was never found in the deeper soils around the lower edges of the boulders.

The van Zijl corms grew for nearly two years under what would normally be considered adverse conditions: plenty of water all year, poor light, and an indoor atmosphere. After being put outside they grew very happily and were apparently trouble free. Rhoda van Zijl reports that they flower freely for several weeks early in the season when one is eager for a flower to brighten up the bulb pots. The flowers are about 0.5 inch (10 mm) across and the leaves are about 2 inches (51 mm) high. Because of their small size the fruits are best retrieved with tweezers. Seed germinates well.

The other species of the genus is *Pauridia minuta*. The leaves are broader than those of *P. longituba,* and while the flowers are similar, the perianth tube is (in spite of the name) longer than its counterpart in *P. longituba,* reaching about 0.75 inch (20 mm). *Pauridia minuta* was described in 1782 as *Ixia minuta* by the son of Linnaeus. Mary Rand (1980) wrote a charming article on *P. minuta*. According to Rhoda van Zijl (1984, page 12), "This is a delightful, rewarding genus especially for those growers interested in miniature species."

Polyxena (Hyacinthaceae)

In Greek mythology, Polyxena was the daughter of Priam, the last king of Troy, and his wife, Hecuba. After the fall of Troy, the ghost of Achilles claimed Polyxena as part of his share of the spoils, and she was put to death at his tomb. In the post-classical version, Achilles, the greatest of the Greek warriors, and Polyxena have a love affair before his death. I much prefer the latter tale.

Polyxena is related to *Massonia* and *Whiteheadia*. According to Jessop (1976), this genus of dwarf plants contains only two species, both endemic to the Cape Province. The small flowers, which range in color from white to pink to mauve or lilac, are in dense racemes at ground level, and the leaves are prostrate or semi-erect. There is considerable variation within each species, accounting for several scientific names that are merely synonyms.

Polyxena ensifolia is a variable species that is widespread from Namaqualand to Port Elizabeth in both sandy and clay soils and may be found in open spaces, or among rocks. The plants usually have two leaves that are initially prostrate with a cluster of stemless flowers in the center, reminiscent of the growth form of *Massonia*. The leaves, which are about one inch (2.5 cm) wide and 4 inches (10 cm) long, become semi-erect as the flowers mature. (See Plate 63.)

Polyxena ensifolia merits attention by more than just the ardent bulb collector. I am fortunate to have a clone of *P. ensifolia* that produces a lovely circle of waxy white flowers that look like jewels against the dark green background of the leaves. The ring is formed by the outer flowers of the cluster, which open first. The blossoms continue to open toward the center of the ring, and in a few days the plant has a central mound of numerous flowers. The flowers have long perianth tubes and may range in color from white to pink to mauve. Their variability is beautifully illustrated by Barbara Jeppe (1989) in her splendid book. The flowers have a delightful hyacinth-like fragrance, so it is not surprising that one synonym of *P. ensifolia* is *P. odorata;* another is *P. pygmaea* because of the small plant size.

Polyxena corymbosa, which is not so earth-hugging as *P. ensifolia,* grows naturally in sandy or stony ground from Clanwilliam to the Cape Peninsula. It was once common but now is rather rare. The flowers vary from white to pale pink or lilac and have a short whitish tube. They bloom in a cluster of about 15 flowers that are no more than 2 to 3 inches (5 to 7 cm) high. *Polyxena corymbosa* is a bit easier to grow than *P. ensifolia,* but I think it is not as attractive and probably is of greatest interest to collectors.

Propagation of *Polyxena* is from offsets or seeds, which are shiny black and produced in abundance. They bloom in their second or third year and are easy to grow if given protection from severe winter frosts. The bulbs are fleshy and should be planted just beneath the surface and close together to make a show. They do best in shallow containers in full sun in a well-drained sandy mix. The flowers are produced during the fall months in the Cape and also in my garden, where they bloom from late September to December.

Rheome (Iridaceae)

Rheome was erected by Goldblatt in 1980 and I know little about it except that it is related to *Homeria;* presumably its use is similar. The genus has three Cape species. The corms have woody tunics, and the leaves are long, trailing, and definitely channeled. The flowers are orange or yellow.

Jeppe (1989) illustrated *Rheome nana*, which grows to about 10 inches (25 cm) high. The flowers are pinkish orange with distinct venation. It may have horticultural merit, but I have not yet tried it because it has not been available.

Rhodohypoxis (Hypoxidaceae)

Rhodohypoxis is not a component of the Cape flora, but it is such a sought after South African container plant that its inclusion here seems justified. According to John Bryan (1989) the name is derived from the Greek *rhodon*, "rose," and *hypo*, "under," referring to some flower relationship that I do not understand.

Rhodohypoxis consists of about six species of dwarf, deciduous, summer-growing plants with fibrous rhizomes and is mostly restricted to the higher elevations of the Drakensberg. The species are reviewed by Hilliard and Burtt (1978) and by Holmes (1979). The species most common in cultivation is *Rhodohypoxis baurii*. It has several varieties and a number of named cultivars.

According to Jim Holmes (1979), the best-known variety is *Rhodohypoxis baurii* var. *platypetala*. Its attractive, long-lasting flowers are usually white, and there is an occasional pink form. It grows naturally on wet slopes and plateaus. *Rhodohypoxis baurii* var. *baurii* has beautiful red flowers and is usually found growing on dripping cliffs or on wet rock faces. *Rhodohypoxis baurii* var. *confecta* is more widespread than the other varieties and is quite variable, the flowers being red, pink, or white. The dwarf plants have hairy leaves about 3 inches (8 cm) long.

I also grow a plant that I believe to be *Rhodohypoxis milloides* (previously known as *R. palustris*). The flowers are red, and the leaves are longer, thinner, and less hairy than those of *R. baurii*. For me it is a bit more robust.

Du Plessis and Graham (1989) consider *Rhodohypoxis* to be ideally suited to cultivation in shallow containers. The rhizomes are planted about 0.5 inch (1 cm) deep and require full sun and a rich, well-drained, peaty medium that should never be allowed to dry out during the growing period. Jim Holmes suggests a mix of equal parts peat and sand in 6-inch pots. Du Plessis and Duncan suggest, as does Jim Holmes, that the container be placed in a saucer permanetly filled with water during the growing period. During dormancy in winter, the tiny rhizomes must be kept dry but should not be stored without soil for any length of time.

Propagation is by offsets and seeds. The fine seed is sown in spring in shallow seed trays and must be kept constantly moist. Jim Holmes had plants flower three months after sowing, but Du Plessis and Duncan say three years are required. Matthews (1991) in Cornwall says that *Rhodohypoxis* does best in an alpine house and does not last long outside in Cornish gardens. She adds that grubs of the vine weevil attack and destroy the rootstock.

Rhodohypoxis is an eye-catching container or rock garden plant that blooms for weeks and performs particularly well in the Pacific Northwest. It is hardy and seems to be free of pests and diseases.

Romulea (Iridaceae)

The genus *Romulea* is concentrated in two separate centers; one is the Mediterranean area, the other is South Africa. Since a number of species grow near Rome, the genus was named in 1772 after Romulus, the legendary founder of the city.

Romulea species are mostly small plants, 6 inches (15 cm) high or less, with tunicated corms (Figure 3-35). The flowers are actinomorphic, funnel shaped, and thermonastic. Their bright colors range from white to yellow, orange, apricot, pink, lilac, and magenta. A few are blue or bright red. Many are reminiscent of *Crocus*, and, in fact, Linnaeus at first assigned a species of *Romulea* to the genus *Crocus*.

There are over 50 species in the Cape flora and about 95 worldwide. They are self-compatible and with few exceptions are scentless.

Romulea sabulosa is one of the showiest of the genus with large, 2-inch (5-cm) wide flowers that increase in size during the five consecutive

FIGURE 3-35.
Romulea setifolia.

days they are in bloom. The flowers have a satiny sheen. The segments are scarlet or currant red with a brownish-black blotch that has a basal yellow mark. This species is more difficult to grow than most other species. (See Plate 64.) A very similar species, equally handsome, is *R. monadelpha*. Its segments are deep claret-red with purplish-black blotches. It is interesting that *R. monadelpha* and *R. sabulosa* are sympatric. While a number of *Romulea* species may grow in close proximity, natural hybrids are rare.

Romulea amoena is another red-flowered species (carmine red to deep rose pink) with large black blotches in the throat. It comes from the same Nieuwoudtville area as *R. sabulosa,* but the flower size is smaller than that of *R. sabulosa.*

Graham Duncan (1989) reported that the brilliantly colored *Romulea unifolia* had great horticultural potential as a container plant. It was first discovered in 1937 but not recorded again until 1979. It was then grown by the van Zijls at their Rust-En-Vrede nursery; they realized that the large, vivid, reddish orange blooms represented a wonderful, new *Romulea*. It was described and named in 1987 by Miriam De Vos, South Africa's expert on the genus.

Romulea atrandra var. *atrandra* is rose pink with dark blotches and a yellow throat. *Romulea atrandra* var. *esterhuyseniae* has paler flowers that are lilac with dark blotches and a yellow throat.

Romulea hantamensis is unlike other *Romulea* species. It has magenta-pink, widely separated segments that have a purplish-black blotch above the middle, a white blotch with three dark lines below the middle. To me they glow like neon lights. This is a rare species found on a plateau on Hantam mountain where it was collected in 1900 and again in 1968. My plants are small, growing to only about 4 inches (10 cm) high. (See Plate 65.)

Romulea tortuosa is bright golden yellow with dark blotches and lines in the throat (Plate 66). The related *R. austinii* is jasmine yellow with dark blotches in the throat.

I grow three color forms of *Romulea flava*. One is sulphur yellow (Plate 67); one is white; and one is said to be blue, but I find it more nearly white. All have yellow in the throat. They are small, 4-inch (10-cm) tall plants.

Another small plant that I find very bright is *Romulea leipoldtii*. Its characteristic flower coloring of yellow in the lower half of the perianth segments and white in the upper half makes it a standout.

I also find *Romulea obscura* var. *campestris* to be a charmer. It has apricot-colored flowers with interesting dark blotches in the throat. A related, polymorphic species is *R. rosea*, which has pink flowers and long grasslike foliage.

I grow many other species of *Romulea* from the southwestern Cape but those listed above are definitely my favorites.

Propagation is by corms or by seeds. Germination of *Romulea campanuloides* is 33 days, *R. kamisensis* is 36–60 days, *R. leipoldtii* is 40 days, and *R. rosea* is 34 days. It is interesting that the flower stalk of some species bends over after flowering so that the seed capsule is near the soil when it matures. All the *Romulea* species prefer sunny sites and, of course, good drainage with a dry summer rest. They are best handled as container plants or in a rockery.

Scadoxus (Amaryllidaceae)

Species of *Scadoxus* were formerly in the genus *Haemanthus,* which has caused considerable confusion in the identification of some spectacular flowers commonly called blood lilies that are listed in garden catalogs as *Haemanthus katherinae* rather than *Scadoxus multiflorus* subsp. *katherinae*. The name change is fully discussed in the *Haemanthus* section.

Scadoxus is rhizomatous, whereas *Haemanthus* has true bulbs. The tubular leaf base of *Scadoxus* forms a pseudostem, and foliage is thin-textured with a distinct midrib. *Scadoxus* flowers are in a dense umbel. Two species are listed in the Cape Flora.

Scadoxus multiflora subsp. *katherinae* is not a Cape species, having a more eastern distribution and ranging northward into Zimbabwe. It has a spectacular inflorescence and highly attractive foliage. It needs a shady site and can take deep shade. The rhizome is just below the ground. It can be grown in large containers and is best left undisturbed. The plants are evergreen, the flowers are scarlet, and the common name is blood lily.

These magnificent flowers thrive in California. William Drysdale (1987) reported that under his conditions at Riverside, stalks held six to eight broad, medium-green leaves over 2 feet (61 cm) above the soil. The sensational flower umbels were on stalks about 36 inches (91 cm) long, which held the inflorescence well above the foliage.

Scadoxus puniceus is a Cape species. It is summer growing, deciduous, and likes partial shade. William Drysdale (1987) claimed the primary reason for its cultivation was for the cranberry-sized seed capsules that are scarlet colored and decorative for months. It is a good container plant.

Propagation of *Scadoxus* is from offsets or from seeds. The offsets are removed just after flowering and should be planted immediately. The seeds are sown as soon as ripe. The pulpy covering is removed, and seeds are sown just below the soil surface. Seedlings bloom in their third year. *Scadoxus* species need rich, well-drained soil and benefit from regular feedings.

Sessilistigma (Iridaceae)

Sessilistigma is a monotypic genus related to *Homeria,* though the filaments of *Homeria* are united, whereas those of *Sessilistigma* are free (Jeppe, 1989).

Sessilistigma radians grows to 10 to 14 inches (25 to 35 cm) tall. The flowers, which are on a branched stalk, are actinomorphic with broad cream-colored segments that are bright yellow at the base. This species is spring flowering with a long summer dormancy and is cultivated in the same manner as *Homeria*.

Sparaxis (Iridaceae)

According to Peter Goldblatt (1969), the name *Sparaxis* is derived from the Greek *sparasein,* meaning "torn," which alludes to the characteristically very dry, papery, and often lacerate bracts.

Sparaxis is a small but showy genus of six species native to the winter-rainfall area of the Cape Province. The plants are usually 8 to 12 inches

(20 to 30 cm) in height, but *S. pillansii* can reach 2 feet (61 cm) in height. They have several sword-shaped leaves and a corm covered with fine, white, netted fibers. The flowers are borne on a spike, face upward, and have six subequal segments. Bulbils are produced in the lower leaf axils at the end of the flowering season in all species of *Sparaxis*. Bulbils are usually long and narrow and sheathed by the leaves.

Sparaxis bulbifera is a widespread species in the Cape with a wide ecological tolerance, occurring on sand as frequently as on clay and growing in both wet and drier situations on flats and lower slopes of mountains. Peter Goldblatt (1979) reported it as common in damp, low-lying areas. At Caledon, in the eastern part of its range, the flowers are cream with rather dirty purple-brown streaks on the outside of the segments. The forms in the western part of its range on the Cape Flats and north to Darling have clear creamy white flowers and are fairly tall. They are always an attractive sight at the Darling Wildflower show.

The species is named *Sparaxis bulbifera* because small but quite prominent bulbils are produced at all the nodes after the flowering season is over. Since *S. bulbifera* grows near Cape Town, the site of the initial European settlement in South Africa, it was early collected and cultivated in Europe. Linnaeus grew it at Uppsala, Sweden, and it was also grown by the English botanist Phillip Miller at Chelsea, London, in the mid-18th century (Goldblatt, 1979).

Sparaxis elegans was originally known as *Streptanthera cuprea*, but Peter Goldblatt incorporated *Streptanthera* into *Sparaxis* in 1969. *Sparaxis elegans* was discovered in 1827 and is one of the three species that grow around the small town of Nieuwoudtville and Neil MacGregor's farm on the plateau above Van Rhyns Pass. The flowers are commonly salmon colored and have interesting coiled anthers (Plate 68). It was the twisting of the anthers that caused the species to be placed originally in the genus *Streptanthera*, which means "twisted flower." There are dark bands with yellow streaks in the center of the flower, and these sharply contrasting markings make *Sparaxis elegans* a striking plant. A rare white form, once thought to be extinct, was rediscovered in 1971 by Neil MacGregor, whose wildflower conservation efforts are described in Chapter 1. According to Goldblatt (1979), this white form occasionally grows among the plants with salmon-colored flowers but also is found in pure stands.

Sparaxis tricolor (Figure 3-36) is one of the three most beautiful and rare species of *Sparaxis,* along with *S. elegans* and *S. pillansii*; all grow around Nieuwoudtville. *Sparaxis tricolor* is somewhat taller than *S. elegans* and has bright orange flowers, dark orange markings in a band around the center of the flower, and a bright yellow throat. The stamens are straight. It was described in 1795 by the Dutchman, George Schneevoght. (See Plate 69.)

The plants of *Sparaxis tricolor* are very scarce in the wild today, owing to the expansion of agriculture. This attractive species is endemic to a very small area. In undisturbed ground the plants occur among low shrubs and are thus lightly shaded. The soil type is a heavy clay that appears to be waterlogged for part of the growing season and later dries to an almost concretelike consistency. Although a rarity in the wild, *S. tricolor* or at least its hybrids and cultivars is the most commonly grown *Sparaxis* on the U.S. Pacific Coast.

Sparaxis pillansii was unknown until 1915, when it was collected by Marloth. Peter Goldblatt (1969) reported that it was later cultivated by specialists who at first thought it a garden hybrid. However, it was not named until 1932 when it was described by the famous Cape botanist Louisa Bolus, who systematically explored the Nieuwoudtville area in the 1930s with a group of students.

Sparaxis pillansii has a rather peculiar and very localized habitat. It occurs plentifully over a few acres on the rocky hills a mile northeast of Nieuwoudtville. It grows in red clay around large boulders where water accumulates in quantity during the short wet season, so it is semi-aquatic during the early stages of its winter growth.

Sparaxis pillansii has flowers of a reddish color (*old rose* was the term used by Louisa Bolus) with a yellow throat. This is the tallest of all the species of *Sparaxis,* often reaching 2 feet (61 cm) high. It is not so brightly colored as is *S. tricolor* nor so strikingly marked as is *S. elegans,* but its

FIGURE 3-36.
Sparaxis tricolor.

color and markings are quite distinctive. The coiled anthers of *S. pillansii* resemble those of *S. elegans*, though the twist is much less noticeable. The former hybridizes easily with *S. tricolor* and is one of the parents of several garden cultivars.

Sparaxis fragrans was described by Austrian Nicholas von Jacquin in 1793. It is a small-flowered species with slender leaves. The flowers are yellow or cream with as many as five on a stalk. It is the only *Sparaxis* with a scent, which is reported to be rather unpleasant. Peter Goldblatt (1979) stated that this odor, together with the plant's small size, made *S. fragrans* the least desirable *Sparaxis* horticulturally. The species grows in the Caledon district of the southwestern Cape, but owing to increased acreage planted with wheat, the habitat of *S. fragrans* is rapidly disappearing, and this plant, which once grew in thousands in dense stands, is on the verge of extinction.

Sparaxis grandiflora was described by the Swiss botanist Daniel de la Roche in 1768. It is widespread and the most variable of all *Sparaxis* species. It grows only in clay soils and especially on wetter slopes and flats. This species has the largest flowers in the genus, and since they are often brilliantly colored, they merit horticultural attention. Distinctive races have evolved in parts of the range, and Goldblatt treated them as subspecies in a revision of *Sparaxis* published in 1969. *Sparaxis grandiflora* subsp. *fimbriata* has cream to white, zygomorphic flowers. *Sparaxis grandiflora* subsp. *grandiflora* has purple or brilliant red-magenta flowers of a quite remarkable shade. It grows only in the Tulbagh valley, and Peter Goldblatt expressed surprise that it is apparently not in cultivation. *Sparaxis grandiflora* subsp. *acutiloba* has large flowers of a bright clear yellow. When well-watered this subspecies grows fairly tall and bears many flowers on several stalks.

Goldblatt (1969) stated that the genera *Dierama*, *Ixia*, and *Synnotia* are related to *Sparaxis* and form a natural group. All have a diploid chromosome number of $2n = 20$. Intergeneric hybrids are reported. Goldblatt crossed *Sparaxis tricolor* with *Synnotia variegata* with no noticeable reduction in seed production or viability. The two genera were also crossed by Johan Loubser, who raised a sturdy hybrid generation. The species of *Sparaxis* readily hybridize among themselves. Christien Malan (1979) reported on the work of Japie Krige, who developed fine garden hybrids between *S. grandiflora* from the Tulbagh valley and *S. elegans* from Nieuwoudtville. Although Krige produced flowers larger and generally considered more attractive than three of the wild species, most of his plants eventually were infected by a fungus and were destroyed.

Propagation of *Sparaxis* is by division of the corms, by the bulbils produced in the leaf axils, or by seeds. *Sparaxis grandiflora* germinates in 22–25 days. As with most other winter-growing Cape bulbs, it prefers a sunny site on well-drained soil and a dry rest during the summer months. It has naturalized in my garden.

The showy species of *Sparaxis*, often called harlequins, make a colorful splash in the garden and are good cut flowers.

Spiloxene (Hypoxidaceae)

According to Mary Rand (1980) *Spiloxene* is derived from the Greek *spilos*, "spot," and *xenos*, "host," referring to the dark, iridescent, peacock-eye at the base of the perianth segments in many species.

Spiloxene is endemic to the Cape, and while there may be as many as 30 species, very few are under cultivation. The genus is in need of revision. The plants are cormous and rather small, reaching only 6 to 10 inches (15 to 25 cm) high. The flowers have six widely separated and pointed segments.

Spiloxene serrata (Figure 3-37) is a rewarding container plant with six-segmented, starlike, bright yellow flowers, accounting for its common name, golden star. The species was first described by Thunberg, the brilliant student of Linnaeus whom Lighton (1973) called the "father of South African botany." The foliage has tiny serrations along the leaf margins, which gives the species its name. It is perhaps the longest blooming Cape bulb in my collection, starting in early fall and blooming through the winter into the spring months. The flowers remain tightly closed on gray days but are very cheery when they open on sunny and bright days.

FIGURE 3-37.
Spiloxene serrata.

The plants grow to about 8 inches (20 cm) high, and the leaves are slender and gracefully curved. The plants need to be kept moist during their growing season; they occur naturally in slightly damp situations.

The only other species I grow is *Spiloxene canaliculata*. It is orange or yellow with a beautiful, maroonish brown, peacock-eye center (Plate 70). It is very similar to the widespread and very beautiful species, *S. capensis*.

Spiloxene capensis is usually a star-shaped, buttercup-yellow flower with a large iridescent brown blotch at the base of each perianth segment. In the spring of 1990 after a winter of heavy and prolonged rains, there was an explosion of *S. capensis* throughout the Cape peninsula (De Villiers, 1991). Not only did plants appear in great numbers in places where they had not been seen in years, but they displayed an array of color forms. There was a white form with blue iridescence and a pink form with plum-colored iridescence. The blotches in all the color forms were quite variable in size and shape. *Spiloxene capensis* is the logo plant for the Indigenous Bulb Growers Association of South Africa. Matthews (1991) claimed that *S. capensis* is easily renewable from seed but is attacked by the vine weevil in England.

Spiloxene minuta is a tiny plant with white flowers similar in size to *Pauridia minuta,* with which it has been confused (Rand, 1980). It can be distinguished by its six stamens and flat-bottomed corm. *Pauridia minuta* has three stamens and a rounded corm.

Spiloxene certainly deserves more recognition and use by gardeners.

Strumaria (Amaryllidaceae)

Strumaria has about ten species and is endemic to the winter-rainfall area from the western Cape northward to southwestern Namibia (Du Plessis and Duncan, 1989). The roostock is a tunicated bulb. The inflorescense is an umbel on a slender stalk. The hysteranthous flowers are fairly long lasting and bloom in mid to late fall.

I grow a single species, *Strumaria truncata*, which has a delicate-appearing inflorescence of pendulous flowers that are white tinged with

FIGURE 3-38.
Strumaria truncata.

pink. The leaves emerge from a distinct, dark maroon cataphyll, while the 8-inch (20-cm) high flower stalk arises from the side of the bulb (Figure 3-38).

Propagation of *Strumaria* is quickest from seeds, which will flower in their third season. Offsets are slow to form. *Strumaria* is best left undisturbed in containers where plants will continue to bloom well even when crowded. When concentrated in a container, these species make a good display. *Strumaria* is certainly not a flamboyant flower but it does have a quiet, understated charm.

Synnotia (Iridaceae)

John Bryan (1989) wrote that *Synnotia* is named in honor of W. Synnot, a collector of South African plants. Bond and Goldblatt (1984) recognized five named species and a sixth unidentified species in the Cape flora. Bryan (1989) suggested that they may all belong to a single variable species, *S. variegata*. Sometimes the genus is included in *Sparaxis*.

From the horticultural standpoint, *Synnotia variegata* is the prime candidate for garden use. Well-grown plants may reach 20 inches (50 cm) in height, but mine are in the one foot (30 cm) range. The best variety is *S. variegata* var. *metelerkampiae,* which is a small plant in the 8 inch (20 cm) range. The top segment is deep purple flanked by two white segments with purple blotches at their base. The three lower segments are white with a bright yellow or orange spot.

The specific epithet in *Synnotia villosa* (Plate 71) means "hairy," but this name is misleading because the plants are without hairs. Its synonym, *S. bicolor*, is more appropriate because the upper segments of the fragrant flowers are flushed with purple while the lower segments are white and have a yellow area at the base.

The species *Synnotia parviflora* is correctly named for its small white and yellow flowers.

Propagation of *Synnotia* is by offsets or by seeds. Germination time is 26 days for *S. parviflora* and 20 days for *S. villosa*. Seedlings flower in their third season. They need extremely well-drained, somewhat sandy soil.

According to Una Van Der Spuy (1976), plants should be crowded to make the best display and therefore she suggested the corms be planted about one inch (2–4 cm) deep and 4 inches (10 cm) apart. Bryan (1989) concurs that *Synnotia* should be planted in bold groupings of 25 or more plants. Sima Eliovson (1980) considered *Synnotia* species to be delightful plants that should be introduced into general cultivation.

Syringodea (Iridaceae)

Syringodea, a genus of dwarf plants related to *Crocus* and *Romulea*, is endemic to South Africa. The corm is tunicated. The flowers are solitary and ephemeral; they have no aerial stem but develop from a long perianth tube arising from the ground. The style branches are entire, which is a diagnostic characteristic. Eight species are native to the Cape.

I grow *Syringodea longituba,* a widespread species. I think it is the species I saw growing in a very rocky, screelike situation north of Springbok in Namaqualand. It has tiny plants only 2 inches (5 cm) high. The flower is violet or blue-violet with an orange-yellow or yellow throat. As the species name indicates, the perianth tube is very long. Flowers appear in late winter. The leaves are slender and curled.

Propagation is by offsets or seeds, which flower in their third season. The dwarf plants are best grown in containers in full sun and in a sandy, well-drained medium. The corms are planted shallowly at a depth of only 0.5 inch (1–2 cm). *Syringodea* has cute little flowers but probably has more appeal to bulb collectors than to conventional gardeners.

Tenicroa (Hyacinthaceae)

I have recently planted seeds of *Tenicroa multifolia* and know little more about it other than the illustration and condensed description by Jeppe (1989). From this I anticipate that it will be a small plant with fragrant, whitish flowers on 8-inch (20-cm) high stalks. The filiform leaves are sheathed at the base. The plants are dormant in summer, grow in the winter, and bloom in the spring. I find no comment on their horticultural merit. Five *Tenicroa* species are native to the Cape.

Tritonia (Iridaceae)

Miriam De Vos, in her revision of *Tritonia* (1982, page 106), said that in 1802 Ker-Gawler named the genus, observing that "the name is derived from Triton, in the signification of a vane or weathercock, in allusion to the variable direction of the stamens of the different species." *Tritonia* is widespread in South Africa with 16 species in the winter-rainfall area of the Cape. Flowers are brightly colored in shades of cream, yellow, orange, reddish orange, tangerine, and pink. The somewhat bowl-shaped flowers are sessile with short to long perianth tubes. The leaves are lance shaped. The plants average about one foot (30 cm) in height.

Tritonia lineata is not from the winter-rainfall area of the Cape, but it has the same growth habit, namely sprouting in the autumn and flowering in the spring or early summer. The leaves, in addition to their prominent middle vein, have a long vein near each margin. The cream to pale apricot to salmon pink flowers are slightly zygomorphic, funnel-shaped, and one inch (2.5 cm) long. Sometimes they have apricot tints outside, especially toward the tips of the segments. They are finely and curiously pencilled with dark lines which accounts for the species name. (See Figure 3-39.)

I grow two forms of *Tritonia securigera,* one yellow the other reddish orange with a yellow throat. They bloom somewhat earlier than the other *Tritonia* species. The three lower segments have a high callus in the yellow, red-margined throat. *Tritonia securigera* was one of the first of the callus-bearing species of *Tritonia* found in South Africa and it was given the appropriate epithet, meaning "axe-bearing."

Tritonia pallida is distinguished by its pale, long-tubed flowers with a low greenish yellow excrescence (callus) on the median or sometimes on all three of the lower perianth segments. It is much like *T. flabellifolia* which has similar long-tubed, zygomorphic flowers and habit. However, *T. flabellifolia* is readily distinguished by its bracts, which elongate considerably after flowering, and by its linear leaves. There are no calli in the throat of *T. flabellifolia.*

FIGURE 3-39.
Tritonia lineata.

Tritonia squalida has a very inappropriate name, for it is a fine flower and is neither dirty nor squalid. The flowers are almost actinomorphic, widely cup-shaped, mauvish pink to pale pink with deeper pink or purplish veins and often deeper pink or yellowish at the base. The lower segments sometimes have a pale yellow or deep pink median line in the throat. It is supposed to be scented, but I cannot detect it.

Tritonia crocata (syn. *T. hyalina*) is closely related to *T. squalida*; the most obvious difference is its color, which is a bright, fiery, orange-red. I find it one of the more prolific *Tritonia* species under the growing conditions of my garden.

Tritonia crocata, T. deusta, and *T. squalida* are all related and are sympatric. Miriam De Vos (1982) recognized *T. deusta* subsp. *deusta* and *T. deusta* subsp. *miniata*, which were once considered to be distinct species. The basic difference is that *T. deusta* subsp. *deusta* has a dark blotch on the outer perianth segment, which *T. deusta* subsp. *miniata* lacks.

Tritonia dubia is placed by De Vos (1982) in the same taxonomic section as *T. crocata, T. deusta,* and *T. squalida*; *T. dubia* has a slightly longer perianth tube. The flowers are salmon-pink or orange-pink with dark veins. It is an undemanding species and a useful garden subject.

Tritonia crispa gives me difficulty and has never bloomed, contrary to my experience with the other species of *Tritonia*, which are so easily cultivated. It is widely distributed in the western and southwestern Cape, so one would think it an easily adaptable species. The leaves of *T. crispa* have crisped margins. The flowers are reported to be zygomorphic and range from cream to pale yellow to shell pink to salmon pink with a red or purple center and a median stripe on the lower segments. I hope eventually to find the key to its successful culture.

Tritonia is related to *Crocosmia* and to *Chasmanthe*, and hybrids between *Tritonia* and *Crocosmia* are reported. There are garden cultivars produced by crossing *Tritonia* species, particularly *T. crocata* and *T. squalida*.

Propagation of *Tritonia* is by separating the corms. The current season corms are on top of last year's (Figure 1-5), and if separated, both age groups will produce new plants. *Tritonia* can also be increased from seeds.

Germination time for *T. crispa* is 33 days. The winter-growing *Tritonia* from the Cape should have a sunny location, well-drained soil, and a dry rest in summer.

Tritonia is especially useful as a bold color group in a sunny border.

Tulbaghia (Alliaceae)

Linnaeus named this purely African genus of about 20 species for Ryk Tulbagh, who was the Dutch governor of the Cape of Good Hope from 1751 until his death in 1771. Tulbagh sent Linnaeus a great many Cape species, and Conrad Lighton (1973) gives a charming account of their sporadic but very valuable correspondence, which was conducted in Latin. A translation of a letter from Linnaeus to Tulbagh that is a memorable tribute to the Cape is set forth in the nomenclature section of this chapter.

Of the 20 or so species of *Tulbaghia*, only two are commonly grown. They are rhizomatious plants about one foot (30 cm) in height and bear umbels of blue or mauve flowers. They tend to be evergreen and flower over a long period. Some have an odor similar to garlic. Propagation of *Tulbaghia* is either by division of the rhizomes or from seeds. The plants do well in a sunny, open site.

The Cape species most frequently seen in gardens is *Tulbaghia violacea* which, because of its odor, has been given the name society garlic. It has narrow, strap-shaped leaves and produces an umbel of as many as twenty clear mauve flowers on a slender 2-foot (61-cm) high stalk. It is easy to grow and the flowers are attractive, but some gardeners consider the odor to be a serious defect.

A somewhat bolder and larger plant is *Tulbaghia simmleri*. It was formerly named *T. fragrans* and instead of the strong garlicy odor of *T. violacea* it has a sweet, hyacinth-like fragrance according to Edith Strout (1948). This species is not from the Cape but from a summer-rainfall area so it does need water. Erens (1948) found that a single plant of *T. simmleri* will vigorously grow to a clump 18 inches (46 cm) across in three to four years.

Both species are good container plants. While *T. violacea* will do well in moist, low positions, Mrs. Archbell (1939) pointed out that it also flourished on a dry, stony hillside among her aloes and succulents, so perhaps it has a place in xeriscapes.

Veltheimia (Hyacinthaceae)

Veltheimia is named in honor of an amateur German botanist and patron of botany, Frederick Augustus Graf von Veltheim. The genus is endemic to South Africa, and there are just two species.

In the garden, the two species are easily distinguished by their bulb form, their leaf color and shape, and their blooming periods. The flowers of *Veltheimia* superficially resemble those of the red hot pokers, *Kniphofia*, though the two are not at all related.

Veltheimia capensis is truly a species from the winter-rainfall area. It grows from the Cape northward into arid Namaqualand, where it favors open, dry, and rocky areas. My flowers, borne on 18-inch (46-cm) high stalks, are a mottled pink (Plate 72). Bond and Goldblatt (1984) also recorded red and yellow forms, and Terry Hatch (1987a) grew one that was a lemon yellow. The flowers are early, beginning in midfall. The large bulbs are mostly above the soil surface. The especially handsome foliage is very striking, for the leaves are a bluish gray-green with heavily undulated margins.

Veltheimia bracteata (Figure 3-40), the forest lily, blooms in the spring. It occurs naturally in the coastal forest at Natal, where it gets some summer rainfall. It is almost evergreen, having only a short dormant season at the end of summer. The *Aloe*-like inflorescence has pink flowers in good light and pinkish-green in the shade or semi-shade, next to shrubs, or under small trees. Its broad, shiny, bright green leaves are slightly undulated. The large, fleshy bulb grows just below ground level; it prefers to be undisturbed for years and will gradually increase by division of its bulbs. *Veltheimia bracteata* has a striking yellow variety given the cultivar name 'Lemon Flame' because of its green-yellow inflorescence. It comes true from seed (Duncan, 1982c).

FIGURE 3-40.
Veltheimia bracteata.

I find the propagation of *Veltheimia* is best from seed because the bulb offsets are somewhat slow to form. The seeds should be planted in autumn in a fine, well-drained medium to which some compost can be added. Germination takes about three weeks, and the seedlings need to be shaded and should be fed with a liquid fertilizer. If well grown, the seedlings will flower in their third season.

Veltheimia bracteata is a valuable plant for shady areas. I have seen it grow handsomely to 2 feet (61 cm) high in a shady, fern garden. *Veltheimia capensis* should be useful in xeriscapes. Both species are highly recommended.

Watsonia (Iridaceae)

Around 1750, Phillip Miller, curator of the Chelsea Physic Garden, recognized that a flower he grew from seed was a new genus. He named it *Watsonia* in honor of Sir William Watson, a physician and scientist. According to Peter Goldblatt (1987), Sir William was an admirer of Linnaeus and was instrumental in introducing the Linnaean system of binomial nomenclature to Britain.

Watsonia is a genus of about 52 species restricted to southern Africa. Most are found in the winter-rainfall area of the Cape and are deciduous. A few species that grow in the summer-rainfall area tend to be evergreen. The species range in height from robust plants of 6 feet (2 m) tall down to dwarfs that are 10 inches (26 cm) high and ideal for pot culture.

Peter Goldblatt (1989) points out that the species with long-tubed, orange-to-red colored flowers are pollinated by the beautiful little sunbirds, whereas the short-tubed, pink flowers are pollinated by bees.

Watsonia marginata is one of the loveliest species. The broad leaves are gray and have a midrib and thickened margins. The handsome foliage forms a single-planed V. The pink flowers are on 5-foot (152-cm) tall stalks. This species grows in seasonally marshy sites or temporary seeps where there is complete summer drought. There are both tall and dwarf forms.

Watsonia borbonica (Figure 3-41) now includes *W. pyramidata* and the white *W. ardernei* as synonyms (Goldblatt, 1987). *Watsonia borbonica*

FIGURE 3-41.
Watsonia borbonica.

is named for Gaston de Bourbon, Duke of Orleans, a 17th-century patron of botany. It is a tall species growing to 6 feet (2 m). The slightly fragrant flowers range from white to pale or deep pink to light purple. The synonymous *W. pyramidata* is known for its spectacular mass flowering in the season following a summer or autumn wildfire. This mass flowering serves to minimize seed predation and the seedlings establish themselves in the favorable post-fire environment according to le Maitre (1984).

Watsonia versfeldii is a rare species and was something of a mystery because there were no records of it in the wild for many years until it was rediscovered by Dee Snijman (1978). The flowers are purplish pink and the plants grow 4 to 5 feet (122 to 153 cm) high.

Watsonia meriana is a variable species with pink, orange, red or even purple flowers. It grows to 4 feet (122 cm) or more in height and is related to the dwarf species *W. humilis* and *W. coccinea*.

Watsonia humilis is also a variable species. The flowers are pink or white flushed with pink. The latter variety was once called *W. roseoalba* but is now recognized as a synonym of *W. humilis*. *Watsonia humilis* is a very nice container plant because it grows to only one foot (30 cm) or less in height.

Another dwarf species is *Watsonia coccinea* (Plate 73). It is about the same size as *W. humilis,* but the distinctive flowers are reddish.

The evergreen species include *Watsonia angusta, W. pillansii*, and *W. wilmaniae*. *Watsonia pillansii* has bright orange or orange-red flowers. It grows 3 to 4 feet (92 to 122 cm) high. The species *W. beatricis* is now considered a synonym.

Watsonia angusta has red to orange flowers that are pollinated by the sunbirds in the Cape. The species grows in more or less permanently wet places, so it needs water most of the year.

Another evergreen species that I grow is *Watsonia wilmaniae*, which has been confused with *W. angusta*. Some of my plants have pink flowers, others have orange flowers. The plants grow over 3 feet (91 cm) high. (See Plate 74.)

My nursery now has seedlings of *Watsonia fourcadei*, *W. laccata*, *W. stenosiphon*, and *W. tabularis,* growing nicely, but they are still a season or two away from flowering so I cannot offer much insight or information about them.

Propagation of *Watsonia* is from corms or from seeds. *Watsonia angusta* germinates in 33 days, *W. marginata* in 32 days, *W. stenosiphon* in 27 days, and *W. tabularis* in 16–22 days. The dwarf species may flower in the seond year, but the larger species require three or even four years to bloom. The corms should be planted about 4 inches (10 cm) deep. Good drainage is important, and while plants will respond to fertilizer, they are not heavy feeders. Occasionally clumps need to be thinned because crowding diminishes flowering.

Watsonia is a tough and hardy genus that is used in South Africa in highway plantings. There are some beautiful plantings of it in the Kirstenbosch garden, and certainly it is suitable for many parks and gardens in North America. It is a good cut flower. Sara Coombs (1936) wrote that it is the least fussy of bulbs and is likely to give good results under indifferent conditions. She considered it an amiable creature, greatly recommended.

Whiteheadia (Hyacinthaceae)

A single species, *Whiteheadia bifolia*, constitutes this Cape genus that is named for Reverend Whitehead of South Africa. This species is rather widespread in the Cape and is found often in shady, damp places. The 5-inch (12-cm) high inflorescence is a dense spike of inconspicuous flowers cupped in large green bracts. The plants have two, large, many-veined, prostrate leaves that resemble those of *Massonia*. *Whiteheadia bifolia* is a simple curiosity. I enjoy having it in my collection but cannot think of any use it would have in most gardens.

Wurmbea (Colchicaceae)

The famous botanist Thunberg named this genus for one of his supporters, F. Van Wurmb, a Dutch merchant and secretary of the Academy of Sciences in Batavia (Bryan, 1989).

It is interesting that there are 13 or more species of *Wurmbea* in South Africa and 18 to 20 in Australia. Was the genus split in two and freighted off with the fragmentation of Gondwanaland?

In the Cape, the species are winter growing with a long summer dormancy. Found in damp situations, the tunicated corms are deep seated. The plants are small, generally under 12 inches (30 cm) tall. The flowers may be white or cream colored with interesting markings. *Wurmbea recurva* has purplish black flowers with reflexed segments. I have no experience with any species of *Wurmbea,* but they certainly intrigue any bulb collector and may have horticultural merit. Because of their small size, they should be good container plants. Bryan (1989) suggested they would fit well in damper areas of rock gardens.

Zantedeschia (Araceae)

The genus *Zantedeschia* was named in 1826 in honor of Professor Zantedeschia. There is a question of whether it was named for Francesco Zantedeschia or Giovanni Zantedeschia; the smart money seems to be on Giovanni.

Cynthia Letty (1973) recognized six species and two subspecies of *Zantedeschia*. More recently, Pauline Perry (1989) described a new, sweetly scented species, *Z. odorata,* from the remarkably rich flora of Nieuwoudtville in Namaqualand.

Zantedeschia has underground tuberous or rhizomatous stems. Characteristically the inflorescence is a large bract, the spathe, enveloping the central spadix on which numerous small flowers are borne. The flowers are unisexual; the male flowers are on the upper part of the spadix, and the female flowers are on the lower portion.

Professor Jackson (1986) wrote that the first known reference to *Zantedeschia aethiopica* was in 1687, and that it was first illustrated in 1697 from plants sent to Europe by Governor Simon van der Stel. This figure was cited by Linnaeus in 1753. The specific epithet, *aethiopica*, given to the plant by Linnaeus, does not refer to northeastern Africa. In classical times it meant "south of the known world," that is, south of Libya and Egypt.

The common name in North America is calla lily (*calla* meaning "beauti-ful"). In the Cape it has several names, including pig lily, probably refer-ring to the fondness the ystervark (the wild iron pig or porcupine) has for the tubers. The tubers have also been used as fodder for domestic pigs.

According to Professor Jackson (1986), the Xhosa people applied the fresh, warmed leaf of *Zantedeschia* to soothe boils, sores, and insect bites. Early colonists used it locally for gout and rheumatism. All vegeta-tive parts of the plant contain bundles of needle-shaped crystals of cal-cium oxalate that are highly irritating to the mucous membrane of the mouth and throat. However, Jackson reported that the young leaves and boiled tubers have been used for human consumption which may ac-count for another common name, Hottentotsbrood.

Zantedeschia aethiopica grows in the Cape wherever there is a wet-land. In this habitat there is a tiny arum frog that climbs into the spathe and presumably feeds on the insects attracted by the faintly scented flow-ers. Another common resident of the spathe is a camouflaged, insect-eat-ing, white crab spider that does not make a web. Since the plants grow in wetlands, they have special water stomata in the leaves to help discharge excess water, a process known as guttation, to prevent water logging.

Zantedeschia aethiopica grows during the winter and blooms in the spring. Well-grown plants reach 2 feet (61 cm) high. If given water they remain evergreen, but their normal pattern is to go dormant for a brief time in the summer, which is the time to divide them. Ordinarily they do not need dividing for three years or so. They will flower in the shade but it is best to grow them in the sun. They are apparently fairly cold hardy; an English gardener allowed the tubers to be frozen in the icy ground, but they bloomed beautifully afterward (Jackson, 1986).

Many people at my local farmers' market find the large white, petaloid spathes of *Zantedeschia aethiopica* attractive and readily purchase the cut flowers. To me they have an early association with funerals, but in a delightful piece, Katherine Whiteside (1991) claimed this morbid link no longer exists. It is now appropriate to use calla lilies for joyous occasions, including wedding decorations.

Zantedeschia albomaculata is not a Cape species. It grows near Natal in a summer-rainfall area. It is deciduous and dormant in winter. The flower colors range from white to cream, lemon, deep golden yellow and even apricot, but all have a dark purple patch in the throat. The arrow-shaped leaves are spotted, and the spots are like little windows: the green pigment is missing and the light shows through. The plant grows to 18 inches (46 cm) high or more.

Zantedeschia pentlandii has golden yellow flowers that are like those of the yellow-flowered forms of *Z. albomaculata*. The leaves of *Z. pentlandii* are also arrow-shaped but not spotted. The natural habitat is also in the summer-rainfall region. Under commercial cultivation, the species produces flowers on stalks 18 to 28 inches (46 to 71 cm) high from three-year-old rhizomes in the open field (Brown, 1990).

According to Cynthia Letty (1973), *Zantedeschia elliotiana* is a provisional species for no plants have ever been found in the wild, and the species may be a hybrid (Plate 75). Brown (1990) reported it produced flowers on 16- to 24-inch (41- to 61-cm) high stalks from three-year-old rhizomes grown in open fields. It is a showy plant with yellow flowers but has no dark patch in the throat. The leaves are wide, glossy, and arrow shaped, and they are splashed with confetti-like markings. *Zantedeschia elliotiana* combined with *Z. rehmannii* in a pot can make a stunning effect when in peak bloom. Both species should be planted about 2 inches (5 cm) deep in fast-draining soil and kept watered during their summer growing season.

Zantedeschia rehmannii is a pink-flowered species that grows about 8 inches (20 cm) high in the open field and up to 14 inches (36 cm) high in a shade house or greenhouse (Brown, 1990). It is also from the summer-rainfall area and is dormant in the winter. The flower color is intensified if the soil is rather acid. It is easily crossed with other species of *Zantedeschia,* so there are a number of hybrids that have become popular commercial cultivars.

The breeding of *Zantedeschia* to achieve a calla as a top container plant and cut flower for the marketplace is discussed by Brown (1990), who listed the qualities of a good bulb pot plant that must be considered in a breeding program, including height, floriferousness, flower size, ease of culture, disease resistance, production cost, and ability to force the plant to flower at the right time. Similarly, the qualities necessary for breeding a good cut flower are stalk length, stalk strength, number of blooms per plant, vase life, flower size, ease of culture, disease resistance, ability to force, and cost of production.

A breakthrough in calla hybridizing was a hybrid yellow, the result of crossing and backcrossing *Zantedeschia elliotiana* with *Z. albomaculata*. According to Brown (1990), however, it is the pink *Z. rehmannii* hybrids that hold the most potential for pot culture.

Propagation of *Zantedeschia* is by division of the rhizome or by seeds. The seedlings take about five weeks to germinate and bloom in their third year. Division of the rhizome or tuber is done when the plants are dormant. For the Cape species *Z. aethiopica*, divisions are made in summer. Division of other species is best done in the winter.

Zantedeschia is very susceptible to a bacterial soft rot, *Erwinia carotovora*, which is difficult to control. In breeding for disease resistance to *Erwinia*, Brown (1990) found that *Z. elliotiana* is the most susceptible calla, *Z. rehmannii* is less so, and *Z. albomaculata* is the most tolerant.

Six or eight rhizomes of the colorful deciduous species of *Zantedeschia* planted about 2 inches (5 cm) deep in a 12-inch pot will make a striking accent in the corner of a patio. Pots can also be taken indoors. The cut flowers of *Zantedeschia* last from two to three weeks in a vase after cutting if cared for properly (Brown, 1990).

Glossary

Actinomorphic. Flower regular, radially symmetrical, divisible in essentially equal halves in more than one plane (see *Zygomorphic*)

Aestivate. Dormant in summer

Anther. Pollen-containing portion of stamen borne at top of filament

Apomixis. Nonsexual process in which seeds are genetically identical to mother plant

Autolysis. Self-dissolution of tissues by action of plant's own enzymes

Axil. Angle at which leaf joins stem

Bract. Usually small, leaflike structures associated with an inflorescence

Bulb. Short, underground stem surrounded by fleshy leaves

Bulbil. Small, bulblike structure in leaf axil

Bulblet. Small bulb at base of mother bulb

Campanulate. Bell shaped

Cataphyll. Collarlike sheath from which leaves emerge

Chaparral. Brushy vegetation produced by the Mediterranean climate of the western United States

Clone. Genetically identical individuals resulting from division of mother corms, rhizomes, bulbs, or tubers

Convergent evolution. Evolutionary response of plants in different parts of the world to similar environmental pressures

Corm. Short, thick, underground stem, surrounded by dry leaves or leaf bases

Cormel. Tiny corm at base of mother corm

Cornicles. In aphids, a characteristic pair of dorsal tubes

Cultivar. Horticultural variety, often a hybrid or selected garden form

Deciduous. Seasonally leafless

Deliquesce. Aging perianth becomes semiliquid

Distichous. Arranged in two vertical rows

Doleritic. Related to mostly undeterminable constituents of dark, igneous rocks

Edaphic. Soil related

Endemic. Native to restricted geographic area

Epithet. Any word following the name of a genus (species, subspecies, variety)

Exserted. Protruded

Filament. Threadlike portion of stamen forming stalk of anther

Filiform. Threadlike—long and very slender

Forb. Any herb other than a grass

Fugacious. Of short duration

Fynbos. Shrubby vegetation produced by the Mediterranean climate in South Africa

Gene. A unit of inheritance; a section of chromosome that determines one or more specific hereditary traits

Genus. A closely related group of plants including one or more species

Geophyte. Plant with modified stem functioning as subterranean storage organ (bulb, corm, rhizome, tuber)

Gibbosity. A swelling (usual on flowers of *Lachenalia*)

Hirsute. Hairy

Hysteranthous. Flowers produced before foliage

Inflorescence. Entire cluster of flowers and associated structures

Infructescence. Inflorescence with maturing fruits, seeds

Klipkoppies (Koppies). Rocky hills, often Precambrian granite, in South Africa

Lacerate. Torn or cut

Lobe. A major division of the perianth (also termed *segment* or *tepal*)

Monocot. Plant with only one seed leaf in the embryo; a major division of the Angiosperms

Monotypic. A genus comprised of a single species

Naturalized. Not native and reproducing without human intervention

N–P–K. Formula of nitrogen–phosphorus–potassium in fertilizer

Octoploid. Having eight sets of chromosomes

Panicle. Branched inflorescence

Pedicel. Stalk of an individual flower

Peduncle. Stalk of an inflorescence

Pendulous. Hanging downward

Perianth. Calyx and corolla indistinguishably combined

Petaloid. Resembling a petal in color and shape

Pistil. Female structure consisting of ovary, style, stigma

Polymorphic. Appearing in several different forms

Raceme. Unbranched inflorescence of pediceled flowers that open from the bottom up

Radicle. Rudimentary root of seed embryo

Recurved. Gradually curved backward

Reflexed. Abruptly curved backward

Rhizome. Underground stem, usually horizontal

Scree. Sloping accumulation of rock fragments; talus

Secund. Flowers arranged on only one side of the flower stalk axis

Segment. A major division of the perianth (also termed *lobe* or *tepal*)

Serrate. Margins toothed

Sessile. Without any kind of stalk

Sheath. A surrounding, often tubular part

Spike. Unbranched inflorescence of sessile flowers opening bottom to top

Stamen. Male structure of flower composed of stalklike filament bearing terminal pollen-producing anther

Stellate. Starlike

Subspecies. A major division of a species between species and variety, often reflecting a special geographic distribution

Subtend. To occur immediately below

Sympatric. Occurring naturally in same area

Taxon. A taxonomic group of any rank (pl. *taxa*)

Tepal. A major division of the perianth (also termed *lobe* or *segment*)

Tetraploid. Having four sets of chromosomes

Thermonastic. Growth response of plant to temperature

Tuber. Short, thick, fleshy underground stem

Tunic. Covering of corm, netted or often hard and woody

Tunicated. Having an outer coat or layer

Umbel. Inflorescence with pedicels radiating from a common point

Urceolate. Urn-shaped

Veld (Veldt). South African wildland

Vleis. Seasonal marshy area, seep, or vernal pool

Xeriscape. Dry landscape or garden of drought tolerant plants

Zygomorphic. Flower irregular, divisible in equal halves in only one plane, or asymetrical (see *Actinomorphic*)

References

Archbell, J. W. 1939. *Tulbaghia* culture. *Herbertia* 6: 228.

Axelrod, D. I., and P. H. Raven. 1978. Late Cretaceous and Tertiary vegetation history. In *Biogeography and Ecology of Southern Africa*. Ed. M. J. A. Werger. *Monographie Biologicae*, vol. 31. The Hague: W. Junk. 77–130.

Barker, W. F. 1969. A new combination in *Lachenalia* with notes on the species. *Journal of South African Botany* 35(5): 321–322.

———. 1972. A new species of *Lachenalia* from the southwestern Cape. *Journal of South African Botany* 38(3): 179–183.

———. 1978. Ten new species of *Lachenalia* (Liliaceae). *Journal of South African Botany* 44(4): 391–418.

———. 1979. Ten more species of *Lachenalia* (Liliaceae). *Journal of South African Botany* 45(2): 193–219.

———. 1980. Victor Stanley Peers, conservationist and cultivator of South African plants. *Veld & Flora* 66(1): 25–27.

———. 1983. Six more new species of *Lachenalia* (Liliaceae). *Journal of South African Botany* 49(4): 423–444.

———. 1984. Three more new species of *Lachenalia* and one new variety of an early species (Liliaceae). *Journal of South African Botany* 50(4): 535–547.

———. 1987. Five more new species of *Lachenalia* (Liliaceae–Hyacin-thoideae)—four from the Cape Province and one from southern South West Africa/Namibia. *Journal of South African Botany* 53(2): 166–172.

Barnard, T. T. 1972. On hybrids and hybridization. In *Journal of South African Botany*. Supplementary vol. 10. Eds. G. Joyce Lewis and A. Amelia Obermeyer. 304–310.

Blackbeard, G. I. 1939. *Clivia* breeding. *Herbertia* 6: 191–193.

Bond, P., and P. Goldblatt. 1984. Plants of the Cape Flora, a descriptive catalogue. *Journal of South African Botany*. Supplementary vol. 13: 1–455.

Boussard, M. 1985. Growing South African Iridaceae. *Veld & Flora* 71(2): 61–63.

Brickell, C. D., D. F. Cutler, and M. Gregory. 1980. Petaloid mono-cotyledons, horticultural and botanical research. *Linnaean Society Symposium*, Series No. 8. Eds. C. Brickell et al. New York and London: Academic Press.

Brown, E. 1976. Bulbs for permanence. *Pacific Horticulture* 37(2): 23–28.

Brown, J. 1990. California calla breeding. *Herbertia* 46(2): 165–168.

Brown, P., and D. Le Maitre. 1990. Fire-lilies, the firebirds of the fynbos. *Veld & Flora* 76(1): 22.

Bryan, J. E. 1989a. *Bulbs, Volume I. A–H*. Portland, OR: Timber Press.

———. 1989b. *Bulbs, Volume II, I–Z*. Portland, OR: Timber Press.

Collett, R. 1982. Why so many plants from the western Cape in our gardens? *Pacific Horticulture* 43(3): 13–16.

Coombes. A. J. 1985. *Dictionary of Plant Names*. Portland, OR: Timber Press.

Coombs, S. V. 1936. *South African Plants for American Gardens*. New York: Frederick A. Stokes Company.

———1948. South African amaryllids as house plants. *Herbertia* 15: 101–112.

Court, G. D. 1983. Wild flower showing. *Veld & Flora* 69(4): 139.

Cowlishaw, G. H. 1935. Notes on amaryllid activities in Australia. 1. The cultivation of Amaryllids in Australia. *Year Book American Amaryllis Society* 2: 43–51.

Creasey, L. B. 1939. *Callicore rosea* in its native habitat. *Herbertia* 6: 214–221.

Crosby, T. S. 1978. Hybridization in the genus *Lachenalia*. *Veld & Flora* 64(3): 87–90.

Dearing, H. P. 1928. South African bulbs in Santa Barbara. *The Santa Barbara Gardener* 3(10): 1, 3, 5.

de Forest, L., and E. de Forest. 1930. Natives of South Africa. *The Santa Barbara Gardener* 5(6): 6–7.

———. 1937. Spring picture. *The Santa Barbara Gardener*. 12(10): 1, 2.

———. 1942. Pink Amaryllis. *The Santa Barbara Gardener* 17(10): 2.

Delpierre, G. R., and N. M. Du Plessis. 1973. *The Winter-growing Gladioli of South Africa*. Cape Town: Tafelberg Publishers Ltd.

DeVilliers, A. T. 1991. Birthplace of the bulbs. *IBSA Bulletin* 39: 1–3.

De Vos, M. P. 1970a. Bydrae tot die morfologie en anatomie van *Romulea:* I. die knol. *Journal of South African Botany* 36(3): 215–228.

———. 1970b. Bydrae tot die morfologie en anatomie van *Romulea*: II die blare. *Journal of South African Botany* 36(4): 271–286.

———. 1970c. Die herontdekte *Romulea monadelpha*. *Journal of South African Botany* 36(1): 1–8.

———. 1971. Bydrae tot die morfologie en anatomie van *Romulea:* III die bloeiwyse en blom. *Journal of South African Botany* 37(1): 57–70.

———. 1972. The genus *Romulea* in South Africa. *Journal of South African Botany*. Supplementary vol. 9: 1–307.

———. 1976. Die Suid-Afrikaanse species van *Homoglossum*. *Journal of South African Botany* 42(4): 301–359.

———. 1979. The African genus *Ferraria*. *Journal of South African Botany* 45(3): 295–375.

———. 1982. The African genus *Tritonia* Ker-Gawler (Iridaceae): Part 1. *Journal of South African Botany* 48(1): 105–163.

———. 1983. The African genus *Tritonia* Ker-Gawler: Part 2. Sections *Subcallosae* and *Montbretia*. *Journal of South African Botany* 49(4):

347–422.

———. 1984. The African genus *Crocosmia* Planchon. *Journal of South African Botany* 50(4): 463–502.

———. 1985. Revision of the South African genus *Chasmanthe*. *Journal of South African Botany* 51(4): 253–161.

———. 1988. Die Suid-Afrikaanse genus *Ixia* L. *Veld & Flora* 74(2): 79–80.

D'Ewes, D. R. 1978. Some easy indigenous bulbs. *Veld & Flora* 64(3): 67–69.

Doutt, R. 1988. Homoglossums for Pacific Coast gardens. *Pacific Horticulture* 49(2): 32.

Drysdale, W. T. 1987. *Haemanthus/Scadoxus*. *Herbertia* 43(1): 42–47.

Duncan, G. 1979. *Cybistetes longifolia:* a bulbous treasure of the Cape. *IBSA Bulletin* 29: 13.

———. 1980. The *Antholyza*—gem of the Sandveld. *Veld & Flora* 66(1): 21.

———. 1981a. *Gladiolus aureus* Bak.—its present position. *Veld & Flora* 67(1): 17–18.

———. 1981b. *Moraea loubseri* Goldbl.—saved through cultivation. *Veld & Flora* 67(1): 18–19.

———. 1982a. *Gladiolus ochroleucus*—a desirable species for pot culture. *Veld & Flora* 68(4): 112–113.

———. 1982b. Ten *Babiana* species for promotion. *Veld & Flora* 68(2): 47–48.

———. 1982c. *Veltheimia bracteata* Lemon Flame—introducing the yellow form. *Veld & Flora* 68(3): 72.

———. 1983a. *Moraea aristata*. *Veld & Flora* 69(4): 143–144.

———. 1983b. The white form of *Agapanthus walshii* L. Bol. *Veld & Flora* 69(1): 21.

———. 1984. *Nerine sarniensis* Kirstenbosch White—the white sport. *Veld & Flora* 70(2): 55.

———. 1985a. *Agapanthus* species—their potential, and the introduction of ten selected forms. *Veld & Flora* 71(4): 122–125.

234

———. 1985b. The *Moraea* collection at Kirstenbosch. *IBSA Bulletin* 35: 1–3.

———. 1985c. Notes on the genus *Clivia* Lindley, with particular reference to *C. miniata* Regel var. *citrina* Watson. *Veld & Flora* 71(3): 84–85.

———. 1986. The re-discovery of *Lachenalia mathewsii* W. Barker. *Veld & Flora* 72(2): 40.

———. 1988. The *Lachenalia* Handbook. *Annals of Kirstenbosch Botanic Gardens* 17: 1–71.

———. 1989a. Cultivation and propagation. *Spring and Winter Flowering Bulbs of the Cape.* Ed. B. Jeppe. Cape Town: Oxford University Press. 5–10.

———. 1989b *Gladiolus alatus* L. *Veld & Flora* 75(2): 33–34.

———. 1989c. *Romulea unifolia* De Vos—an exciting new Cape irid. *Veld & Flora* 75(4): 98–99.

———. 1990a. *Cyrtanthus*—its horticultural potential—part 1. *Veld & Flora* 76(1): 18–21.

———. 1990b. *Cyrtanthus*—its horticultural potential—part 2. *Veld & Flora* 76(2): 54–56.

———. 1990c. *Cyrtanthus*—its horticultural potential—part 3. *Veld & Flora* 76(3): 72–73.

Du Plessis, N., and G. Duncan. 1989. *Bulbous Plants of Southern Africa.* Cape Town: Tafelberg Publishers Ltd.

Dyer, R. A. 1939. A review of the genus *Cyrtanthus. Herbertia* 6: 65–103.

Eliovson, S. 1967. *Bulbs for the Gardener in the Southern Hemisphere.* Cape Town: Citadel Press.

———. 1980. *Wild Flowers of Southern Africa.* 6th ed. Johannesburg: MacMillans South Africa Publishers (Pty) Ltd.

Erens, J. 1948. Notes on amaryllids cultivated in the Transvaal. *Herbertia* 15: 91–101.

Everett, T. H. 1981. *Dierama. The New York Botanical Garden Illustrated Encyclopedia of Horticulture.* New York and London: Garland Publishing. 4: 1070–1071.

Field, D. V. 1971. The identity of *Gloriosa simplex* L. (Liliaceae). *Kew Bulletin* 25: 243–245.

Friis, I. B., and I. Nordal. 1976. Studies on the genus *Haemanthus* (Amaryllidaceae) IV. Division of the genus into *Haemanthus* and *Scadoxus* with notes on *Haemanthus*. *Norwegian Journal of Botany* 23: 63–77.

Genders, R. 1973. *Bulbs, A Complete Handbook*. New York: The Bobbs-Merrill Co. Inc.

Gethyllis. 1983. *IBSA Bulletin* 33: 1–2.

Goemans, R. A. 1980. The history of the modern *Freesia*. In *Linnaean Society Symposium*, Series No. 8. Eds. C. Brickell et al. New York and London: Academic Press. 161–170.

Goldblatt, P. 1969. The genus *Sparaxis*. *Journal of South African Botany* 35(4): 219–252.

———. 1971. Cytological and morphological studies in the southern African Iridaceae. *Journal of South African Botany* 37(4): 317–460.

———. 1972. A revision of the genera *Lapeirousia* Pourret and *Anomatheca* Ker in the winter rainfall region of southern Africa. *Contributions from the Bolus Herbarium* 4: 1–74.

———. 1973. Biosystematics and taxonomic studies in *Homeria* (Iridaceae). *Journal of South African Botany* 39(2): 133–140.

———. 1978. An analysis of the flora of southern Africa: its characteristics, relationships, and origins. *Annals of the Missouri Botanical Garden* 65: 369–436.

———. 1979a. Biology and systematics of *Galaxia* (Iridaceae). *Journal of South African Botany* 45(4): 385–423.

———. 1979b. The *Homeria* species of Thunberg's herbarium. *Annals of the Missouri Botanic Garden* 66: 588–590.

———. 1979c. New species of Cape Iridaceae. *Journal of South African Botany* 45(1): 81–89.

———. 1979d. The species of *Sparaxis* and their geography. *Veld & Flora* 65(1): 7–9.

———. 1980. Systematics of *Gynandriris* (Iridaceae), a Mediterranean–

southern African disjunct. *Botaniska Notiser* 133: 239–260.

——. 1981a. Moraeas—one lost, one saved. *Veld & Flora* 67(1): 19–20.

——. 1981b. Systematics and biology of *Homeria* (Iridaceae). *Annals of the Missouri Botanical Garden* 68: 413–503.

——. 1981c. Systematics, phylogeny and evolution of *Dietes* (Iridaceae). *Annals of the Missouri Botanical Garden* 68: 132–153.

——. 1982a. Corm morphology in *Hesperantha* (Iridaceae, Ixioideae) and a proposed infrageneric taxonomy. *Annals of the Missouri Botanical Garden* 69: 370–378.

——. 1982b. A synopsis of *Moraea* (Iridaceae) with new taxa, transfers, and notes. *Annals of the Missouri Botanical Garden* 69: 351–369.

——. 1982c. Systematics of *Freesia* Klatt (Iridaceae). *Journal of South African Botany* 48(1): 49–91.

——. 1984a. New species of *Galaxia* (Iridaceae) and notes on cytology and evolution in the genus. *Annals of the Missouri Botanical Garden* 71: 1082–1087.

——. 1984b. A revision of *Hesperantha* (Iridaceae) in the winter rainfall area of southern Africa. *South African Journal of Botany* 50(1): 15–141.

——. 1985. Systematics of the southern African genus *Geissorhiza* (Iridaceae—Ixioideae). *Annals of the Missouri Botanical Garden* 72: 277–447.

——. 1986. The moraeas of Southern Africa. *Annals of Kirstenbosch Botanic Gardens* 14: 1–224.

——. 1987a. Notes on the variation and taxonomy of *Watsonia borbonica* (*W. pyramidata*, *W. ardernei*) (Iridaceae) in the southwestern Cape, South Africa. *Annals of the Missouri Botanic Garden* 74: 590–592.

——. 1987b. Systematics of the southern African genus *Hexaglottis* (Iridaceae–Iridoideae). *Annals of the Missouri Botanical Garden* 74: 542–569.

——. 1989. The genus *Watsonia*. *Annals of Kirstenbosch Botanic Gardens* 19: 1–148.

Goldblatt, P., and D. Snijman. 1985. Notes on the southern African genus

Ixia L. (Iridaceae). *Journal of South African Botany* 51(1): 66–70.

Goldblatt, P., and J. H. J. Vlok. 1989. New species of *Gladiolus* (Iridaceae) from the southern Cape and the status of *G. lewisiae*. *South African Journal of Botany* 55(2): 259–264.

Hall, L. 1986. *Bulbine* Linn. (Liliaceae). *IBSA Bulletin* 36: 5–6.

Hannibal, L. S. 1952a. ×*Crinodonna corsii* clone Dorothy Hannibal. *Plant Life 8:* 97–98.

———. 1952b. The heat factor in relation to amaryllid flower color. *Plant Life* 8(1): 142.

———. 1980. Amar-Bruns-Crinum. *IBSA Bulletin* 30: 2–4.

———. 1983. *Amaryllis belladonna. IBSA Bulletin* 33: 4–5.

———. 1984. *Clivia* hybrids. *Herbertia* 40: 102–105.

———. 1986. *Cybistetes longifolia* and its many names. *IBSA Bulletin* 36: 4–5.

Hardman, C. 1976. Nerines, just waiting for a chance. *Pacific Horticulture* 37(2): 34–36.

———. 1985a. Communicating with plants, or Am I getting the message? *American Plant Life Society Newsletter*. Quarters 3 & 4: 1–2.

———. 1985b. Nerines in the U.S.A. *Herbertia* 41: 76–82.

Hartmann, H. T., and D. E. Kester. 1975. *Plant Propagation, Principles and Practices*. Englewood Cliffs, NJ: Prentice Hall.

Hatch, T. 1987a. Cultivation of a rare, pale lemon form of *Veltheimia capensis. Herbertia* 43(1): 23.

———. 1987b. Production of *Haemanthus albiflos* from leaf cuttings. *Herbertia* 43(1): 22.

Hauser, K. 1978. Die Kukumakranka (*Gethyllis afra*). *Veld & Flora* 64(1): 19–20.

Hilliard, O. M., and B. L. Burtt. 1978. Notes on some plants from Southern Africa chiefly from Natal: VII. *Notes from the Royal Botanic Garden, Edinburgh* 36(1): 43–70.

———. 1986. Notes on some plants of southern Africa chiefly from Natal; Part 12. *Notes from the Royal Botanic Garden, Edinburgh* 43(2): 190–191.

———. 1991. Dierama, *the Hairbells of Africa*. Johannesburg and London: Acorn Books CC.

Holmes, J. 1979. *Rhodohypoxis*. Gem from the Drakensberg. *IBSA Bulletin* 29: 10.

———. 1981. *Engysiphon. IBSA Bulletin* 31: 2–3.

———. 1983. *Geissorhiza* (the wine cups). *Veld & Flora* 69(1): 9–10.

Hoog, T. M. 1935. *Belladonna* lily hybrids and *Pamianthe peruviana. Year Book American Amaryllis Society* 2: 114.

Ingram, C. 1977. Homoglad, a new plant for Pacific horticulture. *Pacific Horticulture* 38(2): 41–42.

Innes, C. 1985. *The World of Iridaceae*. Ashington, Sussex, England. Holly Gate International Ltd.

Jackson, W. P. J. 1986. The Cape white arum lily, *Zantedeschia aethiopica. Veld & Flora* 72(2): 44–45.

Jackson, W. P. U. and J. McW. Macgregor. 1985. What's in a name? *Veld & Flora* 71(4): 120.

———. 1987. What's in a name? *Veld & Flora* 73(3): 109–110.

———. 1989. What's in a name? *Veld & Flora* 75(1): 33

James, D. 1935. Notes on *Babiana. The Santa Barbara Gardener* 10(4): 5.

———. 1937. Coomb's *South African Plants for American Gardens*. Book review in *The Santa Barbara Gardener* 12(3): 7.

Jeppe, B. 1989. *Spring and Winter Flowering Bulbs of the Cape*. Cape Town: Oxford University Press.

Jessop, J. P. 1976. Studies in the bulbous Liliaceae in South Africa: 6. The taxonomy of *Massonia* and allied genera. *Journal of South African Botany* 42(4): 401–437.

———. 1977. Studies in the bulbous Liliaceae in South Africa: 7. The taxonomy of *Drimia* and certain allied genera. *Journal of South African Botany* 43(4): 265–319.

King, L. 1978. The geomorphology of central and southern Africa. In *Biogeography and Ecology of Southern Africa*. Ed. M. J. A. Werger. *Monographie Biologicae*, vol. 31. The Hague: W. Junk. 3–17.

Klatt, F. W. 1866. Revisio Iridearum: *Freesia* Eckl. *Linnaea* 34: 672–674.

Koopowitz, H. 1986a. Conservation problems in the Amaryllidaceae. *Herbertia* 42: 21–25.

——. 1986b. Horticultural potential of *Cyrtanthus* (Amaryllidaceae). *Herbertia* 42: 75–81.

——. 1990. Conservation and bulbous plants. *Herbertia* 46(1): 22

Koopowitz, H., and H. Kaye. 1983. *Plant Extinction: A Global Crisis.* Washington, DC: Stone Wall Press.

Lane, W. 1976. *Clivia*, the triple dividend plant. *Pacific Horticulture* 37(2): 5–8.

Lawder, E. 1978. Seeds to sow. *Veld & Flora* 64(4): 106.

Lehmiller, D. J. 1987. A South African *Crinum* Safari. *Herbertia* 43(2): 50–59.

Leighton, F. M. 1965. The genus *Agapanthus* L'Heritier. *Journal of South African Botany.* Supplementary vol. 4: 1–50.

le Maitre, D. C., 1984. A short note on seed predation in *Watsonia pyramidata* (Andr.) Stapf in relation to season of burn. *Journal of South African Botany* 50(4): 407–415.

Letty, C. 1973. The genus *Zantedeschia. Bothalia* 11(1 & 2): 5–26.

Lewis, G. J. 1959. The genus *Babiana. Journal of South African Botany.* Supplementary vol. 3: 149.

——. 1962. The genus *Ixia. Journal of South African Botany* 28: 45–195.

Lewis, G. J., and A. A. Obermeyer, with T. T. Barnard. 1972. *Gladiolus*, a revision of the South African species. *Journal of South African Botany.* Supplementary vol. 10: 1–316.

Lighton, C. 1973. *Cape Floral Kingdom.* Cape Town: Juta & Company, Ltd.

Loubser, J. W. 1981a. Intergeneric hybrids in the Amaryllidaceae. *IBSA Bulletin* 31: 9–10.

——. 1981b. The story of *Ferraria densepunctulata* De Vos. *Veld & Flora* 67(3): 88.

——. 1982. The germination time of seed of bulbous plants. *IBSA Bulletin* 32: 6–7.

——. 1983. *Brunsvigia marginata* — my favourite Amaryllid. *IBSA Bul-*

letin 33: 8.

——. 1985. My favourite *Gladiolus*. *IBSA Bulletin* 35: 3.

McLean, F. T., W. D. Clark, and E. N. Fischer. 1927. *The Gladiolus Book*. Garden City, NY: Doubleday Page & Company.

McNeil, P. G. 1985. Hybridising *Clivia*. *Herbertia* 41: 24–29.

Malan, C. 1979. Oom Japie Krige—*Sparaxis*-teler. *Veld & Flora* 65(1): 9–11.

Martley, J. 1939. *Ammocharis falcata*. *Herbertia* 6: 225–228.

Matthews, Y. S. 1991. South African bulbs in Cornwall. *IBSA Bulletin* 39: 4–6.

Metelerkamp, W., and J. Sealy. 1983. Some edible and medicinal plants of the Doorn Karoo. *Veld & Flora* 69(1): 4–8.

Meyer, F., R. J. Griesbach, and H. Koopowitz. 1990. Inter- and intraspecific hybridization in the genus *Ornithogalum*. *Herbertia* 46 (1 & 2): 129–139.

Morris, B. 1990. A true breeding strain of yellow *Clivia*. *Herbertia* 46(2): 95–96.

Narain, P. 1988. *Gloriosa*: cultivars and natural species. *Herbertia* 44(1): ?–1?

Norris, C. A. 1980. The search for *Nerine*. *Veld & Flora* 66(2): 51–53.

Obermeyer, A. A. 1978. *Ornithogalum*: a revision of the southern Africa species. *Bothalia* 12(3): 323–376.

Olivier, W. 1980. The genus *Cyrtanthus* Ait. *Veld & Flora* 66(3): 78–81.

——. 1981. The genus *Boophane*. *IBSA Bulletin* 31: 5–8.

——. 1983. Rare Amaryllidaceae from southern Africa. *Veld & Flora* 69(4): 162–165.

Onderstall, J. 1976. The fabulous flame lily. *Veld & Flora* 62(3): 24–25.

Orpet, E. O. 1939. *Callicore rosea* and brunsdonnas. *Herbertia* 6: 221–223.

Patterson, F. 1984. *Namaqualand—Garden of the Gods*. Toronto: Key Porter Books.

Perry, P. 1985. The restructuring of the family Liliaceae. *Veld & Flora* 71(3): 66–68.

——. 1987. A synoptic review of the genus *Bulbinella* (Asphodelaceae) in South Africa. *South African Journal of Botany* 53(6): 431–444.

——. 1989. A new species of *Zantedeschia* (Araceae) from the western Cape. *South African Journal of Botany* 55(4): 447–451.

——. 1991. Growing geophytes at the Karoo gardens. *Veld & Flora* 77(3): 87–89.

Perry, P. L., and M. B. Bayer. 1980. Flora of the Karoo Botanic Garden. 4. *Albuca* L. *Veld & Flora* 66(2): 58–60.

Perry, P. L., M. B. Bayer, and L. A. Wilbraham. 1979. Flora of the Karoo Botanic Garden. 2. Geophytes. *Veld & Flora* 65(3): 79–81.

Poindexter, R. W., Jr. 1931. *Gladiolus tristis* again. *The Santa Barbara Gardener* 6(5): 2–3.

Rand, M. 1980. A shower of brilliant little stars. *Veld & Flora* 66(3): 81–82.

Richfield, L. 1984. Problems in growing *Cyrtanthus*. *IBSA Bulletin* 34: 10–11.

Rix, M. 1983. *Growing Bulbs*. Portland, OR: Timber Press.

Rourke, J. P. 1985. From threatened species to invasive weed: the strange case of *Gladiolus caryophyllaceus*. *Veld & Flora* 71(4): 126.

Roux, J. P. 1980. Studies in the genus *Watsonia*. *Journal of South African Botany* 46(4): 365–378.

Scholtz, E. 1985. South African bulbs. *Plants & Gardens* 37(3): 52–54.

Schulze, R. E., and O. S. McGee. 1978. Climatic indices and classifications in relation to the biogeography of southern Africa. In *Biogeography and Ecology of Southern Africa*. Ed. M. J. A. Werger. *Monographie Biologicae*, vol. 31. The Hague: W. Junk. 19–52.

Scott, G. 1989a. *Cyanella*—one for the pot (or the rockery). *Veld & Flora* 75(3): 65–68.

——. 1989b. Preliminary investigations of *Cyanella hyacinthoides* (Tecophilaceae) as an edible crop plant. *South African Journal of Botany* 55(5): 533–536.

Smith, C. A. 1966. Common names of South African plants. *Botanical Research Institute*. Botanical Survey Memoir, No. 35: 1–641.

Smithers, Sir P. 1984. The enigma of hybrid nerines. *Herbertia* 40: 82–93.

Snijman, D. A. 1978. The genus *Watsonia. Veld & Flora* 64(3): 93.

——. 1981. *Haemanthus.* A curiosity of early Cape botany. *Veld & Flora* 67(1): 4–7.

——. 1984. A revision of the genus *Haemanthus* L. (Amaryllidaceae). *Journal of South African Botany.* Supplementary vol. 12: 1–139.

Snifman, D., and P. Perry. 1987. A floristic analysis of the Nieuwoudtville Wild Flower Reserve, north-western Cape. *South African Journal of Botany* 53(6): 445–454.

Stephens, E. L. 1939. Notes on *Gethyllis. Herbertia* 6: 112–117.

Stirton, C. H. 1980. Aspects of research on South African petaloid monocotyledons of horticultural importance. In *Linnaean Society Symposium*, Series No. 8. Eds. C. Brickell et al. New York and London: Academic Press. 191–197.

Strout, E. B. 1948. Growing amaryllids in pots. *Herbertia* 15: 145–163.

Thompson, M. F. 1979. Studies in the Hypoxidaceae. III. The genus *Pauridia. Bothalia* 12(4): 621–625.

Tompsett, A. A. 1985. Dormancy breaking in bulbs by burning over. *The Plantsman* 7: 40–51.

Traub, H. P. 1963. *The Genera of Amaryllidaceae.* La Jolla, CA: The American Plant Life Society.

Van Der Spuy, U. 1976. *Wild Flowers of South Africa for the Garden.* Johannesburg: Hugh Keartland (Publishers) (Pty) Ltd.

van Zyjl, R. 1984. *Pauridia*—a tiny genus. *IBSA Bulletin* 34: 12.

Verity, D. S. 1976. *Cyrtanthus purpureus* in containers. *Pacific Horticulture* 37(2): 57–58.

Vosa, C. G. 1980. Notes on Tulbaghia: 2. *Journal of South African Botany* 46(2): 109–114.

Walters, K. 1988. Clivias. *Herbertia* 44(1): 29–32.

Watt, J. M., M. G. Breyer-Brandwijk. 1962. *Medicinal and Poisonous Plants of Southern and Eastern Africa.* Edinburgh and London: E. & S. Livingstone Ltd.

Welch, W. R. P. 1982. Experiences with *Brunsvigia* hybrids. *Plant Life* 38(1): 92–95.

Whiteside, K. 1991. *Classic Bulbs, Hidden Treasures for the Modern Garden*. New York: Villard Books.

Wilson, M. C. 1982. Pollen storage. *Plant Life* 38: 67–68.

Wrinkle, G. 1984. An introduction to the genus *Boophane*. *Herbertia* 40: 77–82.

Zimmerman, E. P. 1935. Culture of hybrid clivias. *Yearbook of American Amaryllis Society* 2: 142–144.

List of Suppliers and Organizations

SUPPLIERS

BioQuest International
P.O. Box 5752
Santa Barbara, CA 93150
USA

Jim Duggan Flower Nursery
1817 Sheridan
Leucadia, CA 92024
USA

Skittone Bulb Company
1415 Eucalyptus Drive
San Francisco, CA 94132
USA

Jim Holmes
P.O. Box 4063
Idas Valley 7609
Republic of South Africa

Rust-En-Vrede Nursery
P.O. Box 753
Brackenfell 7560
Republic of South Africa

Imbali Bulbs
P.O. Box 267
Aukland Park 2006
Republic of South Africa

Silverhill Seeds
18 Silverhill Crescent
Kenilworth 7700
Republic of South Africa

BULB ORGANIZATIONS

International Bulb Society
University of California
    Arboretum
Irvine, CA 92717
USA

The Executive Secretary
Botanical Society of South Africa
Kirstenbosch
Claremont 7735
Republic of South Africa

The Secretary
Indigenous Bulb Growers of
    South Africa (IBSA)
3 The Bend
Edgemead 7441
Republic of South Africa

Index

247